RANDOM
HOUSE
LARGE
PRINT

Bittersweet

Bittersweet

HOW SORROW AND LONGING
MAKE US WHOLE

SUSAN CAIN

RANDOM HOUSE
LARGE PRINT

Cover design: Evan Gaffney
Art direction: Jackie Phillips
Cover illustration: Qweek/Getty Images

The Library of Congress has established a
Cataloging-in-Publication record for this title.

ISBN: 978-0-593-55957-4

www.penguinrandomhouse.com/large-print-format-books

FIRST LARGE PRINT EDITION

Printed in the United States of America

1st Printing

This Large Print edition published in accord
with the standards of the N.A.V.H.

In memory of Leonard Cohen

There is a crack, a crack in everything
That's how the light gets in

—L. C., "ANTHEM"

Gregory the Great (ca. 540–604) spoke about **compunctio,** the holy pain[,] the grief somebody feels when faced with that which is most beautiful. . . . The bittersweet experience stems from human homelessness in an imperfect world, human consciousness of, and at the same time, a desire for, perfection. This inner spiritual void becomes painfully real when faced with beauty. There, between the lost and the desired, the holy tears are formed.

—OWE WIKSTRÖM, PROFESSOR IN PSYCHOLOGY OF RELIGION AT THE UNIVERSITY OF UPPSALA

AUTHOR'S NOTE

I've been working on this book officially since 2016, and unofficially (as you'll soon read) for my whole life. I've spoken to, read, and corresponded with hundreds of people about all things Bittersweet. Some of these people I mention explicitly; others informed my thinking. I would have loved to name them all, but this would have produced an unreadable book. So, some names appear only in the Notes and Acknowledgments; others, no doubt, I've left out by mistake. I'm grateful for them all.

Also, for readability, I didn't use ellipses or brackets in certain quotations, but made sure that the extra or missing words didn't change the speaker's or writer's meaning. If you'd like to quote these written sources from the original, the citations directing you to most of the full quotations appear in the Notes at the back of the book.

Finally, I've changed the names and identifying details of some of the people whose stories I tell. I didn't fact-check the stories people told me about themselves, but included only those I believed to be true.

Sarajevo Requiem by Tom Stoddart, © Getty Images

The Cellist of Sarajevo

One night, I dreamed that I was meeting my friend, a poet named Mariana, in Sarajevo, the city of love. I woke up confused. Sarajevo, a symbol of love? Wasn't Sarajevo the site of one of the bloodiest civil wars of the late twentieth century?

Then I remembered.

Vedran Smailović.

The cellist of Sarajevo.

. . .

It's May 28, 1992, and Sarajevo is under siege. For centuries, Muslims, Croats, and Serbs have lived together in this city of streetcars and pastry shops, gliding swans in parkland ponds, Ottoman mosques and Eastern Orthodox cathedrals. A city of three religions, three peoples, yet until recently no one paid too much attention to who was who. They knew

but they didn't know; they preferred to see one another as neighbors who met for coffee or kebabs,
took classes at the same university, sometimes got
married, had children.

But now, civil war. Men on the hills flanking the
city have cut the electricity and water supply. The
1984 Olympic stadium has burned down, its playing fields turned into makeshift graveyards. The
apartment buildings are pockmarked from mortar
assaults, the traffic lights are broken, the streets are
quiet. The only sound is the crackling of gunfire.

Until this moment, when the strains of Albinoni's
Adagio in G Minor* fill the pedestrian street outside
a bombed-out bakery.

Do you know this music? If not, maybe you
should pause and listen to it right now: youtube
.com/watch?v=kn1gcjuhlhg. It's haunting, it's ex-
quisite, it's infinitely sad. Vedran Smailović, lead
cellist of the Sarajevo opera orchestra, is playing it
in honor of twenty-two people killed yesterday by
a mortar shell as they lined up for bread. Smailović
was nearby when the shell exploded; he helped take
care of the wounded. Now he's returned to the scene
of the carnage, dressed as if for a night at the opera
house, in a formal white shirt and black tails. He sits
amidst the rubble, on a white plastic chair, his cello

---

* This work is commonly attributed to Tomaso Albinoni, but was
probably composed by Italian musicologist Remo Giazotto, possibly
based on a fragment of an Albinoni composition.

propped between his legs. The yearning notes of the adagio float up to the sky.

All around him, the rifles fire, the shelling booms, the machine guns crackle. Smailović keeps on playing. He'll do this for twenty-two days, one day for each person killed at the bakery. Somehow, the bullets will never touch him.

This is a city built in a valley, ringed by mountains from which snipers aim at starving citizens in search of bread. Some people wait for hours to cross the street, then dart across like hunted deer. But here's a man sitting still in an open square, dressed in concert finery, as if he has all the time in the world.

You ask me am I crazy for playing the cello in a war zone, he says. **Why don't you ask THEM if they're crazy for shelling Sarajevo?**

His gesture reverberates throughout the city, over the airwaves. Soon, it'll find expression in a novel, a film. But before that, during the darkest days of the siege, Smailović will inspire other musicians to take to the streets with their own instruments. They don't play martial music, to rouse the troops against the snipers, or pop tunes, to lift the people's spirits. They play the Albinoni. The destroyers attack with guns and bombs, and the musicians respond with the most bittersweet music they know.

We're not combatants, call the violinists; **we're not victims, either,** add the violas. **We're just humans,** sing the cellos, **just humans: flawed and beautiful and aching for love.**

...

A few months later. The civil war rages on, and the foreign correspondent Allan Little watches as a procession of forty thousand civilians emerges from a forest. They've been trudging through the woods for forty-eight hours straight, fleeing an attack.

Among them is an eighty-year-old man. He looks desperate, exhausted. The man approaches Little, asks whether he's seen his wife. They were separated during the long march, the man says.

Little hasn't seen her but, ever the journalist, asks whether the man wouldn't mind identifying himself as Muslim or Croat. And the man's answer, Little says years later, in a gorgeous BBC segment, shames him even now, as he recalls it across the decades.

"I am," said the old man, "a musician."

CONTENTS

PART I

Sorrow and Longing

How can we transform pain into creativity,
transcendence, and love?

PART II

Winners and Losers

How can we live and work authentically
in a "tyranny of positivity"?

PART III

Mortality, Impermanence, and Grief

How should we live, knowing that we and
everyone we love will die?

Portrait of a Young Woman, 2021, Ukraine,
© Tetiana Baranova (Instagram: @artbytaqa)

The Power of Bittersweet

Homesick we are, and always, for another
And different world.

—VITA SACKVILLE-WEST,
THE GARDEN

Once, when I was a twenty-two-year-old law student, some friends picked me up in my dorm on the way to class. I'd been happily listening to bittersweet music in a minor key. Not the Albinoni, which I hadn't heard back then; more likely a song by my all-time favorite musician, Leonard Cohen, aka the Poet Laureate of Pessimism.

It's hard to put into words what I experience when I hear this kind of music. It's technically sad, but what I feel, really, is love: a great tidal outpouring of it. A deep kinship with all the other souls in the world who know the sorrow the music strains to express. Awe at the musician's ability to transform pain into beauty. If I'm alone when I'm listening, I often make a spontaneous prayer gesture, hands to face, palm to palm, even though I'm deeply agnostic and don't formally pray. But the music makes my heart open: literally, the sensation of expanding chest muscles. It even makes it seem okay that everyone I love, including me, is going to die one day. This equanimity about death lasts maybe three minutes, but each time it happens, it changes me slightly. If you define transcendence as a moment in which your self fades away and you feel connected to the all, these musically bittersweet moments are the closest I've come to experiencing it. But it's happened over and over again.

And I could never understand why.

Meanwhile, my friends were amused by the incongruity of mournful songs blasting from a dorm room stereo; one of them asked why I was listening to funeral tunes. I laughed, and we went to class. End of story.

Except that I thought about his comment for the next twenty-five **years.** Why **did** I find yearning music so strangely uplifting? And what in our culture made this a fitting subject for a joke? Why, even as I write this, do I feel the need to reassure you that I love dance music, too? (I really do.)

At first, these were just interesting questions. But as I searched for answers, I realized that they were **the** questions, the big ones—and that contemporary culture has trained us, to our great impoverishment, not to ask them.

. . .

Two thousand years ago, Aristotle wondered why the great poets, philosophers, artists, and politicians often have melancholic personalities. His question was based on the ancient belief that the human body contains four humors, or liquid substances, each corresponding to a different temperament: melancholic (sad), sanguine (happy), choleric (aggressive), and phlegmatic (calm). The relative amounts of these liquids were thought to shape our characters. Hippocrates, the famed Greek physician, believed that the ideal person enjoyed a harmonious balance of the four. But many of us tend in one direction or another.

This book is about the melancholic direction, which I call the "bittersweet": a tendency to states of longing, poignancy, and sorrow; an acute awareness of passing time; and a curiously piercing joy at the beauty of the world. The bittersweet is also about the recognition that light and dark, birth and death—bitter and sweet—are forever paired. "Days of honey, days of onion," as an Arabic proverb puts it. The tragedy of life is linked inescapably with its splendor; you could tear civilization down and rebuild it from scratch, and the same dualities would rise again. Yet to fully inhabit these dualities—the dark as well as the light—is, paradoxically, the only way to transcend them. And transcending them is the ultimate point. The bittersweet is about the desire for communion, the wish to go home.

If you see yourself as a bittersweet type, it's hard to discuss Aristotle's question about the melancholia of the greats without sounding self-congratulatory. But the fact is that his observation has resonated across the millennia. In the fifteenth century, the philosopher Marsilio Ficino proposed that Saturn, the Roman god associated with melancholy, "has relinquished the ordinary life to Jupiter, but he claims for himself a life sequestered & divine." The sixteenth-century artist Albrecht Dürer famously depicted Melancholy as a downcast angel surrounded by symbols of creativity, knowledge, and yearning: a polyhedron, an hourglass, a ladder ascending to the sky. The nineteenth-century poet Charles Baudelaire could "scarcely conceive of a type of beauty" in which there is no melancholy.

This romantic vision of melancholia has waxed and waned over time; most recently, it's waned. In an influential 1918 essay, Sigmund Freud dismissed melancholy as narcissism, and ever since, it's disappeared into the maw of psychopathology. Mainstream psychology sees it as synonymous with clinical depression.*

---

* This conflation of melancholy and depression follows a long tradition in Western psychology. Freud used the term "melancholia" to **describe** clinical depression: "a profoundly painful dejection, cessation of interest in the outside world, loss of the capacity to love, inhibition of all activity." The influential psychologist Julia Kristeva wrote

But Aristotle's question never went away; it can't. There's some mysterious property in melancholy, something essential. Plato had it, and so did Jalal al-Din Rumi, so did Charles Darwin, Abraham Lincoln, Maya Angelou, Nina Simone . . . Leonard Cohen.

But what, exactly, did they have?

I've spent years researching this question, following a centuries-old trail laid by artists, writers, contemplatives, and wisdom traditions from all over the world. This path also led me to the work of contemporary psychologists, scientists, and even management researchers (who have discovered some of the unique strengths of melancholic business leaders and creatives, and the best ways to tap them). And I've concluded that bittersweetness is not, as we tend to think, just a momentary feeling or event. It's also a quiet force, a way of being, a storied tradition—as dramatically overlooked as it is brimming with human potential. It's an authentic and elevating response to the problem of being alive in a deeply flawed yet stubbornly beautiful world.

Most of all, bittersweetness shows us how to respond to pain: by acknowledging it, and attempting to turn it into art, the way the musicians do, or healing, or innovation, or anything else that nourishes

---

in 1989 that "the terms melancholy and depression refer to a composite that might be called the melancholy/depressive, whose borders are in fact blurred." Try typing "melancholy" into today's PubMed search engine and you pull up articles on . . . depression.

the soul. If we don't transform our sorrows and longings, we can end up inflicting them on others via
abuse, domination, neglect. But if we realize that all
humans know—or will know—loss and suffering,
we can turn **toward** each other.*

This idea—of transforming pain into creativity,
transcendence, and love—is the heart of this book.

...

The ideal community, like the ideal human, would
embody all four Hippocratic temperaments. But just
the way many people tend in one direction or another, so do our societies. And, as we'll see in chapter 5, we've organized American culture around the
sanguine and the choleric, which we associate with
buoyancy and strength.

This sanguine-choleric outlook is forward leaning and combat ready; it prizes cheerful goal orientation in our personal lives, and righteous outrage
online. We should be tough, optimistic, and assertive; we should possess the confidence to speak our
minds, the interpersonal skills to win friends and
influence people. Americans prioritize happiness
so much that we wrote the pursuit of it into our
founding documents, then proceeded to write over
thirty thousand books on the subject, as per a recent

* No one has expressed this idea better than the musician Nick Cave,
in his Red Hand Files: theredhandfiles.com/utility-of-suffering.

Amazon search. We're taught from a very young age to scorn our own tears ("Crybaby!"), then to censure our sorrow for the rest of our lives. In a study of more than seventy thousand people, Harvard psychologist Dr. Susan David found that one-third of us judge ourselves for having "negative" emotions such as sadness and grief. "We do this not only to ourselves," says David, "but also to people we love, like our children."

Sanguine-choleric attitudes have many advantages, of course. They help us throw a ball to second base, pass a bill through Congress, fight the good fight. But all this vigorous cheer and socially acceptable anger disguises the reality that all humans—even, say, online influencers with impressive dance moves or the fiercest "takes"—are fragile and impermanent beings. And so we lack empathy for those who disagree with us. And so we're blindsided when our own troubles come.

The bittersweet-melancholic mode, in contrast, can seem backward leaning, unproductive, and mired in longing. It yearns for what could have been, or what might yet be.

But longing is momentum in disguise: It's active, not passive; touched with the creative, the tender, and the divine. We long for something, or someone. We reach for it, move toward it. The word **longing** derives from the Old English **langian,** meaning "to grow long," and the German **langen**—to reach, to extend. The word **yearning** is linguistically associated with hunger and thirst, but also desire. In Hebrew, it comes from the same root as the word for passion.

The place you suffer, in other words, is the same place you care profoundly—care enough to act. This is why, in Homer's **Odyssey**, it was homesickness that drove Odysseus to take his epic journey, which starts with him weeping on a beach for his native Ithaca. This is why, in most every children's story you've ever loved, from Harry Potter to Pippi Longstocking, the protagonist is an orphan. Only once the parents die, transforming into objects of yearning, do the children have their adventures and claim their hidden birthrights. These tales resonate because we're all subject to illness and aging, breakups and bereavement, plagues and wars. And the message of all these stories, the secret that our poets and philosophers **have been trying to tell us for centuries,** is that our longing is the great gateway to belonging.

Many of the world's religions teach the same lesson. "Your whole life must be one of longing," writes the anonymous author of **The Cloud of Unknowing,** a fourteenth-century mystical work. "Those who constantly cherish only intense longing to encounter the essential face of their lord will attain complete realization," reads the Qu'ran, 92:20–21. "God is the sigh in the soul," said the thirteenth-century Christian mystic and theologian Meister Eckhart. "Our heart is restless 'til it rests in thee" is the most quoted line of Saint Augustine.

You can feel this truth during those out-of-time

moments when you witness something so sublime—
a legendary guitar riff, a superhuman somersault—
that it seems to come from a more perfect and beautiful world. This is why we revere rock stars and
Olympic athletes the way we do—**because** they
bring us a breath of magic from that other place.
Yet such moments are fleeting, and we want to live
in that other world for good; we're convinced that
there is where we belong.

At their worst, bittersweet types despair that the
perfect and beautiful world is forever out of reach.
But at their best, they try to summon it into being.
Bittersweetness is the hidden source of our moon
shots, masterpieces, and love stories. It's because of
longing that we play moonlight sonatas and build
rockets to Mars. It's because of longing that Romeo
loved Juliet, that Shakespeare wrote their story, that
we still perform it centuries later.

It doesn't matter whether we arrive at these truths
via Pippi Longstocking, Simone Biles, or Saint
Augustine—whether we're atheists or believers. The
truths are the same. Whether you long for the partner who broke up with you, or the one you dream
of meeting; whether you hunger for the happy childhood you'll never have, or for the divine; whether
you yearn for a creative life, or the country of your
birth, or a more perfect union (personally or politically); whether you dream of scaling the world's
highest peaks, or merging with the beauty you saw
on your last beach vacation; whether you long to

ease the pain of your ancestors, or for a world in which life could survive without consuming other life; whether you yearn for a lost person, an unborn child, the fountain of youth, or unconditional love: These are all manifestations of the same great ache.

I call this place, this state that we're longing for, "the perfect and beautiful world." In the Judeo-Christian tradition, it's the Garden of Eden and the Kingdom of Heaven; the Sufis call it the Beloved of the Soul. There are countless other names for it: for instance, simply, home, or "Somewhere Over the Rainbow," or, as the novelist Mark Merlis puts it, "the shore from which we were deported before we were born." C. S. Lewis called it "the place where all the beauty came from." They're all the same thing—they're the deepest desire of every human heart, they're what Vedran Smailović conjured into being when he played his cello in the streets of a war-ravaged city.

During the past decades, Leonard Cohen's "Hallelujah," a ballad of spiritual longing, became a staple—even a cliché—of TV talent shows such as **American Idol.** But this is why tears of joy streamed down audience faces as all those contestants performed it for the thousandth time. It doesn't matter whether we consider ourselves "secular" or "religious": in some fundamental way, we're all reaching for the heavens.

• • •

Around the same time those friends picked me up in my law school dorm and I started wondering about sad music, I came across the Buddhist idea that, as the mythologist Joseph Campbell put it, we should strive "to participate joyfully in the sorrows of the world." I couldn't stop thinking about this: What did it mean? How could such a thing be possible?

I understood that this injunction wasn't to be taken literally. It wasn't about dancing on graves, or a passive response to tragedy and evil. Quite the opposite; it had to do with a sensitivity to pain and transience, and embracing this world of suffering (or of dissatisfaction, depending on how you interpret the Sanskrit in the First Noble Truth of Buddhism).

Still, the question persisted. I suppose I could have gone to India or Nepal to try to answer it, or enrolled in an East Asian Studies program at a university. But I didn't. I just went out and lived life, with this question, and related ones, never far from mind: Why would sadness, an emotion that makes us glum and Eeyore-like, have survived evolutionary pressures? What's really driving our longing for "perfect" and unconditional love (and what does it have to do with our love of sad songs, rainy days, and even the sacred)? Why does creativity seem to be associated with longing, sorrow—and transcendence? How should we cope with lost love? How did a nation founded on so much heartache turn into a culture of normative sunshine? How can we live and work authentically in a culture of enforced positivity? How should we live, knowing that we and everyone we love will die? Do we inherit the pain of our parents and ancestors, and if so, can we also transform **that** into a beneficent force?

Decades later, this book is my answer.

It's also an account of my passage from agnosticism to . . . what? Not faith, exactly; I'm no more or less agnostic than when I started. But to the realization that you don't have to believe in specific conceptions of God in order to be transformed by spiritual longing. There's a Hasidic parable in which a rabbi notices that an old man in his congregation is indifferent to his talk of the divine. He hums for the man a poignant melody, a song of yearning. "Now I understand what you wish to teach," says the old man. "I feel an intense longing to be united with the Lord."

I'm a lot like that old man. I started writing this book to solve the mystery of why so many of us respond so intensely to sad music. On its face, this seemed a small subject for a years-long project. Yet I couldn't let it go. I had no idea, then, that the music was just a gateway to a deeper realm, where you notice that the world is sacred and mysterious, enchanted even. Some people enter this realm through prayer or meditation or walks in the woods; minor-key music was the portal that happened to entice me. But these entryways are everywhere, and they take endless forms. One of the aims of this book is to urge you to notice them—and to step through.

Bittersweet Quiz

Some of us inhabit the bittersweet state instinctively, always have; some of us avoid it as much as we can; some of us arrive there when we reach a certain age, or after facing life's trials and triumphs. If you're wondering how inclined you are to this sensibility, you can take this quiz, which I developed in collaboration with research scientist Dr. David Yaden, a professor at Johns Hopkins Medicine, and cognitive scientist Dr. Scott Barry Kaufman, director of the Center for the Science of Human Potential.*

To find out how bittersweet you are, at this particular moment in time, please ask yourself the following questions, and indicate your level of agreement on a scale from 0 (not at all) to 10 (completely).

___ Do you tear up easily at touching
TV commercials?

___ Are you especially moved by old photographs?

___ Do you react intensely to music, art,
or nature?

* Note to psychologists and other scholars interested in exploring the bittersweet construct: While the exploratory pilot studies conducted by Yaden and Kaufman assessed preliminary aspects of the items, they didn't yet include other ways of validating them, such as focus groups, expert review, and larger sample exploratory and confirmatory factor analysis. They encourage interested scholars to conduct more research on the survey items to further ascertain their psychometric properties.

__ Have others described you as an "old soul"?

__ Do you find comfort or inspiration in a rainy day?

__ Do you know what the author C. S. Lewis meant when he described joy as a "sharp, wonderful stab of longing"?

__ Do you prefer poetry to sports (or maybe you find the poetry **in** sports)?

__ Are you moved to goosebumps several times a day?

__ Do you see "the tears in things"? (This phrase comes from Virgil's **Aeneid.**)

__ Do you feel elevated by sad music?

__ Do you tend to see the happiness and sadness in things, all at once?

__ Do you seek out beauty in your everyday life?

__ Does the word **poignant** especially resonate with you?

__ When you have conversations with close friends, are you drawn to talking about their past or current troubles?

__ And this: Do you feel the ecstatic is close at hand?

This last item may seem an odd question for an inventory of the bittersweet. But I'm not talking about an optimistic outlook or an easy smile. I mean the strange exaltation that yearning can bring. According to recent research by Yaden, self-transcendence (as well as its milder cousins, such as gratitude and flow states) increases at times of transition, endings, and death—at the bittersweet times of life.

In fact, you could say that what orients a person to the bittersweet is a heightened awareness of finality. Children splashing joyfully in puddles brings tears to grandparents' eyes because they know that one day the children will grow up and grow old (and they won't be there to see it). But those aren't tears of sorrow, exactly; at heart, they're tears of love.

To score yourself on the Bittersweet Quiz, add up your responses and divide that total by 15.

If your number is lower than 3.8, you tend toward the sanguine.

If your number is above 3.8 and below 5.7, you tend to move between sanguine and bittersweet states.

If you score above 5.7, you're a true connoisseur of the place where light and dark meet.

Readers of my book **Quiet: The Power of Introverts in a World That Can't Stop Talking** will be interested to know that exploratory studies by Yaden and Kaufman show a high correlation between high scorers on the Bittersweet Quiz and the trait identified by psychologist and author Dr. Elaine Aron as "high sensitivity."* Yaden and Kaufman also found a high correlation with the tendency to "absorption"—which predicts creativity—and a moderate correlation with awe, self-transcendence, and spirituality. Finally, they found a small association with anxiety and depression—which isn't surprising. Too **much** melancholy can lead to what Aristotle called the diseases of black bile (**melaina kole,** from which melancholy takes its name).

This is not a book about those afflictions, real and devastating though they are; and it's certainly not a celebration of them. If you think you're experiencing depression or severe anxiety, or even post-traumatic stress disorder, please know that help is out there— and seek it out!

This book is about the riches of the bittersweet tradition—and how tapping into them can transform the way we create, the way we parent, the way we lead, the way we love, and the way we die. I hope it will also help us to understand each other, and ourselves.

---

* Interestingly, they found no correlation with introversion.

Maya Angelou, © Craig Herndon/**The Washington Post**

PART I

Sorrow and Longing

How can we transform pain into creativity, transcendence, and love?

CHAPTER 1

What is sadness good for?

Before you know kindness as the deepest thing inside, you must know sorrow as the other deepest thing.

—NAOMI SHIHAB NYE

In 2010, celebrated Pixar director Pete Docter decided to make an animated film about the wild and woolly emotions of an eleven-year-old girl named Riley. He knew the rough outlines of the story he wanted to tell. The film would open with Riley, uprooted from her Minnesota hometown and plunked down in a new house and school in San Francisco, while also caught in the emotional storm of incoming adolescence.

So far, so good. But Docter faced a creative puzzle. He wanted to depict Riley's feelings as lovable animated characters running a control center in her brain, shaping her memories and daily life. But which feelings? Psychologists told him that we have up to twenty-seven different emotions. But you can't tell a good story about so many different characters. Docter needed to narrow it down, and to pick one emotion as the main protagonist.

He considered a few different emotions for the starring role, then decided to place Fear at the center of the movie, alongside Joy; partly, he says, because Fear is funny. He considered Sadness, but this seemed unappealing. Docter had grown up in Minnesota, where, he told me, the sanguine norms were clear: "The idea that you'd cry in front of people was very uncool."

But three years into the development of the film—with the dialogue already done, the movie partially animated, the gags with Fear already in place, some of them "quite inspired"—he realized that something was wrong. Docter was scheduled to screen the film-in-progress for Pixar's executive team. And he was sure it was a failure. The third act didn't work. According to the film's narrative arc, Joy should have learned a great lesson. But Fear had nothing to teach her.

At that point in his career, Docter had enjoyed two mega-successes—**Up** and **Monsters, Inc.** But he started to feel sure that these hits were flukes.

"I don't know what I'm doing," he thought. "I should just quit."

His mind spun into dark daydreams of a post-Pixar

future in which he'd lost not only his job but also his career. He went into preemptive mourning. The thought of living outside his treasured community of creatives and business mavericks made him feel he was drowning—in Sadness. And the more despondent he grew, the more he realized how much he loved his colleagues.

Which led to his epiphany: The real reason for his emotions—for all our emotions—is to connect us. And Sadness, of all the emotions, was the ultimate bonding agent.

"I suddenly had an idea that we needed to get Fear out of there," he recalls now, "and Sadness connected with Joy." The only problem was, he had to convince John Lasseter, who ran Pixar at the time, to place Sadness at the heart of the movie. And he was worried that this would be a tough sell.

Docter tells me this story as we sit in the airy, light-filled atrium designed by Steve Jobs for Pixar's Emeryville, California, campus. We're surrounded by larger-than-life sculptures of Pixar characters—the Parr family from **The Incredibles,** Buzz from **Toy Story,** all of them striking poses by sky-high glass windows. Docter enjoys cult status at Pixar. Earlier that day, I'd led an executive session on harnessing the talents of introverted filmmakers, and a few minutes into the proceedings, Docter had bounded into the conference room, instantly lighting up the room with his warmth.

Docter resembles an animated character himself,

drawn mainly of rectangles. He has a gangly six-foot-four frame and a long face, half of which is forehead. Even his teeth are long and rectangular, the beanpoles of the dental world. But his most salient feature is the animation of his facial expressions. His smiles and grimaces convey a bright, winsome sensitivity. When he was a kid, his family moved to Copenhagen so his father could research a Ph.D. on Danish choral music. Docter didn't speak the language and had no idea what the other kids were saying. The pain of that experience drew him to animation; it was easier to draw people than talk to them. Even now, he's apt to create characters who live in treehouses and float away into a wordless dreamscape.

Docter was concerned that the executive team would find Sadness too glum, too dark. The animators had drawn the character as dowdy, squat, and blue. Why would you place a figure like that at the center of a movie? Who would want to identify with **her**?

Throughout this process, Docter had an unlikely ally: Dacher Keltner, an influential University of California, Berkeley, psychology professor. Docter had called in Keltner to educate him and his colleagues on the science of emotions. They became close friends. Keltner's daughter was suffering the slings and arrows of adolescence at the same time as Docter's, and the two men bonded over vicarious angst. Keltner taught Docter and his team the functions of each major emotion: Fear keeps you safe. Anger protects you from getting taken advantage of. And Sadness—what does Sadness do?

Keltner had explained that Sadness triggers compassion. It brings people together. It helps you see just how much your community of quirky Pixar filmmakers means to you.

The executive team approved the idea, and Docter and his team rewrote the movie—which ultimately won the Oscar for Best Animated Feature and was the highest grossing original film in Pixar history—with Sadness in the starring role.*

...

When you first meet Dacher Keltner—who has flowing blond locks; the relaxed, athletic aura of a surfer; and a lighthouse-beam smile—he seems an unlikely ambassador for Sadness. His default state seems more like Joy. He radiates warmth and caring, and has a sincere politician's gift for seeing and appreciating others. Keltner runs the Berkeley Social Interaction Lab and the Greater Good Science Center, two of

* Keltner told **The New York Times** that he did have "some quibbles" with the ultimate portrayal of Sadness in the movie. "Sadness is seen as a drag, a sluggish character," he said. "In fact, studies find that sadness is associated with elevated physiological arousal, activating the body to respond to loss. And in the film, Sadness is frumpy and off-putting."

the world's most influential positive psychology labs, where his job is to study the emotional goodies of being alive: wonder, awe, happiness.

But spend some time with Keltner and you notice that the corners of his eyes turn down like a basset hound's, and that he describes himself as anxious and melancholic—as a bittersweet type. "Sadness is at the core of who I am," he tells me. In my book **Quiet,** I described the research of psychologists Jerome Kagan and Elaine Aron, which found that 15 to 20 percent of babies inherit a temperament that predisposes them to react more intensely to life's uncertainty as well as its glory. Keltner considers himself what Kagan would call a born "high-reactive," or what Aron would call "highly sensitive."

Keltner was raised in a wild and starry-eyed 1970s household. His father was a firefighter and painter who took him to art museums and taught him Taoism, his mother a literature professor who read him Romantic poetry and was especially fond of D. H. Lawrence. Keltner and his younger brother, Rolf, who were very close, roamed around nature at all hours of the day and night. Their parents encouraged them to figure out their core passions, and to build a life around them.

But in their quest to experience life in all its intensity, Keltner's parents moved the family at a dizzying pace: from a small town in Mexico, where he was born in a tiny clinic; to Laurel Canyon, a countercultural California neighborhood in the Hollywood

Hills, where they lived next door to Jackson Browne's pianist and Keltner went to second grade at a school called Wonderland; to a rural farm town in the Sierra foothills, where few of his fifth-grade classmates were destined for college. By the time the family arrived in Nottingham, England, when Keltner was in high school, his parents' marriage had imploded. His father fell in love with the wife of a family friend; his mother started traveling back and forth to Paris to study experimental theater. Keltner and Rolf, left on their own, got drunk and threw parties. They were never a foursome again.

On the outside Keltner seemed—seems still—like a golden child. But the abrupt shattering had what he describes as a "long, enduring sad effect" on him and his family. His father mostly disappeared; his mother became clinically depressed; Keltner suffered three years of full-blown panic attacks. Rolf, who would grow up to be a dedicated speech therapist in an impoverished community, and a devoted husband and father, battled the demons of what one physician diagnosed as bipolar disorder: insomnia, binge eating, and regular consumption of beer and marijuana to calm his nerves.

Of all these unravelings, it was Rolf's struggles that shook Keltner most. Partly because his brother had been his anchor from the time they were small: In every neighborhood into which they crash-landed, they were boon companions, fellow explorers of the new terrain, tennis partners who never lost a doubles match. When the family fell apart, they fended for themselves, together.

But Rolf was also his exemplar. He was only a year younger, but, by Keltner's account, he was bigger, braver, kinder: the most "morally beautiful" person he ever knew. He was modest and humble, in contrast with Keltner's more driven and competitive nature; he never met an underdog he didn't love. In one of their many hometowns lived a girl named Elena, who grew up in a ramshackle house with a front lawn that looked like a junkyard. Elena was underfed, her hair stringy and unwashed, the favorite target of local bullies. And Rolf, who was neither the largest nor the strongest kid in his grade, defended her constantly from her many tormentors. **That guy is courageous out of compassion,** Keltner thought. **I want to be like him.**

When Keltner emerged from adolescence and began to survey the family wreckage, he suspected that it was his parents' commitment to high passion that had caused their family so much trouble. And even though he had an artistic, romantic temperament, he was also a born scientist—one who decided to study human emotions when he grew up. Emotions like the awe, wonder, and joy that had always been so central to him, Rolf, and his parents. And emotions like the sadness inside Keltner and his family, and inside so many of us.

. . .

One of the cornerstones of Keltner's research, which he summarized in his book **Born to Be Good,** is what he calls "the compassionate instinct"—the idea that we humans are wired to respond to each other's troubles with care. Our nervous systems make little distinction between our own pain and the pain of others, it turns out; they react similarly to both. This instinct is as much a part of us as the desire to eat and breathe.

The compassionate instinct is also a fundamental aspect of the human success story—and one of the great powers of bittersweetness. The word **compassion** literally means "to suffer together," and Keltner sees it as one of our best and most redemptive qualities. The sadness from which compassion springs is a pro-social emotion, an agent of connection and love; it's what the musician Nick Cave calls "the universal unifying force." Sorrow and tears are one of the strongest bonding mechanisms we have.

The compassionate instinct is wired so deeply throughout our nervous system that it appears to trace back to our earliest evolutionary history. For example, if someone pinches you or burns your skin, this activates the anterior cingulate region of your cortex (ACC)—the more recently developed, uniquely human part of the brain responsible for your ability to perform high-level tasks such as paying your taxes and planning a party. And your ACC activates in the same way when you see someone **else** get pinched or burned. But Keltner also found the compassionate instinct in the more instinctive and evolutionarily ancient parts of our nervous system: in the mammalian region known as the periaqueductal gray, which is located in the center of the brain, and causes mothers to nurture their young; and in an even older, deeper, and more fundamental part of the nervous system known as the vagus nerve, which connects the brain stem to the neck and torso, and is the largest and one of our most important bundles of nerves.

It's long been known that the vagus nerve is connected to digestion, sex, and breathing—to the mechanics of being alive. But in several replicated studies, Keltner discovered another of its purposes: When we witness suffering, our vagus nerve makes us care. If you see a photo of a man wincing in pain, or a child weeping for her dying grandmother, your vagus nerve will fire. Keltner also found that people with especially strong vagus nerves—he calls them vagal superstars—are more likely to cooperate with others and to have strong friendships. They're more likely (like Rolf) to intervene when they see someone being bullied, or to give up recess to tutor a classmate who's struggling with math.

Keltner's isn't the only research to show this connection between sadness and unity. The Harvard psychologist Joshua Greene and the Princeton neuroscientist and psychologist Jonathan Cohen, for example, found that people asked to consider the suffering of victims of violence displayed activation of the same brain region as a previous study had shown of besotted mothers gazing at pictures of their babies. The Emory University neuroscientists James Rilling and Gregory Berns found that helping people in need stimulates the same brain region as winning a prize or eating a delicious meal. We also know that depressed (and formerly depressed) people are more likely to see the world from others' points of view and to experience compassion; conversely, high-empathy people are more likely than others to enjoy sad music. "Depression deepens our natural empathy," observes Tufts University psychiatry professor Nassir Ghaemi, "and produces someone for whom the inescapable web of interdependence . . . is a personal reality, not a fanciful wish."

These findings have enormous implications. They tell us that our impulse to respond to other beings' sadness sits in the same location as our need to breathe, digest food, reproduce, and protect our babies; in the same place as our desire to be rewarded and to enjoy life's pleasures. They tell us, as Keltner explained to me, that "caring is right at the heart of human existence. Sadness is about caring. And the mother of sadness is compassion."

If you want to experience Keltner's findings viscerally, watch this brilliant four-minute video that went unexpectedly viral: youtube.com/watch?v=cDDWvj _q-o8. Produced by the Cleveland Clinic as part of a campaign to instill empathy in its caregivers, the video takes you on a short walk through the hospital corridors, the camera lingering on the faces of random passersby, people we'd normally walk past without giving a second thought—except that this time there are subtitles telling us their unseen trials (and occasional triumphs): "Tumor is malignant." "Husband is terminally ill." "Visiting Dad for the last time." "Recently divorced." And: "Just found out he's going to be a dad."

...

So. What happened? Maybe a tear came to your eyes? Maybe a lump in your throat, maybe the physical sensation of an opening heart? Maybe soaring feelings of love for this random swath of humanity, followed by an intellectual commitment to start paying attention to the people you pass every day, not only in the corridors of a hospital but also the guy at the gas pump and your overly talkative co-worker? Those reactions were likely influenced by your vagus nerve, your anterior cingulate cortex, your periaqueductal gray: processing people you've never met as if their pain is your own. As, in fact, it is.

Many of us have long perceived the power of sadness to unite us, without fully articulating it, or thinking to express it in neuroscientific terms. Years ago, when this book was still a gleam in my eye, I gave a blog interview to author Gretchen Rubin on what I then called "the happiness of melancholy." A young woman responded with her own blogpost, reflecting on her grandfather's funeral, and the "union between souls" she experienced there.

> My grandfather's barbershop chorus sang him a tribute and, for the first time in my fourteen years, I witnessed tears cascading down my father's face. That moment—with the lilting sound of men's voices, the hushed audience, and my father's sadness—is permanently etched on my heart. And when our family first had to euthanize a pet, the love in that room—shared by my father, brother, and me—took my breath away. You see, when I think of these events, it is not the sadness that I most remember. **It is the union between souls.** When we experience sadness, we share in a common suffering. It is one of the few times when people allow themselves to be truly vulnerable. It is a time when our culture allows us to be completely honest about how we feel. [Emphasis added.]

Feeling deprived of the ability to express these insights in her daily life, the young woman turned to art:

> My affinity for serious movies and thought-provoking novels is all an attempt to recreate the beauty of my life's most honest moments. I recognize that, in order to function in society, we cannot all walk around with our hearts

constantly overflowing, so I visit these moments in my mind, re-experience them through art, and appreciate the occurrence of new, utterly vulnerable moments when they come.

But maybe we **need** to move these moments into everyday life—and to understand their evolutionary underpinnings. We're living, famously, through a time in which we have trouble connecting with others, especially outside our "tribes." And Keltner's work shows us that sadness—Sadness, of all things!— has the power to create the "union between souls" that we so desperately lack.

. . .

But if we're going to fully grasp the power of sadness, there's one more piece of our primate heritage we need to understand. Have you ever wondered why we react with such visceral intensity to media images of starving or orphaned children? Why does the thought of children separated from their parents cause such deep and universal distress?

The answer lies deep in our evolutionary history. Our compassionate instinct appears to originate not just with any connection between humans, but with the mother-child bond—with the all-consuming desire of mothers to respond to their crying infants. From there it radiates outward, to other beings in need of care.

Human babies are, as Keltner puts it, "the most vulnerable offspring on the face of the Earth," unable to function without the help of benevolent adults. We're born this fragile to accommodate our enormous brains, which would be too big to fit through the birth canal if we arrived after they fully developed. But our "premature" birth date turns out to be one of the more hopeful facts about our species. It means that the more intelligent our species grew, the more sympathetic we had to become, in order to take care of our hopelessly dependent young. We needed to decipher their inscrutable cries. We needed to feed them, we needed to love them.

This might not mean so much if our compassion extended strictly to our own offspring. But because we were primed to care for small and vulnerable infants in general, says Keltner, we also developed the capacity to care for anything infant-**like**—from a houseplant to a stranger in distress. We aren't the only mammals to do this. Orca whales will circle a mother who has lost her calf. Elephants soothe each other by gently touching their trunks to the faces of fellow elephants. But humans, Keltner told me, "have taken compassion to a whole new level. There's nothing like our capacity for sorrow and caring for things that are lost or in need."

Our horror at the news of suffering children, in other words, comes from our impulse to protect the young. If we can't cherish kids, we know instinctively, we can't cherish anyone.

Of course, we shouldn't be too impressed with this nurturing instinct of ours. It's still our **own** babies' cries that sound most urgent to us; we seem to have a lot less sympathy for other people's infants, for other adults, and even for our own grumpy adolescents. The fact that our compassion seems to dwindle the further we get from our own offspring's cradles—not to mention our species' appetite for cruelty—is as dispiriting as Keltner's findings are encouraging.

But Keltner doesn't see it this way. This is partly because of his brother, Rolf, who taught him to care for the vulnerable. This is also partly because he practices loving-kindness meditation, which (as we'll see in chapter 4) teaches us to treasure others as we do our beloved children. ("And I think we can get close," Keltner says.) But it's also because of what he learned from Charles Darwin.

Darwin is associated, in the popular imagination, with bloody zero-sum competition, with Tennyson's "nature, red in tooth and claw"—with the motto "survival of the fittest." But this wasn't actually his phrase. It was coined by a philosopher and sociologist named Herbert Spencer and his fellow "social Darwinists," who were promoters of white and upper-class supremacy.

For Darwin, says Keltner, "survival of the kindest" would have been a better moniker. Darwin was a gentle and melancholic soul, a doting husband and adoring father of ten, deeply in love with nature from earliest childhood. His father had wanted him to be a doctor, but when at age sixteen he witnessed his first surgery, performed in those days without anesthesia, he was so horrified that for the rest of his life he couldn't stand the sight of blood. He retreated to the woodlands and studied beetles instead. Later, he described his encounter with a Brazilian forest as "a chaos of delight, out of which a world of future & more quiet pleasure will arise."

Early in Darwin's career, he lost his beloved ten-year-old daughter, Annie, to scarlet fever—an event that may have shaped his worldview, according to biographers Deborah Heiligman and Adam Gopnik. He was so grief-stricken that he couldn't attend her burial. Annie had been a joyous child who loved to snuggle with her mother and to spend hours arranging her father's hair, as Darwin tenderly recorded in his diary. "Oh Mamma, what should we do, if you were to die," Annie had cried when she had to separate from her mother. But it was her mother and father, Emma and Charles Darwin, who had to endure that tragedy. "We have lost the joy of the Household," wrote Darwin in his diary, upon Annie's death, "and the solace of our old age."

In what many consider one of Darwin's greatest books, **The Descent of Man,** which he wrote some two decades later, he argued that compassion is our strongest instinct:

The social instincts lead an animal to take plea-sure in the society of his fellows, to feel a certain amount of sympathy with them, and to perform various services for them. . . . **Such actions as the above appear to be the simple result of the greater strength of the social or maternal instincts than that of any other instinct or motive;** for they are performed too instantaneously for reflection, or for pleasure or pain to be felt at the time. [Emphasis added.]

Darwin noted example after example of beings reacting viscerally to the suffering of other beings: The dog who took care, every time he passed it, to lick a sick cat in his household. The crows who patiently fed their blind and elderly companion. The monkey who risked his life to save a beloved zookeeper from a hostile baboon. Of course, Darwin didn't know about the vagal nerve, the anterior cingulate cortex, or the periaqueductal gray. But he intuited their compassionate function, some 150 years before Dacher Keltner would demonstrate it in his lab. "We are impelled to relieve the sufferings of another," wrote Darwin, "in order that our own painful feelings may at the same time be relieved."

Like Keltner, Darwin also intuited that these behaviors evolved from the instinct of parents to care for their young. We shouldn't look for sympathy in animals that have no contact with their mothers or fathers, he said.

Darwin was no naïf, blind to nature's brutality. On the contrary, he was consumed by these observations precisely because, in the words of one biographer, "he felt the world's pain so acutely, and so persistently." He knew that animals often behave viciously, as when they "expel a wounded" member from their troop or gore it to death. He knew that compassion is strongest within families and weaker with out-groups; that it's often absent altogether; and that it's difficult for humans to see other species as "fellow creatures" deserving of sympathy. But he also saw that extending the compassionate instinct as far out as we could, from our own family to humanity in general, and ultimately to all sentient beings, would be "one of the noblest" moral achievements of which we're capable.

Indeed, when the Dalai Lama heard about this aspect of Darwin's work, he was astonished by its similarity to Tibetan Buddhism. ("I will now call myself a Darwinian," he said.) Both Darwinism and Buddhism view compassion as the greatest virtue, and the mother-infant bond as the heart of sympathy. As the Dalai Lama put it, in a dialogue with the University of California, San Francisco, psychology professor emeritus Dr. Paul Ekman, "In the human mind, seeing someone bleeding and dying makes you uncomfortable. That's the seed of compassion. In those animals, like turtles, not dealing with a mother, I don't think they have a capacity for affection."

How to explain what Ekman calls this "amazing coincidence, if it is a coincidence," between

Darwinian and Buddhist thought? Perhaps, says Ekman, Darwin was exposed to Tibetan Buddhism by his friend Joseph Hooker, a botanist who spent time in Tibet studying its flora. Maybe Darwin developed these ideas in the church of the Galapagos wilderness, on his famous voyage of the **Beagle.** Or, possibly, he forged them in the crucible of his own experience—of loving and losing his daughter Annie.

. . .

We tend to place compassion on the "positive" side of the ledger of human emotions, notwithstanding this decidedly bittersweet view of it as the product of shared sorrow. Indeed, Keltner's life work is grounded in the field of "positive psychology," the study of human flourishing. The term was coined by Abraham Maslow in 1954, and later championed and popularized by psychologist Martin Seligman, as an antidote to what both men believed was psychology's excessive focus on mental illness rather than strength. They wanted to discover the practices and mindsets that would make our hearts sing, and our lives well-lived. Seligman was hugely successful in this quest. The countless articles you've likely read urging you to start a gratitude journal or take up mindfulness meditation can be traced to his movement, and to the vast army of practitioners inspired by it.

But the field has also drawn criticism for ignoring

an important swath of human experience—such as sorrow and longing. Critics have charged that it's biased toward an American sensibility that, as the psychologist Nancy McWilliams puts it, "subscribe[s] to . . . the comic rather than the tragic version of human life, the pursuit of happiness rather than the coming to terms with inevitable pain."

This isn't surprising; the entire field of psychology hasn't paid much attention to the human potential in bittersweetness. If you're a melancholic type, you might expect to find your deepest stirrings reflected **somewhere** in the discipline. But other than the "high sensitivity" paradigm, the closest you'll come is the study of a personality trait called "neuroticism," which is about as appealing as the name sounds. According to modern personality psychology, neurotics are fretful and insecure. They're prone to illness, anxiety, and depression.

Neuroticism does have upsides. Despite their stressed immune systems, neurotics may live longer because they're vigilant types who take good care of their health. They're strivers, driven by fear of failure to succeed, and by self-criticism to improve. They're good scholars because they turn concepts over in their minds and consider them at great length, from every angle. For an entrepreneur, the psychiatrist Amy Iversen told a publication called **Management Today,** the tendency to ruminate "can be channeled into obsessively thinking through a user experience, advertising strategy, or how to pitch a new idea, in the same way a creative could use this energy to memorise every line of a film script, or hone the finest detail of a play's production."

Experts like Iversen present these upsides as useful adaptations to an undesirable condition. But there's nothing **inherently** elevating in this view, no notion of Baudelaire's beautiful melancholy, or of a great, transformative longing at the heart of human nature (and in the hearts of some humans in particular). There's also little awareness that, as we'll continue to explore, these states are some of the great catalysts of human creativity, spirituality, and love. Many psychologists are not religious themselves, so it doesn't occur to them to look for spiritual answers to humanity's greatest mysteries.

Recently, though, positive psychology has begun to make room for the bittersweet. Psychologists such as Dr. Paul Wong, the president of Toronto's Meaning-Centered Counselling Institute, and University of East London lecturer Tim Lomas have documented the emergence of a "second wave" that, as Lomas says, "recognizes that well-being actually involves a subtle, dialectical interplay between positive and negative phenomena." And, through his influential book **Transcend,** cognitive psychologist Scott Barry Kaufman is reviving Maslow's original concept of positive psychology, which recognized a bittersweet personality style Maslow called "transcenders": people who "are less 'happy' than the [conventionally] healthy ones. They can be more ecstatic, more rapturous, and experience greater heights of 'happiness,' but they are as prone—or maybe more prone—to a kind of cosmic sadness."

All of which bodes well for our ability, as individuals and as a culture, to realize the transformative potential of Keltner's work. If we could honor sadness a little more, maybe we could see **it**—rather than enforced smiles and righteous outrage—as the bridge we need to connect with each other. We could remember that no matter how distasteful we might find someone's opinions, no matter how radiant, or fierce, someone may appear, they have suffered, or they will.

. . .

Keltner, and the Greater Good Science Center that he co-founded, have developed many science-tested practices that can help us do exactly this.

An important first step is to cultivate humility. We know from various studies that attitudes of superiority prevent us from reacting to others' sadness—and even to our own. "Your vagus nerve won't fire when you see a child who's starving," says Keltner, "if you think you're better than other people." Amazingly, high-ranking people (including those artificially given high status, in a lab setting) are more likely to ignore pedestrians and to cut off other drivers, and are less helpful to their colleagues and to others in need. They're less likely to experience physical and emotional pain when holding their own hands under scalding water, when excluded from a game, or when witnessing the suffering of others. They're even more likely to take more than their fair share of candy handed out by the lab staff!

How then to achieve humility (especially if you find yourself in a relatively fortunate socio-economic position)? One answer is to practice the simple act of bowing down, as the Japanese do in everyday social life, and as many religious people do before God. This gesture actually activates the vagus nerve, according to Keltner. "People are starting to think about the mind-body interface in these acts of reverence," he explained in a 2016 Silicon Valley talk.

Of course, many Americans are irreligious, or uncomfortable with expressions of submission, or both. But we can think of these gestures as devotion rather than capitulation. Indeed, many of us practice yoga, which often includes a bowing element; and when we behold an awe-inspiring work of art, or vista in nature, we instinctively lower our heads.

We can also take to our keyboards. The social psychologist and Leavey School of Business management professor Dr. Hooria Jazaieri suggests a writing exercise in which we describe a time when someone showed us compassion, or we felt it for someone else. If formal writing doesn't appeal to us, we can try keeping a simple log of when we feel more or less engaged with the sadness of others. "Collect your own data," advises Jazaieri on the Greater Good Science Center website. "For example, you could notice when compassion comes easily or spontaneously for you throughout the day (e.g., watching the evening news). You could notice when you resist acknowledging or being with suffering (your own or others') throughout the day (e.g., when passing someone on the street who is asking for money or an extended family member who is challenging). . . . We often notice suffering (our own and that of others) but quickly dismiss it and thus do not allow ourselves to be emotionally touched or moved by the suffering."

But perhaps none of this is possible without first cultivating **self**-compassion. This may sound like the opposite of what you'd do to encourage humility. But many of us engage, without even realizing it, in a constant stream of negative self-talk: "You're terrible at this." "Why did you screw that up?" But, as Jazaieri observes, "There's no empirical evidence to suggest that beating ourselves up will actually help us change our behavior; in fact, some data suggests that this type of criticism can move us **away** from our goals rather than towards them."

Conversely, the more gently we speak to ourselves, the more we'll do the same for others. So the next time you hear that harsh internal voice, pause, take a breath—and try again. Speak to yourself with the same tenderness you'd extend to a beloved child—literally using the same terms of endearment and amount of reassurance that you'd shower on an adorable three-year-old. If this strikes you as hopelessly self-indulgent, remember that you're not babying yourself, or letting yourself off the hook. You're taking care of yourself, so that your self can go forth and care for others.

. . .

Keltner—the psychologist-phenom with the golden locks, surfer aura, and sad eyes, who'd worked with Pete Docter and his band of Pixar filmmakers—has had plenty of cause to practice his own self-compassion. When I caught up with him recently, his youngest daughter had just left for college, leaving his home too quiet and empty. His mother was lonely, depressed, and had a heart condition. And Rolf, his adored younger brother, had died of colon cancer, at age fifty-six, after a long struggle with the disease.

Keltner was reeling, and suffering a profound sense of rootlessness. He felt as if he were missing part of his soul. "There's no doubt my life will be full of sadness for however many more decades I get," he told me. "I'm not sure I'll get a sense of place and community in this life."

I knew how much he loved his brother, but I was surprised anyway when he put it like that. Keltner runs one of the most influential labs in one of academia's most meaningful fields. He's a popular professor at one of the most vibrant universities in the world. He has a wife of thirty years and two grown daughters and countless friends he loves. If **he** didn't have a sense of place and community, then who would?

But Keltner also knew that sadness gives rise to compassion—for others, and for oneself. Throughout his brother's illness and death, he'd followed the practices he'd always known. Inspired by Rolf's natural kindness, he'd long volunteered with convicted criminals at nearby San Quentin prison. "I become most clear when I'm engaged in suffering," he explains. "Sadness is like a meditation on compassion. You have this burst of: There's harm there, there's need there. Then I leave the prison. I think about my brother, and it's like a meditative state. I've always felt that way about the human condition. I'm not a tragic person. I'm hopeful. But I think sadness is beautiful and sadness is wise."

During Rolf's last month, Keltner also performed a daily exercise of gratitude toward his brother: "the things he's done, the gleam in his eye, the funny tenderness he shows to underdogs." He thought about him as he walked across campus, as he decided which research studies to pursue; he saw how all the work he's done and will likely ever do traces back to his kid brother, whose loss will always cause him pain even as it deepens the same well of compassion from which his brother taught him to draw, back when they were kids.

"Him being gone, I've just got all these parts of how I see the world extracted out of me," he told me now. "But they're still there."

I asked Keltner whether the part of him that's drawn to awe, wonder, and connection is separate from or intertwined with the sad part. "That question gives me goosebumps," he replied. "They're intertwined."

Eventually, Keltner started to realize that, after the implosion of his childhood family, he'd never **allowed** himself to feel at home. But maybe it was time to start. Every year at the Berkeley graduation ceremony, he'd instinctively scanned the crowd for the kids who looked lost, the way he once was, the kids floating on their own without a family, who would see their classmates gathered at the picnic tables with a cheerful collection of relatives and wonder why their family couldn't do that, too.

But he'd been at Berkeley since he was thirty-four; he was fifty-seven now; he wasn't one of those kids anymore. And he knew that those students, too, those refugees from broken families, wouldn't be kids forever, either. They would go out into the world the way he once did; they would do their work and have their adventures; they would live in the shadow of their losses and in the light of new loves; and maybe they'd repeat their childhood family patterns and maybe they wouldn't; but all of them would be touched by the people they'd loved most, and all of them would have the capacity, just like Keltner, who learned it from his younger brother, to walk the bridge of sadness, and find the joy of communion waiting on the other side. Just like Keltner, they would make their way home.

CHAPTER 2

Why do we long for "perfect" and unconditional love? (And what does this have to do with our love of sad songs, rainy days, and even the divine?)

> The sweetest thing in all my life has been the longing—to reach the Mountain, to find the place where all the beauty came from—my country, the place where I ought to have been born.
>
> —C. S. LEWIS

An elegant Italian woman, worldly, sophisticated. Francesca. At the end of World War II, she meets and marries an American soldier, moves with him to his small Iowan farm town of good people who bring carrot cakes to their neighbors, look after the elderly, and ostracize those who flout norms by, say, committing adultery. Her husband is kind, devoted, and limited. She loves her children.

One day her family leaves town for a week, to show their pigs at a state fair. She's alone in the farmhouse for the first time in her married life. She relishes her solitude. Until a photographer for **National Geographic** knocks on the door, asking directions to a nearby landmark . . . and they fall into a passionate, four-day affair. He begs her to run away with him; she packs her bags.

Until, at the last minute, she unpacks them.

Partly because she's married, and she has children, and the town's eyes are on them all.

But also because she knows that she and the photographer have already taken each other to the perfect and beautiful world. And that now it's time to descend to the actual one. If they try to live in that other world for good, it will recede into the distance; it will be as if they'd never been there at all. She says goodbye, and they long for each other for the rest of their lives.

Yet Francesca is quietly sustained by their encounter, the photographer creatively renewed. On his deathbed years later, he sends her a book of images he made, commemorating their four days together.

If this story sounds familiar, it's because it comes from **The Bridges of Madison County,** a 1992 novel by Robert James Waller that sold more than twelve million copies, and a 1995 movie, starring Meryl

Streep and Clint Eastwood, that grossed $182 million. The press attributed its popularity to a rash of women trapped in unhappy marriages and pining for handsome photographers.

But that's not what the story was really about.

...

In the frenzy after the book came out, there were two camps: one that loved it because the couple's love was pure and endured over the decades. The other camp saw this as a cop-out—that real love is working through the challenges of an actual relationship.

Which was right? Should we learn to let go of the dream of fairy-tale love, and to fully embrace the imperfect loves we know? Or should we believe Aristophanes, as told in Plato's **Symposium:** that once we were all conjoined souls, two people in a single body, so ecstatic and powerful in our oneness that we aroused the fear of the Titans, who made Zeus break us apart; and now we naturally devote our lives, as author Jean Houston puts it, to yearning for our missing half?

As a citizen of the contemporary world of practicality, you know the right answer to such questions: Of course, you have no missing half. There's no such thing as a soul mate. One person can't satisfy all your needs. The desire for boundaryless, effortless, endless fulfillment will not only disappoint: It's neurotic, immature. You should grow up, get over it.

But another view has existed for centuries, one that we rarely hear. It suggests that our longing for "perfect" love is normal and desirable; that the wish to merge with a beloved of the soul is the deepest desire of the human heart; that longing is the road to belonging. **And it's not just about romantic love:** We're visited by this same yearning when we hear "Ode to Joy" or behold Victoria Falls or kneel on a prayer mat. And, therefore, the proper attitude toward novels about transformative four-day romances with **National Geographic** photographers is not to dismiss them as sentimental nonsense, but to see them for what they really are: equal to, no different from, the music, the waterfall, and the prayer. Longing itself is a creative and spiritual state.

And yet, the case for renouncing Plato is very strong.

. . .

In 2016, the erudite and prolific Swiss-born writer-philosopher Alain de Botton published an essay in **The New York Times** called "Why You Will Marry the Wrong Person." It was the most widely read op-ed of the year, and it argued that we, and our marriages, would be better off if we'd renounce the Romantic idea that, as De Botton put it, "a perfect being exists who can meet all our needs and satisfy our every yearning."

De Botton followed this with a series of seminars

offered by his organization, the School of Life, which is headquartered in a London storefront and operates across the world, from Sydney to Los Angeles, where I sit now at the Ebell Theater alongside three hundred classmates. De Botton's class is grounded in the idea that "one of the gravest errors we make around relationships is to imagine that they aren't things we can get wiser or better at." This means that we should stop longing for the unconditional love of our missing half; we should come to terms with our partners' imperfections and focus instead on fixing ourselves.

Alain is tall and professorial and speaks in the plummiest of Oxbridge accents. He's breathtakingly fluent and witty, and he reads the room with the sensitivity of a psychoanalyst, noticing when someone's too uncomfortable to complete an exercise he's set them, lending encouragement in just the right dose when someone makes a halting confession of feeling like a "selfish bitch" because she left her husband. Despite the impeccable performance, his posture is a bit bendy, as if he feels unentitled to be so tall. He refers to himself jokingly as a "bald weirdo trying to teach others things he doesn't reliably know himself." Alain has written on the wisdom of melancholy, and just as the Bittersweet Quiz would predict, his favorite word seems to be **poignant.** To him, it's poignant that we tend to choose lovers who have the same difficult traits that our parents had. It's poignant that we get cross with people when really we're anxious that we don't matter to them enough. And a Ferrari owner is not shallow and greedy, but animated by a poignant need for love.

"Does anyone here think they're easy to live with?" Alain asks, the first order of business being to see our own faults.

A few hands go up.

"This is **very** dangerous," he says cheerfully. "I don't know you, but I know you're not easy to live with. If you insist on believing that you are, you won't live with anyone! We've got some mics and some lovely honest people and no social media; let's hear all the ways you're difficult to live with."

The hands go up:

"I'm moody and loud."

"I overanalyze everything."

"I'm messy and I have music on all the time."

"You've been warned, everyone!" cries Alain. "You could build a pile to the ceiling with all your difficulties. But we forget this when dating. There is a traditional trope of laughing at how badly our dates go. We think: 'I'm a still circle of perfection in a sea of madness.'

"Who in this room wants to be loved for who they are?" he continues. "Put your hand up if you want to be loved for who you are."

The hands raise again.

"Oh, my goodness," chides Alain. "We have work to do still. Have you not been listening to **anything** I've been saying? How can you possibly be loved for who you are? You're a deeply flawed human being! Why would anyone love you just as you are? You've got to grow, and you've got to develop!"

These lessons are punctuated with short films illustrating couples in various forms of mutual incomprehension. The couples (or the people they're secretly fantasizing about) tend to be comprised of thoughtful young men reading novels on park benches, or sweet-faced women in cardigans about to board a train: bittersweet types. Melancholic piano music plays in the background. The School of Life students, who seem a mix of freelance designers, soulful engineers, and unemployed seekers, look a lot like these couples: earnest, courteous, reasonably but not intimidatingly up-to-date in their fashion choices. Alain's own pants are from the Gap, he mentions from the stage.

Then, the reminder that we have no missing half. "Here's a little bit of darkness," he warns. "We need to accept that there **is** no partner who would understand the whole of us, who will share all of our tastes in large and small areas. Ultimately, it is always a percentage of compatibility we will only ever achieve. Let's go back to Plato and kill, once and for all, as a group, his charming, but insane, love-destroying piece of naivety. WE HAVE NO SOUL MATE."

In fact, says Alain, it's the fantasy of the missing half that prevents us from appreciating the partners we do have; we're forever comparing their flawed selves to "the amazing things we imagine about strangers, especially in libraries and trains." He demonstrates this problem with an exercise called "The Anti-Romantic Daydream," in which we're taught to imagine the deficits of attractive strangers. We're shown four images of potential mates, two men and two women.

"Pick the person of the four who most appeals to you," instructs Alain. "Imagine in detail five ways in which they might turn out to be very challenging after three years together. Look deep into their eyes."

One audience member, a young man with stylish glasses and a charming Irish accent, picks a photo of a woman in a red headscarf with a wistful expression on her face. "She has exactly the same look my dog has when I leave him, so she may be quite needy."

A blonde in a paisley dress chooses a photo of a slender young woman in a library. "She might be a book reader," my classmate offers. "But whatever she reads, you have to also. And you have to validate all her choices."

A woman says about a prosperous-looking man in a suit and tie: "I was attracted to his beautiful hair, but it turns out he's quite vain, and when I run my hands through it, he says: 'Don't touch my hair.'"

. . .

Alain is brilliant, I think, not for the first time (I've admired his work for decades): a droll and insightful author and speaker, and now he can save marriages, too. But even as we apply his insights to our love lives, there remains the question of Francesca's longing—of **our** longing. What should we do about it? What does it even mean?

The bittersweet tradition has much to say about these questions. It teaches that yearning flourishes in the realm of romantic love—**but it doesn't derive from it.** Rather, the yearning comes first, and exists on its own; romantic love is just one expression of it. It happens to be the manifestation that preoccupies our culture. But our longing shows up in myriad ways—including the way that I've been wondering about all my life: the riddle of why so many of us love sad music.

My favorite YouTube video shows a two-year-old boy, with round cheeks and blond hair so fine you can see the pink of his scalp, hearing "Moonlight Sonata" for the first time. He's attending a piano recital, and the young player off-screen is doing her best with the Beethoven. You can tell that the two-year-old knows this is a solemn occasion and he's supposed to be quiet. But he's so moved by the haunting melody that his whole face strains with the doomed effort not to cry. He lets loose a whimper, and then the tears stream silently down his cheeks. There's something profound, almost sacred, in his reaction to the music.

The video went viral, with the many commenters trying to figure out the meaning of the boy's tears. The occasional snarky comment aside ("I'd cry too listening to all those wrong notes"), most people seemed to sense that the best of humanity, and its deepest questions, lay written like a secret code in the boy's sorrow.

Is **sorrow** even the right word? Some commenters spoke of the boy's sensitivity, some of his empathy; others spoke of rapture. One marveled at his reaction to "the paradoxical and mysterious mix of intense joy and sadness" in the music: "Such things have made the lives of generations of people worthwhile."

This idea seemed, to me, closest to the mark. But what is it, exactly, that makes bittersweet music like "Moonlight Sonata" so exalting? How can the same stimulus speak simultaneously of joy and sorrow, love and loss—**and why are we so keen to listen**?

It turns out that lots of people feel the way this child (and I) do. Sad music is much more likely than happy to elicit what the neuroscientist Jaak Panksepp called that "shivery, gooseflesh type of skin sensation" otherwise known as "chills." People whose favorite songs are happy listen to them about 175 times on average. But those who favor "bittersweet" songs listen almost 800 times, according to a study by University of Michigan professors Fred Conrad and Jason Corey, and they report a "deeper connection" to the music than those whose favorites made them happy. They tell researchers that they associate sad songs with profound beauty, deep connection, transcendence, nostalgia, and common humanity—the so-called sublime emotions.

Think how many beloved musical genres tap into longing and melancholy: Portuguese fado, Spanish flamenco, Algerian raï, the Irish lament, the American blues. Even pop music is increasingly written in the minor key—about 60 percent of songs today, compared with only 15 percent in the 1960s, according to researchers E. Glenn Schellenberg and Christian von Scheve. Many of Bach's and Mozart's best-known pieces were also written in a minor key—the keys of "joyous melancholy," as one musician describes them.* In one of America's favorite lullabies, "Rock-a-Bye Baby," an infant falls from a cradle; an Arabic lullaby sings of life as a stranger with "no friends in this world." The Spanish poet Federico García Lorca collected many of his country's lullabies and concluded that Spain uses its "saddest melodies and most melancholy texts to tinge her children's first slumber."

This phenomenon extends to other aesthetic forms, too. So many of us love tragic drama, rainy days, tearjerker movies. We adore cherry blossoms—we even hold festivals in their honor—preferring them to equally lovely flowers **because** they die young. (The Japanese, who love **sakura** flowers most of all, attribute this preference to **mono no aware,** which

---

* A musicologist in 1806 described the key of C minor as a "declaration of love and at the same time the lament of unhappy love. All languishing, longing, sighing of the lovesick soul lies in this key." (In contrast, the key of C major is "completely pure. Its character is: innocence, simplicity, naivety, children's talk.")

means a desired state of gentle sorrow brought about by "the pathos of things" and "a sensitivity to impermanence").

Philosophers call this the "paradox of tragedy," and they've puzzled over it for centuries. Why do we sometimes welcome sorrow, when the rest of the time we'll do anything to avoid it? Now psychologists and neuroscientists are considering the question, too, and they've advanced various theories: A moonlit sonata can be therapeutic for people experiencing loss or depression; it can help us to accept negative emotions rather than ignoring or repressing them; it can show us that we're not alone in our sorrows.

One of the more compelling explanations comes from a recent study by researchers at the University of Jyväskylä in Finland, who found that of all the variables influencing whether a person is likely to be moved by sad music, the strongest is empathy. In this study, 102 people listened to sad music from the **Band of Brothers** soundtrack. Those who reacted to the music the way the toddler did to his sister's recital tended to be high in empathy, "sensitivity to social contagion," and other-focused "fantasy"—in other words, they looked at the world through other people's eyes. They had the ability to lose themselves in fictional characters in books and movies, and they responded to others' troubles with compassion, rather than with personal discomfort or anxiety. For them, sad music was likely a form of communion.

Another longstanding explanation, dating back to Aristotle, is catharsis: Perhaps watching Oedipus gouge out his eyes on an Athenian stage helped the Greeks to release their own emotional entanglements. More recently, neuroscientists Matthew Sachs and Antonio Damasio, along with psychologist Assal Habibi, reviewed the entire research literature on sad music, and posited that yearning melodies help our bodies to achieve homeostasis—a state in which our emotions and physiologies function within optimal range. Studies even show that babies in intensive care units who listen to (often mournful) lullabies have stronger breathing, feeding patterns, and heart rates than infants hearing other kinds of music!

Yet the moonlight sonatas of the world don't simply discharge our emotions; they **elevate** them. Also, it's only sad music that elicits exalted states of communion and awe. Music conveying other negative emotions, such as fear and anger, produces no such effect. Even happy music produces fewer psychological rewards than sad music, concluded Sachs, Damasio, and Habibi. Upbeat tunes make us want to dance around our kitchens and invite friends for dinner. But it's sad music that makes us want to touch the sky.

. . .

But I believe that the grand unifying theory that explains the paradox of tragedy is (like most such theories) deceptively simple: We don't actually welcome tragedy per se. What we like are sad **and** beautiful things—the bitter together with the sweet. We don't thrill to lists of sad words, for example, or slide shows of sad faces (researchers have actually tested this). What we love is elegiac poetry, seaside cities shrouded in fog, spires reaching through the clouds. In other words: **We like art forms that express our longing for union, and for a more perfect and beautiful world.** When we feel strangely thrilled by the sorrow of "Moonlight Sonata," it's the yearning for love that we're experiencing—fragile, fleeting, evanescent, precious, transcendent love.

The idea of longing as a sacred and generative force seems very odd in our culture of normative sunshine. But it's traveled the world for centuries, under many different names, taking many different forms. Writers and artists, mystics and philosophers, have long tried to give voice to it. García Lorca called it the "mysterious power which everyone senses and no philosopher explains."

The ancient Greeks called it **pothos,** which Plato defined as a yearning desire for something wonderful that we can't have. **Pothos** was our thirst for everything good and beautiful. Humans were lowly beings imprisoned in matter, inspired by **pothos** to reach for a higher reality. The concept was associated with both love and death; in Greek myth, Pothos (Longing) was the brother of Himeros (Desire) and the son of Eros (Love). But because **pothos** had that quality of aching for the unattainable, the word was also used to describe the flowers placed on Grecian tombs. The state of longing strikes contemporary ears as passive, gloomy, and helpless, but **pothos** was understood to be an activating force. The young Alexander the Great described himself as "seized by **pothos**" as he sat on a riverbank and gazed into the distance; it was **pothos** that set Homer's Odyssey in motion, with the shipwrecked Odysseus longing for home.

The author C. S. Lewis called it the "inconsolable longing" for we know not what, or **Sehnsucht,** a German term based on the words **das Sehnen** ("the yearning") and **sucht** ("an obsession or addiction"). **Sehnsucht** was the animating force of Lewis's life and career. It was "that unnameable something, desire for which pierces us like a rapier at the smell of bonfire, the sound of wild ducks flying overhead, the title of **The Well at the World's End,** the opening lines of 'Kubla Khan,' the morning cobwebs in late summer, or the noise of falling waves." He'd felt it first as a young boy, when his brother brought him a toy garden in the form of an old biscuit tin filled with moss and flowers, and he was overcome by a joyous ache he couldn't understand, though he would try for the rest of his life to put it into words, to find its source, to seek the company of kindred spirits who'd known the same wondrous "stabs of joy."

Others describe this longing as the answer to a

cosmic mystery. "I feel that the secret of life, love, death, life's paths taken or not taken—the Universe itself—is somehow embraced in its achingly beautiful promise," writes the artist Peter Lucia of **Sehnsucht.** My favorite musician, Leonard Cohen, said that **his** favorite poet, García Lorca, taught him that he was "this aching creature in the midst of an aching cosmos, and the ache was okay. Not only was it okay, but it was the way that you embraced the sun and the moon."

As we saw with Francesca and her **National Geographic** photographer, longing often shows up in the form of carnal love. In this extraordinary passage, the novelist Mark Merlis describes the mysterious pain that comes from meeting someone irresistible:

Do you know how sometimes you see a man, and you're not sure if you want to get in his pants or if you want to cry? Not because you can't have him; maybe you can. But you see right away something in him beyond having. You can't screw your way into it, any more than you can get at the golden eggs by slitting the goose. So you want to cry, not like a child, but like an exile who is reminded of his homeland. That's what Leucon saw when he first beheld Pyrrhus: as if he were getting a glimpse of that other place we were meant to be, the shore from which we were deported before we were born.

Longing is also the ultimate muse. "My artistic life," says songwriter-poet Nick Cave, "has centered around the desire or, more accurately, need to articulate the feelings of loss and longing that have whistled through my bones and hummed in my blood." The pianist and singer Nina Simone was called the "high priestess of soul" because her music was full of longing for justice and love. The Spanish call it **duende:** the yearning, burning center of flamenco dance and other art forms of the inflamed heart. Portuguese speakers have the concept of **saudade,** a sweetly piercing nostalgia, often expressed musically, for something deeply cherished, long gone, that may never have existed in the first place. In Hinduism, **viraha**—the pain of separation, usually from the beloved—is said to be the source of all poetry and music. Hindu legend says that Valmiki, the world's first poet, was moved to verse after watching a bird weeping for her mate, who'd been making love to her when he was killed by a hunter. "Longing itself is divine," writes the Hindu spiritual leader Sri Sri Ravi Shankar. "Longing for worldly things makes you inert. Longing for Infinity fills you with life. The skill is to bear the pain of longing and move on. True longing brings up spurts of bliss."

At the heart of all these traditions is this pain of separation, the longing for reunion, and, occasionally, the transcendent achievement of it. But separation from what, exactly? From our soul mates, the location of whom is one of our great life tasks, the Platonic tradition suggests. From the womb, if you take a psychoanalytic view. From comfort in our own skin, usually because of some past hurt or trauma we're struggling to heal. Or, perhaps, all of these are just metaphors for, or different expressions of, separation from the divine. Separation, longing, and reunion are the beating heart of most religions. We long for Eden, for Zion, for Mecca; and we long for the Beloved, which is the beautiful way the Sufis refer to God.

. . .

I met my dear friend Tara, who grew up in a Sufi meetinghouse in Toronto, when I attended a talk she gave on meaning and transcendence. Tara has a bell-like voice and kind eyes that tilt downward. Italian painters used to paint the Madonna with eyes like hers, to signify empathy; it was the friendship version of love at first sight.

I didn't know much about Sufism at the time—just a vague sense that it was the mystical branch of Islam. Onstage that night, Tara described how she'd grown up at the meetinghouse, serving Persian tea to the elders, who came twice a week to meditate and share stories. Their practice also involved service through acts of love. Later, Tara and her parents moved from Toronto to the United States, the land of success and positivity. At first, she embraced her new world: In college she was president of this and editor in chief of that; she thirsted for the perfect grades, career, boyfriend, apartment. But without Sufism in her daily life, she started to feel unmoored, thrust into what became a lifelong quest for meaning.

She gave her talk at a small auditorium, and afterward there was wine, hors d'oeuvres, and conversation. I asked Tara's father, Edward, a white-bearded homebuilder, whether he knew the Yiddish word **kvelling.** It means "bursting with pride and joy for someone you love," I explained, "especially a child." It was the first time that Tara had given a talk, and I was referring to how he must feel about her newly public role. I expected him to say, "Yes, that's it, that's exactly it." But instead he said that it was a joyful experience, but also a melancholic one: "She's out from under my wing. I'm not the one telling her stories anymore. Now she's telling them to me, and to a whole audience."

I was struck by how quickly and openly he talked about his empty-nest feelings, how close to the surface these longings were for him—and how rarely we admit such emotions over cocktails. But there's something about Edward that makes you feel that you could share these kinds of observations, even though you've only just met. So I did.

"Longing is what Sufism is all about," he exclaimed, lighting up. "The whole practice is based on longing—longing for union, longing for God, longing for the Source. You meditate, practice loving-kindness, serve others, because you want to go home." The most famous Sufi poem, he said, **The Masnavi,** written by the thirteenth-century scholar Jalal al-Din Rumi, is all about longing: "Listen to the story told by the reed," it begins, "of being separated. . . . Anyone pulled from a source longs to go back."

Edward told me the story of how he met Tara's mother, Afra, at a Sufi gathering in Toronto. He was American born, without much religion, and had stumbled across Rumi's poetry serendipitously. Afra had grown up Muslim, in Iran, but had never met a Sufi until she moved to Canada at nineteen. She walked into the gathering and sat next to Edward, and he knew instantly that he'd marry her. But she lived in Toronto, he in Chicago. When they said goodbye, he told her that when he got home, he'd send her his favorite English translation of Rumi's poetry. He started to visit on weekends, and eventually met and came to love her two-year-old daughter, Tara, too.

"I've never felt such longing as I did in those days," he told me. "I was in Chicago and would stare in the direction of Toronto. I would go to see them by train. It got so hard to say goodbye that I had to stop taking the train. I drove. The train was too painful. When you talk about longing, it's so huge, I don't know where it stops. Home isn't a place. Home is where that longing is, and you don't feel good

until you're there. In the end, it's one big yearning.
In Sufism, they call it the pain. In Sufism, they call
it the cure."

By the following May, they were married, and
Edward adopted Tara. Two years later, Edward
and Afra were running the meetinghouse together,
and Tara was growing up in an atmosphere of service and love that she would try to reclaim for the
rest of her life.

At the time of this conversation, I was just as agnostic as ever, but I was also deep into the writing
of this book, and something was opening up in me.
I was starting to understand—not only intellectually, but also viscerally—what the religious impulse
was. I was losing my lifelong dismissiveness of it.
The intense and transformative reaction that I had to
minor-key music was apprehension of the transcendent, I was realizing; it was transformation of the
consciousness. It wasn't belief in God, exactly, or at
least not the specific God of the ancient books. But
it was the spiritual instinct come alive.

I was also beginning to perceive that music is only
one of many manifestations of this instinct, that it
was there equally—for example—in the moment
Edward met Afra. The music is an expression of
that which we long for, but what is "that"? We can
say "½" or "0.5" or "one-half," and these are all expressions of the same thing, but what is the thing
itself? The fractions, decimals, and words describe
the essence of a mathematical concept that remains

just as ineffable after we express it. Every flower we arrange in a vase, every painting we hang just so in the art museum, every newly dug grave over which we weep, are all expressions of the same elusive yet wondrous thing.

. . .

Soon after meeting Tara and her parents, the feelings of sweet sorrow that I've known all my life reached a crescendo. One evening, I googled the words **longing** and **Sufism.** This called up a YouTube video featuring the lilting, Welsh-accented voice of a Sufi teacher named Dr. Llewellyn Vaughan-Lee, set against soaring images of Burmese temples and the Sydney skyline, Brazilian favelas and a Japanese geisha with a single tear running down her white-painted cheek. The video was called "The Pain of Separation," and Vaughan-Lee (or LVL, as I'll call him) was talking about longing. "It's time to go home," he said. "It's time to go back to where you belong. It's time to discover what you really are."

Sufism is practiced in many forms and by many types of people all over the world, many of them Muslim, some not. All religions have their mystical branches, meaning those who seek a direct and intense communion with the divine, outside of traditional rituals and doctrines. Conventional religious leaders sometimes dismiss mystics as woolly-headed or heretical or both—perhaps fearing that anyone who bypasses religious institutions and heads straight to God could put them out of business. Since 2016, the Islamic State has killed many Sufi worshippers in mass executions.

Fortunately, most mystics, like LVL, a U.S.-based teacher, practice undisturbed, and I soon encountered him all over the Internet. Here he was, telling Oprah that we long for the Beloved but the Beloved also longs for us, and there was Oprah, looking like she might jump out of her chair with recognition. Here he was in 2016, giving a talk on "Separation and Union," and there he was, a few years later, warning of a coming spiritual darkness in the world. Always he spoke with an utter lack of desire for the spotlight. He always appeared the same, dressed in white, untouched by time. A soft-spoken, unostentatiously handsome man in round, wire-rimmed spectacles, speaking of the pain of the heart. Speaking of love.

"Longing is the sweet pain of belonging to God," he writes. "Once longing is awakened within the heart it is the most direct way Home. Like the magnet, it draws us deep within our own heart where we are made whole and transformed. This is why the Sufi mystics have always stressed the importance of longing. The great Sufi Ibn Arabi prayed, 'Oh Lord, nourish me not with love but with the desire for love,' while Rumi expressed the same truth in simple terms, 'Do not seek for water, be thirsty.'"

He also recasts the pain of separation as a spiritual opening rather than a psychological event: "If we follow the path of any pain, any psychological wounding," he writes, "it will lead us to this one primal pain: the pain of separation. Being born into this world, we . . . are banished from paradise and carry the scars of this separation. But if we embrace the suffering, if we allow it to lead us deep within ourselves, it will take us deeper than any psychological healing."

Often he quotes Rumi, who left behind reams of ecstatic poetry and who today is the bestselling poet in the United States (though some dispute the accuracy of the most popular English translations). Rumi had famously adored his friend and teacher Shams al-Din of Tabriz; when Shams disappeared (possibly murdered by Rumi's jealous students), Rumi was almost destroyed by grief. But as his heart broke open, the poetry poured out of him. And from all these poems (and indeed from all of Sufism, and from all the world's mystic traditions)* came the central

---

* At the heart of mysticism is the idea that God's absence is not so much a test of faith as the road to divine love; longing brings you closer to that for which you long. For the sixteenth-century Christian mystic Saint Teresa of Avila, God "wounds the soul," but "the soul longs to die of this beautiful wound." The sixteenth-century Hindu mystic Mirabai wrote poetry about "send[ing] letters to [her] Beloved, / The dear Krishna," even though "He sends no message of reply." The modern mystic George Harrison wrote about longing in his iconic song "My Sweet Lord": "I really want to see you / Really want to be with you / Really want to see you, Lord / But it takes so long, my Lord."

insight that "Longing is the core of the mystery / Longing itself brings the cure."

One of Rumi's poems resonated in particular with my agnostic, skeptical self. It's called "Love Dogs," and it describes a man calling for Allah, until a cynic asks why he bothers: "I have heard you calling out, but have you ever gotten any response?"

The man is shaken; he falls asleep and dreams of meeting Khidr, the guide of souls, who asks why he stopped praying.

"Because I never heard an answer back," says the man. Maybe it was a waste of time, maybe he was calling into the void.

But Khidr tells him:

This longing you express
is the return message.

The grief you cry out from
draws you toward union.

Your pure sadness
that wants help
is the secret cup.

Listen to the moan of a dog for its master.
That whining is the connection.

There are love dogs
no one knows the names of.

Give your life
to be one of them.

I saw myself in the cynic, but also in the man who dreams of meeting Khidr. If the poem spoke to me so profoundly, I thought, maybe LVL would do the same; I wanted to meet him in person. Also, I had a consuming question that I thought he could answer. I'd been reading about Buddhism as well as Sufism, and many of its teachings seemed to contradict the Sufi idea that longing is spiritually valuable. Buddhism starts with the observation that life is suffering (or, depending on your interpretation of the Sanskrit word **dukkha,** dissatisfaction). The cause of suffering is our attachment to craving (for wealth, status, possessive love, and so on) and to aversion (for example, to hurt feelings, discomfort, pain). Freedom (or nirvana) comes from extinguishing attachment, a process aided by practices such as mindfulness and loving-kindness meditation. In this nonattached ideal, longing seems a highly problematic condition. As one Buddhist website put it, "After a lot of training with the Buddha's teachings, we tend to recognize longing as an unproductive mindstate and just move on from it to whatever is actually present."

How to square this view with Sufi poetry? Were Rumi and Buddha offering contradictory teachings? Was longing in Sufism different from what Buddhists call craving? I was, at best, a casual student of both traditions. But I felt I needed to know.

I found out that LVL ran an organization called the Golden Sufi Center, and he was holding a retreat in Burlingame, California, called "Journey of the Soul." Before long, I'd booked a flight across the country.

. . .

The retreat is held at the thirty-nine-acre home to the Sisters of Mercy, a Catholic convent adorned with stained glass windows and sober-hued paintings of Jesus and Mary. I'm housed in a thin rectangle of a private room fit for a nun. It's scrupulously clean, a little stuffy, with sensible gray carpet, a wooden desk, and an institutional sink affixed to a bare wall. I want to change out of my airplane clothes, but everything in my bag is wrinkled and there's no iron in the minuscule closet. Is my sundress too creased to wear in public? The only mirror is the size of the rearview one in my car, and it's hanging high above the sink. **Maybe I can see how I look if I stand on this stool?** But the stool turns out to be a rocking chair and I catapult to the floor, landing on all fours on the coarse carpeting. I give up and wear the wrinkled dress.

I make my way to a large and airy hall where we're to gather—about three hundred of us. I'm early, but there are very few seats left. Rows of chairs are jammed together, as on a discount airline, and I take an empty seat smooshed between two women. We're packed so close that it's hard, even sitting still, not to touch each other, or to see the modest stage, where LVL sits, low to the ground and flanked by Japanese screens and vases of flowers. Most sit with eyes closed, and no one's talking, even though the retreat won't start for another fifteen minutes.

But LVL's eyes are open. He sits in an armchair, regarding us peacefully, stroking his salt-and-pepper beard. Those same round, wire-rimmed glasses, the same expression of gentle intelligence, the same white clothes I've seen in all his videos. The atmosphere in the room is quiet yet charged.

When LVL finally speaks, it's of many things, but especially of what Sufis call "the journey." This, he says, is his deepest interest, and really there are three of them. The first journey is **from** God—the journey where you forget that you ever had a divine union in the first place. (This, I suppose, is where I've been until recently.) The second, of remembrance, is the moment of grace in which "you begin to look for the light. You look for prayers and practices to help you. In the West, this is known as spiritual life. Many techniques have come from East to West to help you connect with soul. Every human has his own way of prayer and glorification. And you need to find a spiritual teacher." The final journey is **in** God—you're taken "deeper and deeper into the divine mystery."

To make this journey, says LVL, you need an energy or power source; you don't have enough on your own. In Taoism, he says, you could cultivate Chi, the life force, or be attuned to the Tao, the primal energy of the universe; in Buddhism, the energy of pure consciousness. And Sufis use the energy of love, "the greatest power in creation."

When he speaks of love, I think of Afra, who comes across as brisk, competent, and practical. But growing up in Iran, though she'd been familiar with the Sufi idea that all of creation is about love, she hadn't known that Sufism was still actively practiced. "I wanted to experience what Rumi did, what Hafiz did," she'd told me dreamily, referring to the great Sufi poets of love and longing. "I felt they were so lucky. They were born during that time, and I had no access to it."

This is part of what drew me here, too, even though I'm constitutionally wary of gurus. LVL sometimes speaks of his devotion to his own teacher, Irina Tweedie, invoking a Sufi saying that "the disciple has to become less than dust at the feet of the teacher." I'm pretty sure he's talking about the teacher's role in helping the student achieve the crucial spiritual task of extinguishing the ego. But I don't like the idea of surrendering authority to a fellow fallible human.

Still: Watching his videos, I've felt this love for LVL, even though he says it can't transmit over the Internet. I start wondering if he could be my teacher; maybe I can get past my guru aversion, maybe I could visit the Golden Sufi Center when I fly out to the Bay Area for work . . . and I'm still thinking these very thoughts when LVL drops a bombshell. It comes with no change in his tone or demeanor. After thirty years, he says, in the same contemplative tone in which he's said everything else, he's too tired to go on teaching. He's done. It's over. Most Sufi teachers work with thirty or forty souls, he explains, one leg curled beneath the other, and they do it for fifteen or twenty years. He'd wanted to reach more; eventually he'd taken on eight hundred.

"My work has been to share the secret of divine transformation that has been known for thousands of years to the Sufis," he tells us. "The masters of love have never worked in North America before, until the last few decades. I tried to keep it as long as I could. But part of me that used to be present has been burned out and used up. You're witnessing a teacher in decline. I spent fifteen years sitting at the feet of my teacher and it created a substance, but now it's used up. I wanted to make sure that everyone to whom I opened the door had what they needed to complete their soul's journey. That was my covenant. But I've given you what you need. Use it now. Live it."

Many here have followed LVL for years, and they erupt now with questions. **You said the path continues. What does that mean, if you'll be gone?**

"I'm betting this will work and the connection will remain," he tells them. "Will I still love you? Yes, of course! I've always loved you! Will I still be the Big Daddy? No."

The questions continue, some calm, some verging on panic. LVL answers patiently, until suddenly he registers his own micro-eruption. "Give the old man space!" he cries. "This is the most introverted spiritual path that exists. With space, something will open up. If you give me space, I will be very grateful; if you come at me, I'll put up barriers and walls and ask the angels of mercy to protect me."

He takes his leave from the morning session, and I notice that he looks older than I'd thought, a little more stout, his features a little more slack. I'm absorbing the group's grief, mingled with my own, at losing LVL just as I found him. Even though my relationship with him has been one-sided and online, I feel the familiar, bittersweet waves of separation pains. There's something about his presence that makes you feel he really could help you access some pure state of love. Maybe he could have been my teacher, but I arrived a generation too late.

. . .

Over lunch, I chat with several of LVL's students. Some had known he was leaving; others are in shock. All agree that he's "the real deal." Unlike many spiritual teachers who fall into scandal and disrepute, they say, LVL never got rich, never went after young women; he was faithful to his wife, Anat; he never became a household name, though he had the charisma to do it. When I first came across his videos, I'd wondered why he wasn't a bigger name, given his soft-spoken magnetism. And now I know: For him, eight hundred people—eight hundred souls—was an enormous number to look after. He deserves to rest. I decide I won't try to meet him, after all.

But at the end of the program, he holds a Q and A session, and I have a chance to stand up and ask my question about the difference between longing in Sufism and Buddhism. I tell him that it was his videos on longing that brought me here in the first place.

He gives me a look of excitement and (so I like to imagine) of kinship.

"Longing is different from craving," he explains. "It's the craving of the soul. You want to go home. In our culture it's confused with depression. And it's not. There's a saying in Sufism: 'Sufism was at first heartache. Only later, it became something to write about.'"

His answer confirms what I'd gleaned from his lectures and writings. In one of my favorite written passages, he describes longing not as an unhealthy craving, but as the feminine expression of love: "Like everything that is created, love has a dual nature, positive and negative, masculine and feminine. The masculine side of love is 'I love you.' Love's feminine quality is 'I am waiting for you; I am longing for you.' For the mystic, it is the feminine side of love, the longing, the cup waiting to be filled, that takes us back to God. . . . Because our culture has for so long rejected the feminine, we have lost touch with the potency of longing. Many people feel this pain of the heart and do not know its value; they do not know that it is their innermost connection to love."

"If you're taken by longing," he tells me now, "live it. You can't go wrong. If you're going to go to God, go with sweet sorrow in the soul."

...

So what does it mean, in the end, that so many millions of people resonated with the story of Francesca and her photographer in **The Bridges of Madison County**?

When you feel these longings arising in your own love life, you're going to think there's something wrong. And maybe there is, maybe there isn't; I don't, of course, know your relationship.

But I do know that the most confusing aspect of romantic love is that most enduring relationships start with the conviction that your longing has now been satisfied. The work is done, the dream is realized: the perfect and beautiful world embodied in the object of your affections. But that was the courtship phase, the idealization phase, the phase in which you and your partner were united in reaching, for a marvelous moment in time, that other place. During this phase, there's little distinction between the spiritual and the erotic. This is why so many pop songs concern the first consummation of romance. But these songs should be heard as not only a depiction of love, but also our longing for the transcendent. (According to LVL, the Western tradition of love songs comes from the troubadours, who went east during the Crusades and were influenced by Sufi songs of longing for God. The Sufis used imagery of a woman's cheek, eyebrows, and hair as metaphors for divine love. The troubadours took these metaphors literally, as expressions of the carnal rather than the divine, and used them to serenade Western maidens under moonlit windows.)

Over the course of love, real life will intervene, in the daily negotiations of managing a partnership and possibly a household, and in the limitations of human psychology: sometimes, in the challenges of incompatible attachment styles and interlocking neuroses. You might find that he instinctively avoids intimacy, while you anxiously chase it. You might discover that you're a neat freak and she's a slob, or that you're a bully and he's a doormat, or that you run late and she's punctual to a fault.

Even in the healthiest relationships, the longing often returns. In these unions, you can raise children, if you want. You can share inside jokes, favorite vacation spots, mutual admiration, and a bed; you can search the streets of a brand-new city for a heating pad when you're traveling and your partner's back goes out. In the best relationships, you can still, every so often, go to the moon and back.

But most likely, your relationship will be an asymptote of the thing you long for. As LVL says, "Those who search for intimacy with others are reacting to this longing. They think another human will fulfill them. But how many of us have actually ever been totally fulfilled by another person? Maybe for a while, but not forever. We want something more fulfilling, more intimate. We want God. But not everyone dares to go into this abyss of pain, this longing, that can take you there."

If you're an atheist or agnostic, such talk of "wanting God" probably makes you uncomfortable or impatient. If you're devout, it might seem obvious—of course we're all longing for something, and the something is God. Or you might be somewhere in between. C. S. Lewis, who heard the call of bittersweetness all his life and became a committed Christian in his thirties, eventually concluded that we have hunger because we need to eat, we have thirst because we need to drink; so if we have an "inconsolable longing" that can't be satisfied in this world, it must be because we belong to another, godly one.

"Our commonest expedient," Lewis wrote, in one of literature's most gorgeous passages:

> is to call [the longing] beauty and behave as if that had settled the matter. . . . But the books or the music in which we thought the beauty was located will betray us if we trust to them; it was not in them, it only came through them, and what came through them was longing. These things—the beauty, the memory of our

own past—are good images of what we really desire; but if they are mistaken for the thing itself they turn into dumb idols, breaking the hearts of their worshippers. For they are not the thing itself; they are only the scent of a flower we have not found, the echo of a tune we have not heard, news from a country we have never yet visited.

As for me, I believe that the bittersweet tradition extinguishes these distinctions between atheists and believers. The longing comes through Yahweh or Allah, Christ or Krishna, no more and no less than it comes through the books and the music; they are equally the divine, or none of them are the divine, and the distinction makes no difference; they are all it. When you went to your favorite concert and heard your favorite musician singing the body electric, that was it; when you met your love and gazed at each other with shining eyes, that was it; when you kissed your five-year-old good night and she turned to you solemnly and said, "Thank you for loving me so much," that was it: all of them facets of the same jewel. And yes, at eleven P.M. the concert will end, and you'll have to find your car in a crowded parking lot; and your relationship won't be perfect because no relationship is; and one day your daughter will fail eleventh grade and announce that she hates you.

But this is to be expected. And this is why Francesca's story couldn't have ended any other way.

She couldn't live happily ever after with the photographer, because he represented not an actual man, not even the "perfect" man; he represented longing itself. **The Bridges of Madison County** was a story about the moments when you glimpse your Eden. It was never just a story about a marriage and an affair; it was about the transience of these sightings, and why they mean more than anything else that might ever happen to you.

CHAPTER 3

Is creativity associated with sorrow,
longing—and transcendence?

**Whatever pain you can't get rid of,
make it your creative offering**.

It's time that we began to laugh and cry and
cry and laugh about it all again.

—LEONARD COHEN,
"SO LONG, MARIANNE"

In 1944, when the poet-musician and global icon Leonard Cohen was nine years old, his father died. Leonard wrote a poem, sliced open his father's favorite bowtie, inserted his elegy, and buried it in the family garden in Montreal. That was his first artistic expression. He would echo it again and again during his six-decade, Grammy Lifetime Achievement Award–winning career, penning hundreds of verses on heartache, longing, and love.

Cohen was famously sensual, romantic, a ladies' man; Joni Mitchell once called him a "boudoir poet." He had a hypnotic baritone, a shy charisma. But none of his love affairs lasted; as an artist he "existed best in a state of longing," as his biographer Sylvie Simmons put it.

Perhaps his greatest love was a Norwegian beauty named Marianne Ihlen. He met her on the Greek island of Hydra in 1960, where a free-spirited international arts community had formed. Cohen was a writer then; it wouldn't occur to him to set his poetry to music for another six years. Every morning he worked on a novel, and in the evenings, he played lullabies for Marianne's son by another man. They lived in domestic harmony. "It was as if everyone was young and beautiful and full of talent—covered with a kind of gold dust," he said later of his time on Hydra. "Everybody had special and unique qualities. This is, of course, the feeling of youth, but in the glorious setting of Hydra, all these qualities were magnified."

But eventually Leonard and Marianne had to leave the island, he to earn a living in Canada, she to Norway for family reasons. They tried to stay together but couldn't make it last. He moved to New York City, became a musician, was swept up in a scene that never really suited him. "When you've lived on Hydra," he said later, "you can't live anywhere else, including Hydra."

He moved on with his life, Marianne with hers. But she inspired some of his most iconic songs—about leave-taking. They had titles like "So Long, Marianne" and "Hey, That's No Way to Say Goodbye." "There are some people that have a tendency towards saying hello," Cohen said of his music, "but I'm rather more valedictory." His last great hit, released three weeks before his death at age eighty-two, was called "You Want It Darker."

Even those who adored his work commented on its somber nature. One of his record companies joked about giving away razor blades with his albums. But that's a limited way to think about him. He was really a poet of dark **and** light—of the "cold and broken Hallelujah," as he put it in his most famous song. **Whatever pain you can't get rid of,** he seemed to say, **make it your creative offering.**

. . .

Is creativity associated with sorrow and longing, through some mysterious force? The question has long been posed by casual observers and creativity researchers alike. And the data (as well as Aristotle's intuition, per his question about the prominence of melancholics in the arts) suggest that the answer is yes. According to a famous early study of 573 creative leaders by the psychologist Marvin Eisenstadt, an astonishingly large percentage of highly creative people were, like Cohen, orphaned in childhood.

Twenty-five percent had lost at least one parent by the age of ten. By age fifteen, it was 34 percent, and by age twenty, 45 percent!

Other studies suggest that even creatives whose parents live to their dotage are disproportionately prone to sorrow. People who work in the arts are eight to ten times more likely than others to suffer mood disorders, according to a 1993 study by the Johns Hopkins psychiatry professor Kay Redfield Jamison. In his study of the artistic psyche, **Tortured Artists,** a 2012 book profiling forty-eight creative outliers from Michelangelo to Madonna, author Christopher Zara found that their life stories share a certain amount of pain and suffering. And in 2017, an economist named Karol Jan Borowiecki published a fascinating study in **The Review of Economics and Statistics** called "How Are You, My Dearest Mozart? Well-Being and Creativity of Three Famous Composers Based on Their Letters." Borowiecki used linguistic analytic software to study 1,400 letters written by Mozart, Liszt, and Beethoven throughout their lives. He traced when their letters referred to positive emotions (using words like **happiness**) or negative ones (words like **grief**), and how these feelings related to the quantity and quality of the music they composed at the time. Borowiecki found that the artists' negative emotions were not only correlated with but also predictive of their creative output. And not just **any** negative emotions had this effect. Just as scholars of minor key music found that sadness is the only negative emotion whose musical expression uplifts us (as we saw in chapter 2), Borowiecki found that it was also **"the main negative feeling that drives creativity."** [Emphasis added.]

In another intriguing study, Columbia Business School professor Modupe Akinola gathered a collection of students and measured their blood for DHEAS, a hormone that helps protect against depression by suppressing the effects of stress hormones such as cortisol. Then she asked the students to speak to an audience about their dream jobs. Unbeknownst to her subjects, she arranged for some of these talks to be greeted supportively, with smiles and nods, and others with frowns and head shaking. After the talk, she asked the students how they were feeling; unsurprisingly, those with receptive audiences were in a better mood than the ones who thought they'd bombed. But she also asked the students to make a collage, which professional artists later rated for creativity. The students who faced disapproving audiences created better collages than the ones who were smiled upon. And those who received negative audience feedback **and** had low levels of DHEAS—that is, the students who were both emotionally vulnerable and suffered rejection from the audience—made the best collages of all.

Other studies have found that sad moods tend to sharpen our attention: They make us more focused and detail oriented; they improve our memories, correct our cognitive biases. For example, University of New South Wales psychology professor Joseph Forgas found that people are better able to recall items they've seen in a store on cloudy days compared to sunny ones, and that people in a bad mood (after being asked to focus on sad memories) tend to have better eyewitness memories of a car accident than those who'd been thinking of happy times.*

There are many possible explanations, of course, for such findings. Perhaps it's the sharpened attention that Forgas's studies suggest. Or maybe emotional setbacks instill an extra degree of grit and persistence, which some people apply to their creative efforts; other studies suggest that adversity causes a tendency to withdraw to an inner world of imagination.

Whatever the theory, we shouldn't make the mistake of viewing darkness as the sole or even primary catalyst to creativity. After all, plenty of creatives are sanguine types. And studies also show that flashes of insight are more likely to happen when we're in a good mood. We also know that clinical depression—which we might think of as an emotional black hole obliterating all light—kills creativity.

---

* Incidentally, Forgas also found that sad people who were eyewitnesses to car accidents were better able to resist misleading questions (such as "Did you see the stop sign?" when, in fact, only a yield sign had been present at the scene). And he showed that sad people are better at watching videotapes of criminal suspects and correctly distinguishing the guilty from the innocent. They're less likely to succumb to the "halo effect," in which we assume that a good-looking person must be kind and intelligent. In general, Forgas found, there's something about sadness that removes the scales from our eyes.

As Columbia University psychiatry professor Philip Muskin told **The Atlantic** magazine, "Creative people are not creative when they're depressed."

Instead, it may be more useful to view creativity through the lens of bittersweetness—of grappling simultaneously with darkness **and** light. It's not that pain equals art. It's that creativity has the power to look pain in the eye, and to decide to turn it into something better. As Cohen's story suggests, the quest to transform pain into beauty is one of the great catalysts of artistic expression. "He . . . felt at home in darkness, the way he wrote, the way he worked," observed Sylvie Simmons. "But in the end, it really was about finding the light."

Indeed, as I mentioned in the introduction, preliminary studies show that high scorers on the Bittersweet Quiz tend to score high on the trait of absorption, which other studies have shown predicts creativity. And University of Washington business school professor Christina Ting Fong found that people who simultaneously experience positive and negative emotions are better at making associative leaps and at seeing connections between apparently unrelated concepts. In one 2006 study, she showed subjects a bittersweet scene from the movie **Father of the Bride** in which a young woman describes the joy of her upcoming wedding and the sorrow of leaving childhood behind. Those who watched that scene performed better on creativity tests than subjects who were shown happy, sad, or neutral movies.

One of the greatest examples of creativity as a dynamic move from dark to light is the composition and debut of Beethoven's "Ode to Joy"—the famous choral finale to his Ninth Symphony, performed for the first time on May 7, 1824, at the Theater am Kärntnertor in Vienna. The story of that opening night is also one of the most moving in classical music history.

For three **decades** Beethoven had worked on setting "Ode to Joy," Friedrich Schiller's poem of freedom and brotherhood, to music. Beethoven had grown up during the American and French revolutions, and he was an ardent believer in Enlightenment values. To him, "Ode to Joy" was the ultimate expression of love and unity; he felt he had to do it justice, composing some two hundred versions before settling on the one he liked best.

But those years had not been kind to him. In 1795, he'd written to his brother of his good fortune: "I am well, very well. My art is winning me friends and respect, and what more do I want?" But over time, he'd loved women who didn't love him back; he'd become the guardian of his nephew Karl, with whom he had a stormy relationship, culminating in Karl's attempted suicide; and he'd lost his hearing. By 1801, his letters to his brother took a much darker tone: "I must confess that I am living a miserable life. For almost two years I have ceased to attend any social functions, just because I find it impossible to say to people: 'I am deaf.'"

On that opening night, Beethoven stood onstage beside the conductor, disoriented and disheveled, his back to the audience, gesturing erratically to the orchestra. He hoped to show them how to play the music the way he heard it in his mind. One of the musicians later described how he "stood in front of the conductor's stand and threw himself back and forth like a madman. At one moment he stretched to his full height, at the next he crouched down to the floor. He flailed about with his hands and feet as though he wanted to play all the instruments and sing all the chorus parts."

When the performance ended, the hall fell silent. But Beethoven didn't know this, couldn't hear it. He stood with his back to the crowd, beating time to music that played only in his own head. It was a twenty-year-old soloist named Caroline Unger who gently turned him around so he could see the audience members, who had risen to their feet, tears of awe streaming down their cheeks. They waved their handkerchiefs, raised their hats, used physical gestures rather than sound to pay homage to the man who had expressed their own yearning. Schiller's poem "Ode to Joy" was a famously exultant work. But the audience reacted the way it did because in Beethoven's rendition, the music was laced with sorrow, which anyone can hear echoing, to this day, in its soaring, triumphant notes.

. . .

This doesn't mean that we should be sad, or go deaf, even if once a century these conditions produce sublime music. Nor must we be great artists in order to view our own struggles as objects of creative transformation. What if we simply took whatever pain we couldn't get rid of, and turned it into something else? We could write, act, study, cook, dance, compose, do improv, dream up a new business, decorate our kitchens; there are hundreds of things we could do, and whether we do them "well," or with distinction, is beside the point. This is why "arts therapy"—in which people express and process their troubles by making art—can be so effective, even if its practitioners don't exhibit their work on gallery walls.

We don't even necessarily need to create art ourselves. According to a study of more than fifty thousand Norwegians, conducted by Koenraad Cuypers at the Norwegian University of Science and Technology, immersing oneself in creativity, whether as creator **or as consumer,** via concerts, art museums, or other media, is associated with greater health and life satisfaction, and lower rates of anxiety and depression. Another study, by Dr. Semir Zeki, a University of London neurobiologist, found that the simple act of **viewing** beautiful art increases activity in the pleasure reward centers of the brain. It feels, says Zeki, a lot like falling in love. "The people who weep before my pictures are having the same religious experience I had when I painted them," observed the artist Mark Rothko.

When the pandemic started, I fell into the habit of "doomscrolling" Twitter and marinating in online toxicity, especially first thing in the morning. This produced a state of mind that was the exact opposite of what Rothko described. I decided to transform my Internet addiction by following art accounts instead: first a few, then a dozen; the next thing I knew, my feed was full of art, and my spirit felt lighter. Soon after that, I found myself starting each morning by sharing a favorite work of art on my social media pages. It's become a cherished daily practice: meditative, restoring, and community-building. The art comes from all over the world, and so does our ever-growing group of kindred spirits who delight in it together.

So let's amend our principle: **Whatever pain you can't get rid of, make it your creative offering—or find someone who makes it for you.** And if you do find yourself drawn to such a person, ask yourself why they call to you. What are they expressing on your behalf—and where do they have the power to take you?

. . .

For me, Leonard Cohen was that person. I'd had a crazy love for him and his music from the first time I heard it, decades ago. He seemed the ultimate kindred spirit, embodying everything I've ever felt about love and life in the minor key, the places it can carry you. His songs contained an essence of something I'd been trying to touch all my life, though I couldn't have said exactly what it was.

So when his son, the musician Adam Cohen, planned a memorial concert for November 6, 2017, a year after his father's death, with celebrity musicians booked to perform Cohen's songs in tribute, our family flew from New York to Montreal for the occasion. My husband had urged me to go, and even offered to make a family holiday out of the trip.

I felt oddly detached and a little ridiculous as we boarded the plane with the kids in tow. I'd had to reschedule an important meeting, plus it seemed extravagant and self-indulgent for the family to fly to another country on a random Monday morning, just so I could attend a concert. The feeling persisted as I arrived that evening at the gigantic Bell Centre, along with a sold-out audience of seventeen thousand Leonard Cohen fans. And when the concert started, it only intensified. Cohen was the one I'd loved: What were all these other musicians doing here? Bored, dispirited, I started doing what I always do: writing things down. "He's really gone," I typed into my phone. "They're not Leonard, and they shouldn't try to be. I'd rather go home and listen to him in private, in his own voice. As if he were still alive."

But then onto the stage came a musician named Damien Rice, to perform "Famous Blue Raincoat," which may be the gloomiest of Cohen's many gloomy songs. It's about a love triangle, narrated by a man whose wife, Jane, sleeps with his best friend. After, their relationships are forever changed: Jane is "nobody's wife," and the man addresses his friend as "my brother, my killer." The song takes the form of a letter, written—significantly, as we'll see—at four A.M., at the end of December, as night turns into day, fall into winter.

Rice's performance was inspired. But at the end, he added an extended flourish of his own—a lamentation, really—a musical howl so naked and magnificent that it brought the audience to its feet. In expressing some nameless sorrow, Rice had suffused the vast, cold arena (which hosted an ice hockey game the very next night) in love and longing; he'd reminded us that we were in a hockey stadium, but it was Eden we wanted. And for me, there it was again: that old heart-opening sensation, the one I'd felt in my law school dorm room all those years ago, the one I've always felt upon hearing sad music, the ecstatic longing that the Sufis write about. But this time it went further. Those few moments it took Damien Rice to sing those particular notes were some of the most profound of my life. I felt taken up and held by a thrilling beauty, connected to Damien, Leonard, everyone.

I'd flown to Montreal feeling bored and unmoved; I flew home as if under a spell. It was a pleasantly disoriented sensation, a cousin to the way you feel during the weeks after a child is born, or you adopt a puppy. But it was a distant cousin; this time, it was mixed with grief. In Judaism, when a parent dies, the mourning period ends after a year. That's why Cohen's son staged the concert twelve months after his father's death. But with Damien Rice's version of "Famous Blue Raincoat," my grief had only just begun. For weeks after, I found, to my astonishment, that I couldn't speak of Cohen without tearing up. I held back tears as I paid the cashier at the Montreal art museum exhibiting his work, and again when I told our babysitter why we'd been away for a few days. Yet I was deeply grateful that my husband had convinced me to go. If I'd stayed home, I would have missed out on one of the great experiences of my life.

But what, exactly, had happened? I started to ask myself the same questions that I just suggested to you. What had Leonard Cohen been expressing, on my behalf, for all these years? And where did his music have the power to take me (and the other seventeen thousand fans who flocked to the Bell Centre to honor him)?

Until now, I'd been content to know him mostly through his songs. Now I started to learn more about his personal story. He came from a prominent Jewish family in Montreal and remained steeped in Judaism all his life, even as he spent five years in a Zen Buddhist monastery on the top of Mount Baldy outside Los Angeles, met the mother of his children during a brief stint as a Scientologist, explored Christian iconography in his lyrics. Though he didn't consider himself religious, he told his rabbi that everything he wrote was liturgy. I found out that he drew especially from the Kabbalah—the mystical version of Judaism which teaches that all of creation was once a vessel filled with holy light. But it shattered, and now the shards of divinity are scattered everywhere, amidst the pain and ugliness. Our task is to gather up these fragments wherever we find them. This philosophy made instant and perfect sense to me.

"It was part of this thesis that he had, that his whole life was about," explained Adam Cohen in an interview with the music producer Rick Rubin, "which is brokenness—the broken Hallelujah, the crack in everything. The whole notion that defeat and imperfection and brokenness was the fabric of the experience. Then, instead of just having a plaintive assertion, the real generosity was to write about it in a way that you hadn't considered, with generosity, with voluptuousness, with inventiveness, and then he could, on top of it, set it to a melody. Like what nicotine is in a cigarette, it's a nicotine delivery system. **He was giving you a transcendence delivery system. That's what he was trying to do every time.**" [Emphasis added.]

I hadn't known all this during the many years that I'd loved Cohen's music. But I'd felt it—especially the part about brokenness giving way to transcendence.

• • •

Later, I described the memorial concert to David Yaden, a professor at the Johns Hopkins Center for Psychedelic and Consciousness Research, and a budding superstar in his field. Yaden is an intellectual heir to the great psychologist William James, author of the seminal **The Varieties of Religious Experience,** and he's dedicated his career to the study of what he calls "self-transcendent experiences," or STEs.

Yaden believes that STEs are defined by transient mental states involving feelings of connection and self-loss. They seem to occur on a spectrum of intensity—from gratitude, flow, and mindfulness on the milder end of the spectrum, to full-blown "peak" or mystical experiences on the other end. He also believes that STEs are one of life's most important and creativity-inducing experiences. And he's amazed by how little we know about the psychological and neurological processes that underlie them.

As is true for most careers fueled by a burning question (research as "me-search"), Yaden's quest began with his own mystifying life event that happened not in a concert hall, but in his dorm room as an undergrad. Not long before, he'd been in high school, living in his parents' house. Now he was on his own, wondering what to do with his life. He lay on his bed early one evening, arms crossed behind his head, staring at the ceiling. The phrase "Come What May" came to his mind. He noticed a heat in his chest. It felt like heartburn at first, but it spread over his entire body. A voice in his mind said: "This is love."

It seemed that he had a 360-degree view of every-thing around him, that there was an intricate fabric stretching out to eternity, and that he was part of it in some undefinable way. The warmth in his chest reached a joyful boiling point and stayed there for what felt like hours, or days, though he thinks it was probably a few minutes. He opened his eyes. Love flooded him. He laughed and cried at the same time. He wanted to call his family and friends and tell them how much he adored them. Everything felt new, his future opened up.

But most of all, he says, "I was wondering what the fuck just happened to me. And that question has stayed with me ever since."

Yaden devoted the rest of his college years—and now his career in psychology, neuroscience, and psychopharmacology—to answering this question. He went on a reading binge: philosophy, religion, psychology. He signed up for intense ritualistic ex-periences, everything from a Zen meditation retreat to Officer Candidates School for the U.S. Marine Corps (he was one of the few candidates to graduate from boot camp). He wrote his honors thesis on rites of passage, suspecting that transitional experiences, involving impermanence, were somehow at the heart of his quest. And early in his career, he teamed up with the influential psychologist Jonathan Haidt to explore states of mind like the one he'd experienced.

Previous generations of Freudian psychologists had viewed the "oceanic feeling"—Yaden's STEs, or what the French author Romain Rolland had described to Freud as "a sensation of eternity" or a feeling of "being one with the external world as a whole"—as a sign of neurosis. But Haidt and Yaden found the exact opposite: that such experiences are associated with higher self-esteem, pro-social behavior, a greater sense of meaning, lower rates of depression, greater life satisfaction and well-being, a decreased fear of death, and overall psychological health. These are "some of life's most positive and meaningful" moments, they concluded, and, as William James had hypothesized a century earlier, a source of "our greatest peace."

So Yaden had plenty of thoughts about my night at the Bell Centre. For one thing, he told me, people go to concerts hoping to have exactly this kind of experience. We're all in search of these states, whether or not we think of them in religious terms; we all want to get to the perfect and beautiful world. Also, said Yaden, some of the same traits that predispose people to loving sad music—from "openness to experience" (receptivity to new ideas and aesthetic experiences) to "absorption" (proneness to mental imagery and fantasy)—also predict a readiness to creativity and transcendence.

But it's also no accident, said Yaden, that my "oceanic" experience happened at a time of bittersweetness and impermanence—at a memorial concert for a beloved figure, during a song about relationships ending, a song that takes place during the winter solstice, just before dawn.

Yaden has found that it's precisely during such times—including career changes, divorces, and the ultimate transition of death—that we're more likely to experience meaning, communion, and transcendence. This is true not only for those whose loved ones are dying, but also for the dying themselves. A surprising number, says Yaden, "experience the most important moments of their entire lives near its very end."

In psychometric surveys, Yaden and his colleagues have asked people to think and write about their intense spiritual experiences, and then to answer questions about them. This allowed the researchers to sort the experiences into various types. Did they feature a sense of Unity? God? A Voice or Vision? Synchronicity? Awe? After classifying the experiences, the researchers asked what triggered them. And of a very long list, they found two items that consistently appeared as major triggers: "transitional period of life" and "being close to death." In other words: an intense awareness of passing time—the hallmark of bittersweetness itself.

Yaden's work explains why "sad" music, like Leonard Cohen's, isn't really sad at all: why it's rooted in brokenness, but points at transcendence.

This research echoes the work of the famous UC Davis creativity researcher Dean Keith Simonton, who found that creativity seems to move in a spiritual direction during midlife and beyond, as artists straddle the intersection between life and death. Simonton studied eighty-one Shakespearean and Athenian plays and concluded that their themes grew more religious, spiritual, and mystical as the playwrights aged. He also studied classical composers, and found that musicologists rated their later works as "more profound."

The great mid-century humanistic psychologist Abraham Maslow perceived a similar phenomenon in himself, noticing that he had more frequent and intense "peak experiences" while dying of heart disease. And, in 2017, when a group of researchers led by the University of North Carolina psychologist Amelia Goranson asked people to **imagine** what death would feel like, they mostly described sadness, fear, and anxiety. But their studies of terminally ill patients and death row inmates found that those **actually** facing death are more likely to speak of meaning, connection, and love. As the researchers concluded: "Meeting the grim reaper may not be as grim as it seems."

According to Yaden, we still don't understand the "scientific" reason—the psychological mechanisms and neurobiological pathways—that apparently painful moments of impermanence, such as death itself, should have such transformative effects. But his research echoes the intuitions of countless cultures that, for centuries, have honored life transitions as doorways to spiritual and creative awakening. As Estelle Frankel explores in her excellent book **Sacred Therapy,** this is why so many societies celebrate coming-of-age rituals (first communions, bar mitzvahs, and so on) in religious contexts; and why so many of those ceremonies involve the death of the childhood self and the birth of the adult one. In some cultures, the child is buried (temporarily!) in the ground, and disinterred as an adult; sometimes he's tattooed, or maimed, or performs some other feat marking the end of childhood and the emergence of a new, adult self. Sometimes this involves a separate physical space, whether an initiation hut or a body of water, a church or a synagogue. The point of these rituals is that X must always give way to Y, and that this process, which involves both sacrifice and rebirth (the ultimate creativity), belongs to the realm of exaltation. The fundamental progression of Christianity—the birth of Jesus, the sacrifice on the cross, the resurrection—tells the same story. (The very word **sacrifice** is from the Latin **sacer-ficere,** which means "to make sacred.")

This is also why transitions from one season to another (equinoxes and solstices) have traditionally been marked as religious ceremonies: from Passover and Easter at the spring equinox, to the pagan Yule festival and Christmas at the winter solstice, to the Chinese Moon Festival and Japanese Buddhist Higan celebration at the fall equinox. In Judaism, even the transition from day into night is sacred, with the holy days starting at sundown and moving into dawn—as if to say that the onset of darkness is not the tragedy we imagine, but rather the prelude to light.

In the modern West, we tend to think that narratives proceed in a straight and finite line: that beginnings give way to endings, and endings are a cause for sorrow. How do you tell your life story? It starts with birth, it ends with death; it starts with happy, it ends with sad. You sing "Happy Birthday" in C major, you compose a funeral march in C sharp minor. But these bittersweet traditions, along with Yaden's recent discoveries, suggest a different cast of mind, in which we **expect** our lives to thrust us through one transformation after another. Sometimes these transitions will be joyous (say, the birth of a child), sometimes bittersweet (walking that child down the aisle); sometimes they'll arrive as full-on cataclysms that tear your life apart (fill in your worst fear here). Endings will give way to beginnings just as much as beginnings give way to endings. Your ancestor's life ended, and yours could begin. Yours will come to an end, and your child's story will take center stage. Even within the course of your life, pieces of you will constantly die off—a job will be lost, a relationship will end—and, if you're ready, other occupations, loves, will arise in their place. What follows may or may not be "better" than what came first. But the task is not only to let the past go, but also to transform the pain of impermanence into creativity—and transcendence.

Leonard Cohen, of course, understood all this, and so did Marianne Ihlen. After their breakup, they never met again—until it was time for their next great passage. In July 2016, four months before Cohen's death from leukemia, a friend of Marianne's told him that she was dying of the same cancer. He sent her a farewell letter.

"Dearest Marianne," it said, "I'm just a little behind you, close enough to take your hand. This old body has given up, just as yours has too, and the eviction notice is on its way any day now. I've never forgotten your love and your beauty. But you know that. I don't have to say any more. Safe travels old friend. See you down the road. Love and gratitude. Leonard"

Marianne's friend read Leonard's note aloud to her. He says that she smiled, and reached out her hand.

. . .

In July 2019, two years after the Leonard Cohen memorial concert, I found myself inside another concert hall, this one at the International Conference Center in Edinburgh, Scotland. This time, I was the one onstage (never my most comfortable spot). I was giving a TED Talk about longing, bittersweetness, and transcendence. But I wasn't all alone up there. My dear friend the violinist Min Kym was in the spotlight with me. And she knew the subject intimately: Her entire life had been an act of turning pain into creativity.

Min had started playing violin at six, skipping lightly from lesson to lesson, learning in weeks the scales and sonatas it took others years to master. At seven, she was the youngest student ever accepted to London's prestigious Purcell School for Young Musicians; at eight, she was told she'd outgrow her adult teacher within the year; by thirteen she made her debut with the Berlin Symphony Orchestra; at sixteen, the legendary Ruggiero Ricci said she was the most talented violinist he'd ever taught. Later, he instructed her for free, saying he would learn as much from her as she from him, and it would be wrong to take payment.

Her talent came with constraints familiar to many child prodigies: She was cosseted, revered, but lived in a gilded cage of demanding, often domineering teachers, a rigid practice schedule, the world's expectations. She also felt a crushing responsibility to her family, who'd suffered terribly during the Korean War, then bucked centuries of tradition to leave South Korea so that Min, the youngest daughter, could pursue her musical training in London.

Still, her genius seemed a form of magic. And, as if that weren't enough, when she turned twenty-one another gift, just as dazzling, was bestowed upon her—in the form of a three-hundred-year-old Stradivarius violin. A violin dealer had presented it to her for sale, at the price of £450,000. She knew instantly that this violin was her soul mate, "the One." Without thinking twice, she remortgaged her flat in order to pay for it.

Overnight, her Strad, as she called it, became her everything: the fulfillment of her promise, the key to her art; but also, her lover, child, twin, self. It was the completion we all seek, the divinity we yearn for, the glass slipper that finally fits.

"The instant I drew the first breath with my bow I knew," Min writes of the day she met her violin for the first time.

> I was Cinderella, with her foot sticking out, the shoe gliding over the instep. It was perfect for me, so slim, so natural. . . . It felt as if three hundred years ago Stradivari had held his hands over a length of wood and fashioned this violin just for me, that all her life, my Strad had been waiting for me as I had been waiting for her. . . . It was love at first sight, love and everything else: honor, obedience, trust, everything. . . .
>
> It came to me then, that this was what my life had been leading up to. . . . All my life had been a rehearsal—the tutors, the frustrations, the loneliness, the pangs of joy: everything leading up to now, when I would meet my violin and we would begin. . . .
>
> This was marriage till death do us part, made in heaven right here on earth. I was set for life.

Violins are delicate creatures, requiring constant repair and upkeep; they need to be fashioned to the preferences of their players. Min's Strad in particular had weathered damage over the centuries. She spent years adjusting its sound post, its bridge, its strings; it took three years of sampling just to find the right bow. She poured all her earnings into the Strad's perfection, living in a tiny shoebox of a flat; no fancy car, no expensive clothes. She was sure that enchantment lay on the other side of all these sacrifices.

From a psychodynamic point of view, we can interpret Min's obsession as the product of a young woman's psyche, made fragile by a family history of war and privation and a childhood of submission to overbearing authorities. Min wouldn't deny this interpretation. But she would also tell you that it's not the full story. Take a minute to understand the otherworldly context of Min's Strad, so you can grasp the enormity of what happened next.

For those under its spell, the violin is a symbol of human creativity and divine grace—"the only instrument that goes all the way up to the heavens," as Min puts it. ("Don't tell the cellists I said that," she adds.) Its body is slim and sensuous, its woodwork glows, it has its own mythology. The most revered violins of all are the ones produced by three Italian men, Stradivari, Amati, and Guarneri, three centuries ago. The Strads in particular are thought to be fashioned from the wood of the so-called musical forest in the Dolomites, where, it is said, Stradivari came every full moon, resting his head against the tree trunks to listen for the precious and elusive sound he sought. No one since has figured out how to make violins quite like his, though countless luthiers have tried.

These violins now trade for millions and are bought up by tycoons and oligarchs in whose homes they sit silently under glass cases. There's also a thriving black market for stolen violins, and a long digital trail of their heartbroken owners. Google the words **stolen violin,** and you'll produce tens of pages of entries: "This instrument has been my voice since I was 14 years old and I am devastated at its loss." "My life has been through pain and heartache. . . . Everything went downhill." "My beautiful violin has been stolen!"

Which is exactly what happened to Min. Though she guarded her Strad 24/7, never letting it out of her sight, there came a day, at a Pret a Manger café at Euston railway station in central London, when she looked away for just a moment, and her Strad was taken. Stolen. Spirited away to the criminal underworld of priceless objects.

The theft made international news; Scotland Yard was assigned to the case. After three long years of detective work, the police would eventually recover the violin, which had been handed off from one criminal group to another. But in the meantime, Min had used her insurance money to buy another, lesser instrument, and the violin market was bid up. Her Strad was now worth millions. She couldn't afford to buy it back. It was purchased by an investor, in whose home it still sits.

She descended into depression, stopped playing altogether. At the time of the theft, she'd been about to release an important album and launch a world-wide concert tour. It was meant to mark her arrival as one of the most talented violinists in the world. Instead she lay in bed, shattered. She stayed that way for years. The only headlines about Min Kym reported the news of her stolen instrument.

Whatever pain you can't get rid of, make it your creative offering. All her life, she'd followed that precept. Her offering had been her willingness to walk with stones in her shoes to the temple of the virtuoso. But now, in the fog of her loss, a new story of her past—and future—materialized. She saw that the great love of her Strad had been real, but so were other things: a crippling perfectionism; a sense that she wasn't allowed to be human; the realization that she had nothing to show for her life apart from her musical talent. She realized that she had other creative offerings to make. She decided to write her story.

At first, she thought that her book, which she called **Gone,** would be about the theft of her Strad. And it was. But she also wrote about her family's struggles during the war, her own compulsion to obey, her descent into depression, and her gradual reemergence into life. And she created a work of transcendent beauty.

Min and I had never met, but we happened to

have the same editor, who sent me her manuscript a few months before it was published. It arrived via email attachment, devoid of enticing cover art or breathless blurbs from famous people. Just a Word document on my laptop. I was traveling for work at the time, I'm not sure where; I just remember the hotel room where I stayed up all night, reading, spellbound by language as lyrical as music itself. After I finished, along with the normal afterglow of literary communion, I developed the fantasy that Min's book would become a mega-bestseller and the readers of the world would unite to buy her violin back from the investor who now possessed it. If I'd had the money, I would've written a check right then and mailed it off to her.

Not long after, I visited London for a book tour, and Min and I met for dinner at the Ivy Kensington Brasserie, a Parisian-style bistro on Kensington High Street. In person, she bore little resemblance to the distraught figure in her book. She was delightful company, cheerful and chatty, her shiny dark hair swinging as she spoke. We were the last to leave the restaurant that evening. I shared my fantasy with Min; I expected her to leap at the idea. But she didn't. Instead, she said something that shocked me. She said that she shouldn't have her Strad back.

It's not the same violin it once was, she said, and she's not the same person, either. She'd met her Strad when she was Min the obedient prodigy, and the violin, which had withstood all those centuries of damage, had reflected that insecurity. Now she was growing into Min who possessed a new creative force. She'd come to know what she calls "the upside of loss."

"I'll never stop loving it," she said of her Strad. "I'm just happy knowing where it is. I'm just glad that it's still alive. But the violin has had its own experiences, and I've had mine."

Since then, Min has had several human love affairs: men she's loved, who have loved her back. She's juggling new creative projects, including an album and collaborations with other composers and artists. And after many years without her own instrument, she's commissioned a violin, a replica of the Guarneri del Gesù owned by her former teacher Ruggiero Ricci.

"The moment my violin was stolen," Min explains, "something died in me. I thought for a very long time, until recently, that it would recover. But it never did. I have to accept that the person I was—at one with that violin in a way that I've never been with another person—it's taken me a long time to accept that the person I was with the violin is gone.

"But I've been reborn. When one door closes, another opens—all the clichés about rebirth are true. There's space now for a new me to emerge. It's not something I would have chosen. I would have happily been a complete unit with my violin for the rest of my life. But when you do recover from any loss—when you heal, when your soul starts to heal from the shock—a new part grows, and that's where I am now. I probably won't ever be a soloist again. But I'll take that loss and create new art forms with it."

One day, Min and I met up in Cremona, the town where Stradivari lived and worked, and which is still the unofficial heart and soul of the world's violin lovers. At the Museo del Violino, which stands on the Piazza Marconi, we took an audio tour together, culminating in a dark room of glass cases holding some of the finest violins in the world. They're precious and magnificent, but Min looked stricken. The violins are "strung up on display as if they're in a torture chamber," she whispered, her hand covering her mouth. "I feel they're being silenced."

We hurried out of the museum and emerged blinking into a sunlit plaza. The bells of Cremona's towers were ringing, people wheeling past on their bicycles. "Seeing those instruments just now," said Min, "I feel like I ran a marathon. I feel winded. In the gut."

And then the moment passed. Min's easy smile returned. I thought for the tenth time that day what a great traveling companion Min is, relaxed and good-natured, with little trace of the lacerating grief she wrote about in **Gone.** If you met her, you'd have no idea. Even I have to remind myself that it's still there. Which makes you realize that the world is full of Mins.

. . .

That night, on that TED stage, I told the story of the cellist of Sarajevo—the same story that opened this book—and Min played Albinoni's Adagio in G Minor. She played, that evening, with a borrowed instrument: her friend's Duke of Edinburgh Stradivarius, perfectly chosen, generously offered for the occasion. She stood up there with me and she played the adagio so movingly that you could feel the audience hold its breath. Maybe she wasn't a classical soloist anymore; maybe she never would be again. But she was something greater. In her music, you could feel her loss and her love, and you could feel your own, too. You could feel her pain, and its transformation. And you could feel each member of the audience transcending their own particularities as they listened in unison, each heart straining not to break, yet close to breaking open.*

* This concluding sentence is inspired, like so much of this book, by Rumi's poetry.

CHAPTER 4

How should we cope with lost love?

Though lovers be lost, love shall not.

—DYLAN THOMAS

One of my earliest memories: First afternoon of kindergarten, age four. I'm sitting at a kidney-shaped table, coloring blissfully. Yellow Crayola for a bright sun, green for the grass below, between them a blue, blue sky. I glance up, and there's my mother, standing with the other moms at the back of the classroom, waiting to take me home. She smiles her loving, endlessly patient smile, and I fill with joy. To me it's as if she wears a halo encircling her curly red hair. To me it's like being picked up from school by an angel, and following her home to the Garden of Eden.

Throughout my childhood, she was like this: ready after school with a dish of chocolate ice cream, happy to chat about fourth-grade social life, always present with a gentle joke or, when things went wrong, to soothe tears. My siblings were much older; my father was a medical school professor who worked long hours. I loved them dearly, but my mother was everything. Did a better, more loving mother exist anywhere on earth? That would have been impossible; all my friends said I was lucky to have a mother like her. She made chicken soup and pot roast and lit candles on Friday nights. She rarely raised her voice, except to encourage things I said and wrote.

She had taught me to read and write when I was three. I soon claimed the floor under the card table as my "workshop" and there, crouched beneath the tabletop, produced plays, stories, and magazines on lined paper stapled together. We didn't know, back then, that this act of writing would tear us apart. And I didn't know how complicated my mother actually was.

She was an only child; her own mother had been very ill throughout my mother's childhood, lying in bed for years, facing the wall. What would it have been like—what might it do to you—to see your mother's back turned, day after day, year after year? My mother was convinced that she'd done something horribly wrong to make her own mother so sick—and tormented by an insatiable desire to be seen.

My mother's father was a rabbi—loving, wise, and twinkly; extremely devoted to his daughter—but mired in heartache. In 1927, at age seventeen, he'd come from Eastern Europe to Brooklyn, on his own, to get married. Only a decade later, when my mother was five, he'd called her to the radio to hear Hitler speak. "Listen, **Mamele**" (meaning "little mother," in affectionate Yiddish), my grandfather told her as the führer's clipped, stentorian tones invaded their narrow sliver of a dimly lit kitchen. "This is a very bad man. We have to pay attention." Soon the bad man had killed his mother, father, sister, aunts, uncles, and cousins back in Europe, every single person he'd ever known and loved. In public, my grandfather lived a vibrant life dedicated to his congregation. At home, the air in their one-bedroom apartment was heavy with his sighs.

The tragedies that surrounded my mother became part of her; later, they became almost all of her. She was consumed by feelings of fear and unworthiness. But she managed to hold them at bay when I was a child. Looking back now, I see the signs of what was to come: how she panicked if I wandered steps away at the supermarket; how she forbade many normal childhood activities—climbing a tree, riding a horse—that she deemed too dangerous; how she said that she loved me so much that she would, if she could, wrap me up in cotton. She meant this as an expression of love. I understood that it was also a prison sentence.

From an early age, we also stood on opposite sides of the fault line of religion. My mother raised me as an Orthodox Jew—no driving, TV, or phone calls on Shabbat; no McDonald's, no pepperoni pizza. But it never stuck. One of my earliest memories is surreptitiously watching **Scooby-Doo** on mute on Saturday mornings; another is eating bacon—profoundly unkosher, deeply delicious bacon—on a school ski trip. This was partly because my family was a confusing grab bag of influences: on the one hand, my beloved grandfather the rabbi, and my mother the staunch loyalist; on the other hand, my father, a tacit atheist whose gods were clearly science and literature. Also, I was a born skeptic. To this day, if you say "X," I automatically think: "What about Y?" As an adult, this tendency is intellectually useful (though sometimes it drives my husband bonkers). As a girl, I couldn't see why we should keep kosher in the name of a God I doubted was real.

But the real conflict between my mother and me didn't start until I was in high school, when the minor restrictions of childhood gave way to an ironclad code of chastity: No suggestive clothing. No unsupervised time with boys, ever. My mother even watched as I got my hair cut, chastising the hairdresser if he styled the angles too provocatively. Theoretically the rules were religious and cultural in nature. But their real function was to serve as an anchor to keep my ship docked in my mother's harbor. When I followed the code, the ship rocked gently in her lapping waves. When I deviated from it, her gale-force anger tore us both to smithereens.

By American standards of the 1980s, I was polite and responsible and a little too straitlaced. But invariably I would break the rules—wear the wrong clothes, make the wrong friends, attend the wrong party—and panicked, hostile accusations would follow. Waves of anger, floods of tears; days, then weeks, of stony silence. During these wordless eternities, it was as if all love had drained from my soul. My stomach churned; I couldn't eat. But the weight I lost was nothing compared to the emotional hunger—and the guilt I bore for making my mother so sad.

My friends were bewildered when I reported these conflicts, and the depths of my reactions to them. To them I seemed, and probably was, the most rule-abiding girl in school, got the highest grades, didn't smoke or do drugs; what more did my mother want? **Why don't you just say you're sleeping at my house,** they would say, if we wanted to stay out late one night. They couldn't understand that my mother and I were so close that she could read my face more accurately than any lie detector test, or that the rules in my house were different from theirs, that to break them was not to commit an adolescent transgression but to destroy my mother's fragile psyche. That if only I would do the right thing, my mother, whom I loved more than anyone and anything, would be happy again. And so would I.

Since neither of us could stand being separated, after each traumatic rupture, we always reconciled; the nurturing mother of my childhood always returned to me. We would hug, shed a few tears; I would lower myself gratefully into her warm bath of love and comfort. With each reunion, I believed the war was behind us. But it was never behind us. Over time, I learned to mistrust the cease-fires. I started to approach our house after school with a stomach-ache, grew skilled at gauging her mood the moment I entered. I felt I mustn't do anything to upset her equilibrium or trigger her rage. I became more aware of her childhood sorrows and of her present, gaping maw of emptiness. I started to dream of escape—of the day I'd go to college and be free of her.

But I also longed to stay. She was still my mother. And I wanted desperately, more than I've ever wanted anything before or since, to fill the chasm inside her, to take away her hurt. I couldn't think of my mother's tears—which I often caused—without crying myself. As the youngest child, I mattered so much to her, I mattered too much, I mattered like the sun. To grow up was to condemn her to darkness. Back then, I still believed that there must be a way out of this conundrum, that somehow, if I did everything right, I could find a way to be myself and still make her happy—the way I'd once done so effortlessly, during my Edenic childhood.

. . .

In our house, getting into a good college was the holy grail. My mother dreaded my departure, but even more she desired my success. So it was that on April 15 of senior year, the momentous day of college decisions, we'd set aside our differences. I was still asleep when the mail came, but she beamed as she brought the large, thick envelope bearing the Princeton University insignia to my bedroom. Together we beheld the precious document, as sixty years earlier my grandfather must have gazed at his ticket, steerage class, for a steamship to America. He was the same age then that I was now.

But my acceptance letter delivered me, the following September, not to the teeming throngs of Ellis Island but to an illuminated landscape of Gothic courtyards and cloistered lawns. Princeton, for better and for worse, was the exact opposite of my childhood home, its students landed and nonchalant. The campus was populated with classmates who possessed a physical grace I was wholly unacquainted with: narrow hips, strong limbs, glossy streams of blond hair. This was the 1980s, and students from diverse heritages were relatively scarce on campus; you could still feel F. Scott Fitzgerald in the air. The most attractive students were known as "BPs"—campus slang for "beautiful people." Even the autumn air was crisp and aristocratic. Everything and everyone shimmered.

There was only one blot on this exalted landscape: the telephone in my dorm room, linking me inescapably with my mother. At first when it rang it was merely incongruous: her voice on the other end, beaming in from the distant planet of childhood. She wanted to know if I was happy at college; she wanted to know if I was adhering to the code which, of course, required saving your virginity until you married one of your own. Uneasily I weighed these rules against the strapping young men of Princeton who devoured bacon cheeseburgers after crew practice. To my mother, it went without saying that such classmates were off-limits. But to me they were irresistible. I saw them, at seventeen, as future presidents, gracing us with this interlude in their lives before they would set policies and wage wars, grow paunches and take mistresses. We enjoyed the best of them, I felt, while they still wore Grateful Dead T-shirts, kissed sweetly under moonlit archways, gazed respectfully in art history class at the classmate who could tell a Rembrandt from a Caravaggio.

My mother sensed all this; she was sure I'd get pregnant, ruin my reputation, and die of AIDS before graduation. As freshman year wore on, she felt every inexorable step of my separation from her. She became increasingly distraught, the way you would if you truly believed that your daughter had agreed to be devoured by a monster. If in high school we'd followed a repeating pattern of separation and reunion, now the mother of my childhood had simply vanished. In her place was a vengeful woman who telephoned daily with accusations of malfeasance, who stood for hours at my bedroom door during college vacations, threatening that if I didn't "wise up," she'd pull me out of Princeton so she could keep an eye on me. I was terrified, not so much by the loss of the Ivy League degree as by the prospect of living again under my mother's watch.

Had she been struck down, at that time, by a ten-wheel truck, or a swift and incurable disease, I would have been one part relieved and three parts devastated; and for this there would have been funeral rituals, there would have been a language for the pain, a way for others to understand it. As it was, it never occurred to me to mourn her. Who would think to grieve a mother who was pulsatingly alive and daily appearing, Gorgon-like, at the other end of a dorm room telephone?

Instead, I confided my shameful desires in my journals, filling notebook after notebook. I wrote that I loved her but also hated her. I wrote in excruciating detail about all the forbidden things I was doing at college. I wrote of my dawning realization that the mother I adored—who adored me—was not dead but gone, and possibly had never existed in the first place, that I was motherless in some existential way. In short, I recorded all the things I couldn't tell her in real life, because I knew that to share them would have been emotional matricide. And in this way, I made it through freshman year.

And now we come to the part of the story that you might have trouble believing. All these years later, I can't believe it myself.

It was the last day of the school year. For some reason I can't recall, I needed to stay on campus for a few extra days, but to send my belongings home. My parents arrived to help with my bags; we greeted each other in my empty, echoing dorm room. I felt ill at ease, that my parents didn't belong here, which only reminded me that neither did I. Down the hall had lived another freshman named Lexa, an architecture student with an entire wardrobe the color of charcoal and a collection of elegant friends from Manhattan and assorted European capitals, whom she described as "nice." It had taken me weeks to decipher that **nice** meant **glamorous.** I couldn't help comparing my mother, who carried the weight of the world on her anxious face, with Lexa's mother, a filmmaker who'd come to pick her up the day before, wearing a slim leather jacket and an armful of silver bangles. I hated myself for noticing the difference between them.

We said goodbye. And that's when it happened. Without having planned it, without conscious awareness of the implications: I handed my diaries to my mother. Handed them to her! Unthinkingly, as an afterthought! I asked her to take them home for me—for safekeeping, I said. For safekeeping, I believed. The story I told myself, at that pivotal moment, was that she was still the angel of my childhood, the mother who would never do anything

wrong, like read someone's diary. Even if that someone handed her that diary . . . for safekeeping.

But of course, upon handing her that stack of notebooks, into which I'd inscribed the story of our great
love and its traumatic unraveling, I'd chosen to sever
our relationship. It's painful for any parent to hear
what their teenager really thinks of them. For my
mother, it must have been unbearable. As indeed she
testified, when I got home the following week and
she stood at my bedroom door, holding my journals
and miming a guillotine blade across her neck. I felt
that she was right; I felt that I was, in some psychologically true point of fact, my mother's killer.

. . .

Childhood will always end; but these weren't the
ordinary pangs of adolescence. For the decades
after I gave my mother my diaries, we still talked
on the phone, still saw each other at holidays, still
said "I love you," and meant it. But she haunted
my dreams, appearing in different guises as a sometimes menacing, sometimes fragile protagonist to
whom I was yoked, someone I loved yet longed to
escape. In waking life, we circled each other, warmly
but warily, many of our conversations still fencing
matches best concluded quickly. I didn't trust her,
and she didn't trust me. I learned to keep my distance, to have stronger boundaries, to understand
our not altogether uncommon situation, in which

the parent tells the child that she can be herself or be loved but she can't be both, in which the child believes that if only she agrees never to grow up, she'll be loved forever. Often, the child conspires with this agreement. Until, one day, she doesn't.

It took me a very long time to forgive myself for breaking my end of the bargain. It took me even longer to do, emotionally, without a mother. But I learned to deal with the sequela of having grown up this way: my tendency to avoid conflict, distrust my own reality, defer to others with stronger opinions. There was one me who marched to her own drummer, who followed her own true north, as I'm constitutionally inclined to do. And there was the other me, who surfaced during times of discord, who assumed that other people's interpretations of events must be correct and should naturally trump mine. I've come such a long way; I'm still working on it; I will always be working on it.

But for a very long time, even after my life had moved on and even soared, even after I had a home of my own, a family of my own, in so many ways the vibrant life I'd dreamed of as a child, even then I couldn't speak of my mother without tears. I couldn't even say a simple thing like "my mother grew up in Brooklyn" without crying. For this reason, I learned not to speak of her at all. The tears felt unacceptable; it made no sense to grieve a mother who was still alive, even a mother as difficult as mine. But I couldn't accept the chasm between the mother I remembered, who'd been my greatest companion, champion, and love, and the one I had now. Yet that childhood mother—if she'd ever existed in the first place—had walked away with the diaries I handed her on the final day of freshman year, and it was, for all intents and purposes, the last I ever saw of her.

. . .

But she never did pull me out of Princeton. And when I got back to campus, I signed up for a creative writing class, and wrote a story about a daughter who desperately loves an impossible mother. About a young woman longing to taste adult life and love. I called it "The Most Passionate Love."

The professor, a seasoned novelist with a gruff manner, read it through and pronounced that I was too close to the material.

"Put it in a drawer and don't take it out again for thirty years," she advised.

The professor was right. But that was over thirty years ago.

. . .

I've told you how I loved and lost my mother, but not because of the particulars of my story. Your stories of love and loss—of bitter and sweet—are different; I'm acutely aware that they might be much more traumatic (but hopefully less so) than this. But

I decided to share this story because, whether you consider it a small loss, in the scale of the world's sufferings, or a big one, because mothers represent love itself (as we just discovered from Darwin and the Dalai Lama), I know that you've lost loves of your own, or you will. And it took me decades to understand the events I just described, let alone to heal (mostly) from them. Maybe I've learned something that could be of use to you.

We're taught to think of our psychic and physical wounds as the irregularities in our lives, deviations from what should have been; sometimes, as sources of stigma. But our stories of loss and separation are also the baseline state, right alongside our stories of landing our dream job, falling in love, giving birth to our miraculous children. And the very highest states—of awe and joy, wonder and love, meaning and creativity—emerge from this bittersweet nature of reality. We experience them not because life is perfect—but because it's not.

What are you separated from; what or whom have you lost? Did the love of your life betray you? Did your parents divorce when you were young, did your father die, was he cruel? Did your family reject you when they discovered your true sexuality, do you miss home, or the country of your birth, do you need to hear its music to fall asleep at night? How are you supposed to integrate this bitter with your sweet, how are you supposed to feel whole again?

To these questions there's an infinity of answers; here are three.

One: These losses shape your psyche; they lay down patterns for all your interactions. If you don't understand them and actively work to form new emotional habits, you'll act them out again and again. They'll wreak havoc on your relationships, and you won't know why. There are many ways to confront them, some of which we're exploring in this book.

Two: No matter how much therapeutic work you do, these may be your Achilles' heels for life: maybe a fear of abandonment, a fear of success, a fear of failure; maybe deep-seated insecurity, rejection sensitivity, precarious masculinity, perfectionism; maybe hair-trigger rage, or a hard nub of grief you can feel like a knot protruding from your otherwise smooth skin. Even once you break free (and you **can** break free), these siren songs may call you back to your accustomed ways of seeing and thinking and reacting. You can learn to block your ears most of the time, but you'll have to accept that they're always out there singing.

The third answer is the most difficult one to grasp, but it's also the one that can save you. The love you lost, or the love you wished for and never had: That love exists eternally. It shifts its shape, but it's always there. **The task is to recognize it in its new form.**

• • •

Remember the linguistic origins of the word
yearning: The place you suffer is the place you care.
You hurt **because** you care. Therefore, the best response to pain is to dive deeper into your caring.
Which is exactly the opposite of what most of us
want to do. We want to avoid pain: to ward off the
bitter by not caring quite so much about the sweet.
But "to open your heart to pain is to open your heart
to joy," as the University of Nevada clinical psychologist Dr. Steven Hayes put it in a **Psychology Today**
article he wrote called "From Loss to Love." "In your
pain you find your values, and in your values, you
find your pain."

Hayes is the founder of an influential therapeutic
technique called acceptance and commitment therapy. ACT, as it's known, teaches people to embrace
their thoughts and feelings, including the difficult
ones: to see them as appropriate responses to the
challenges of being alive, and of their own particular
hardships. But it also teaches us to use our pain as
a source of information about what matters most to
us—and then to act on it. ACT, in other words, is
an invitation to investigate the bitter, and commit
to the sweet.

"When you connect with things that you deeply
care about that lift you up, you've just connected
yourself into places where you can and have been
hurt," Hayes explains. "If love is important to you,
what are you going to do with your history of betray-
als? If the joy of connecting to others is important to

you, what are you going to do with the pain of being misunderstood or failing to understand others?"

Hayes and his colleagues have distilled these insights into seven skills for coping with loss. In more than a thousand studies over thirty-five years, they've found that the acquisition of this skill set predicts whether people facing loss fall into anxiety, depression, trauma, substance abuse—or whether they thrive.

The first five skills involve **acceptance** of the bitter. First, we need to acknowledge that a loss has occurred; second, to embrace the emotions that accompany it. Instead of trying to control the pain, or to distract ourselves with food, alcohol, or work, we should simply feel our hurt, sorrow, shock, anger. Third, we need to accept **all** our feelings, thoughts, and memories, even the unexpected and seemingly inappropriate ones, such as liberation, laughter, and relief. Fourth, we should expect that sometimes we'll feel overwhelmed. And fifth, we should watch out for unhelpful thoughts, such as "I should be over this," "It's all my fault," and "Life is unfair."

Indeed, the ability to accept difficult emotions— not just observe them, not just breathe through them, but actually, nonjudgmentally, **accept** them— has been linked repeatedly to long-term thriving. In a 2017 study by University of Toronto professor Brett Ford, subjects were asked to give an impromptu speech describing their communication skills to an imaginary job interviewer. Those who'd been prescreened as habitual "negative emotion acceptors"—even people who'd recently experienced major stresses, such as losing a job or being cheated on—suffered less stress. Another study found that habitual negative emotion acceptors had a greater sense of well-being than their peers, even when they experienced stresses such as an argument with a significant other, or a phone call from a son in prison.

But it's the final two of the seven skills—connecting with what matters, and taking committed action—that move us from bitter to sweet, from loss to love. "Connecting with what matters" is realizing that the pain of loss can help point you to the people and principles that matter most to you—to the meaning in your life. "Taking committed action" is **acting** on those values. "Your loss can be an opportunity to carry what is most meaningful toward a life worth living," writes Hayes. "After having identified what is truly close to your heart, act on it."

So now, ask yourself that question again: **What are you separated from, what or whom have you lost?** And also ask: Where is your particular pain of separation pointing you? What matters most deeply to you? And how can you bring it into being?

These skills, of connecting and committing, can take many forms. The architect and engineer Buckminster Fuller was so devastated after his business failed and he lost his four-year-old daughter to meningitis in 1922 that he almost died by suicide. But he took his belief that life wasn't worth living and turned it on its head, asking what would make life worthwhile after all—what a single human could do to benefit humanity. Quite a lot, it turned out. The inventor of the geodesic dome and many other designs, Fuller became known as the "Leonardo da Vinci of the twentieth century."

For the poet and author Maya Angelou, it was her voice that she lost, along with her dignity and self-love. But later she reconnected with that voice, and committed to it, in new and powerful forms. She tells the story of her early years in her powerful memoir **I Know Why the Caged Bird Sings.** How she was sent with her brother, when they were very small, to live with their grandmother in Arkansas, a sign pinned to their chests reading "To Whom It May Concern." How, when she was five, she was supposed to recite an Easter poem in front of her church, but felt too big, awkward, and unworthy to say the words; she hadn't yet awakened, as she put it, from her "black ugly dream," and she fled the church crying and wetting herself. How she was raped at age eight by her mother's boyfriend, and testified against him in court, after which he was kicked to death by an angry mob. How she believed that anyone else she talked to might die, too.

And so she stopped speaking, to anyone but her brother. For five long years.

Through it all, she took refuge in reading. At age thirteen, Maya was invited to the home of a woman named Mrs. Bertha Flowers. Mrs. Flowers was gentle, graceful, educated; she seemed to Maya perfect, but she must have had sorrows and longings of her own—she smiled often, writes Angelou, but never laughed. She gave Maya a book of poems, asked her to memorize one and recite it on her next visit. But first she read to her from **A Tale of Two Cities:** "It was the best of times, it was the worst of times." Mrs. Flowers spoke these words, but it seemed to Maya that she sang them. She'd read the book before, but now she wanted to examine its pages. "Were they the same that I had read?" she wondered. "Or were there notes, music, lined on the pages, as in a hymn book?"

She started to speak again. At first, through the words of others; later, through her own. Poetry, essays, memoirs. Before long, she was speaking **for** others. Including for one young girl, twenty-six years her junior, a voracious reader growing up in Mississippi, who stumbled across Angelou's book at age fifteen, stunned to see herself in its pages. "How could this author, Maya Angelou, have the same life experiences, the same feelings, longings, perceptions, as a poor black girl from Mississippi—as me?" writes Oprah, in the foreword to **Caged Bird.** "I was that girl who had recited Easter pieces. . . . I was that girl who loved to read. I was that girl raised by my Southern grandmother, I was that girl raped at nine, who muted the telling of it. I understood why Maya Angelou remained silent for years."

One young woman tells the truth about her

sorrows, and another young woman, a generation later, is uplifted. **There's someone else like me. I'm not alone with my story.**

And this healing process doesn't require a shared life history; as Oprah writes, "We can all be stirred when the caged bird sings." There's something about the act of speaking—of singing—the truth-telling language of sorrow and longing. Why did W.E.B. Du Bois call the "Sorrow Songs" sung by the enslaved people of the American South "the most beautiful expression of human experience born this side of the seas"? Why did Oprah see in Angelou's writing not only a mirror reflecting her own life but also, in her own words, a "revelation"? When she read Angelou's memoir, she writes, she was "in awe." The book became her "talisman." When she had the chance to meet Angelou ten years later, it was "Providence." These aren't ordinary terms of enthusiasm. This is the language of transformation. Of a lost self, returned in another form.

. . .

As Angelou's story suggests, many people respond to loss by healing in others the wounds that they themselves have suffered. Angelou did this through writing, but the process takes many forms. Indeed, the "wounded healer," a term coined by the psychologist Carl Jung in 1951, is one of humanity's oldest archetypes. In Greek myth, the centaur Chiron was injured by a poisoned arrow that gave him terrible pain, but also curative powers. In shamanistic cultures, often healers must first undergo an initiation process involving great misery. In Judaism, the Messiah's powers derive from his own suffering; he surrounds himself with the poor and the sick **because** he's one of them. And in Christianity, Jesus is the wounded healer who cures bleeding women, hugs lepers, and dies on a cross to save us all.

In modern times, wounded healers take more recognizable forms. The bereaved mother of a teen girl dead on the highway founds Mothers Against Drunk Driving. A nine-year-old whose father dies of brain cancer grows up to be a grief counselor. The survivor of a mass shooting starts a gun control organization.

Wounded healers also appear in studies finding that mental health counselors personally affected by mental illness tend to be more engaged in their work. After the national trauma of September 11, 2001, record numbers of Americans applied for careers as firefighters, teachers, and healthcare workers. At Teach for America, applications tripled in the six weeks after 9/11, according to **The New York Times,** and half of those applicants said they were motivated by the disaster. One New York City firefighter explained to the **Times** that he'd been " 'on the fence' about joining" the squad because of how time-consuming it was. "Then, after 9/11, all I wanted to do was help." Actor Amy Ting, who came close to dying that day in the World Trade Center, left the film industry and joined the Air Force Medical Service. "After September 11, my perspective on life changed," she told **Airman** magazine. "I have always wanted to help people, so I decided to go back to pursuing the medical field."

Another inspiring example of a wounded healer is author and public defender Rene Denfeld, who has written about her horrific childhood of sexual abuse and neglect. Denfeld's mother was an alcoholic, her stepfather a pimp, her home a magnet for pedophiles. She tried to report the abuse, but no one believed her. She ran away to live on the streets of Portland, Oregon, where she was preyed upon by a grotesque collection of predators.

There were many possible responses to this kind of family life. Denfeld's mother, herself a victim of rape and violence, racked by guilt at having failed to protect her children, died by suicide. Denfeld's brother tried to escape his history by becoming what Denfeld calls, in her searing essay "The Other Side of Loss," "the king of normal." He wore a button-down shirt, carried a pocket protector, tried to wipe away the stains of their childhood. He tried in vain, and he died by suicide, too. "I just wanted to be a good boy," he said before he left.

No one would have been surprised if Denfeld took the same path. But she became the chief investigator at a public defender's office in Portland, where she helped rape victims escape their traffickers and defended the accused from death row. She wrote three novels about characters who suffered their own trauma. And she adopted three kids from foster care, children with pasts as horrific as her own, children who, like Denfeld herself, seemed beyond the reach of love. At first, these children raged at her, stared at her glassy-eyed. But she persevered. For over twenty years now, she has loved their unlikely family into being.

"My kids bring me joy and redemption and a sense of purpose," she writes in her essay.

> Every laugh we share, every touch, is a reminder to me that reality can, indeed, change. From trauma rises the soul, incandescent and perfect. It was always there, waiting to be embraced. . . .
>
> The best way to heal yourself? Heal others.
>
> I don't believe we can escape our past. My brother and mother tried it, and it didn't work. We have to make friends with sadness. We have to hold our losses close, and carry them like beloved children. Only when we accept these terrible pains do we realize that the path across is the one that takes us through.

Most of us haven't been through trials like Buckminster Fuller, Maya Angelou, and Rene Denfeld; and if we have, we aren't going to respond by inventing the geodesic dome, writing transformative memoirs, or loving a family of abused children into being. But many of us **are** wounded healers, and our active moves toward love needn't be so heroic or inventive. Maybe we adopt a dog and lavish it with care. Maybe we find work as a teacher, or midwife, or firefighter. Maybe we simply put down our phones and pay closer attention to our friends and families.

Or maybe, as I recently did, we take up loving-kindness meditation.

. . .

Loving-kindness meditation—known in the Pali language as **metta**—is the practice of wishing well to others. Its name "sounds phony, sentimental, and gooey" to many people, as Sharon Salzberg, one of its leading American teachers, told me. This is one reason that it's not as fashionable in the West as mindfulness. But **metta** is an ancient Buddhist practice that has many benefits—from increased feelings of awe, joy, and gratitude, to decreased migraines, chronic pain, and PTSD. It's also a time-honored way of moving actively toward love. If you're a person who has lost an important love and who realizes that love matters to you deeply, then **metta** is—to use the language of acceptance and commitment therapy—a form of "taking committed action" and "connecting with what matters."

Today, Salzberg is a world authority on **metta.** She popularized the practice in the United States; she's the bestselling author of eleven books, including

Lovingkindness and **Real Happiness;** she's the co-founder of Insight Meditation Society in Barre, Massachusetts, one of the most influential meditation centers in the West.

But she was also, once, a child who suffered one lacerating separation after another. It started with her father, who'd been "her person," the one she adored. He had a nervous breakdown when she was four, and left the family. Her mother died when she was nine. She went to live with her grandparents, whom she barely knew. Her grandfather died when she was eleven. Her father returned, to her brief joy, then overdosed on sleeping pills and spent the rest of his short life in a mental institution. By the time Sharon was sixteen, she'd lived in five different family configurations, each brought to an abrupt end by trauma, loss, or death.

She felt different, less than, ashamed. At home, no one talked about what happened to her father; they pretended the sleeping pills were an accident. At school, the kids asked "What does your father do?" and she didn't know the answer. Her classmates had intact families; the people who loved them didn't go away. She was the only one she knew who'd experienced loss and abandonment; she knew this marked her as different and inferior. Never did it occur to her to question this conclusion. And she might never **have** questioned it—if when she got to college she hadn't serendipitously signed up for a class on Asian philosophy.

She hadn't been seeking Eastern wisdom; she was just looking for a class that fit her schedule. But what she learned changed her life, and later the lives of the countless thousands Sharon has since taught. She learned that everyone faces the pain of separation, that no one is spared, that the real question is how to respond to this unchanging truth.

She was incredulous: **You mean you're** supposed **to feel this way? You mean this is normal? You mean, just because you're in pain doesn't mean you're weird, doesn't mean you don't belong?**

She went to India to learn more, and stayed for almost four years. After her childhood of family secrets, she loved the openness and transparency she found there. She studied with one of India's most revered teachers, Dipa Ma, whose name means Mother of Dipa—Dipa being the teacher's only surviving child. Dipa Ma had suffered, too: an arranged marriage at the age of twelve, years of infertility, then, finally, three children in quick succession, two of whom died along with her husband; everyone gone except for little Dipa, whose mother, Dipa Ma, was too heartbroken to raise her. Dipa Ma suffered from heart disease and hypertension; the doctor told her she would die of a broken heart. You should learn how to meditate, he said. She was so weak that she had to crawl up the stairs of a nearby temple. But she learned quickly, and managed to transform her grief into compassion. She raised little Dipa, moved to Calcutta, and became one of India's greatest teachers.

From Dipa Ma, Sharon Salzberg learned the practice of loving-kindness meditation, in which you send out love to yourself, to your loved ones, and to all the people in the world. She also taught her the classic Buddhist story of the mustard seed. In the story, a woman loses her only child. Grief-stricken, she staggers across the town, her son's corpse in her arms, searching for a doctor or sage who can bring him back to life. Finally, she meets the Buddha. He tells her that her wish will be granted; all she has to do is bring him a mustard seed. But just one thing, he adds. The seed must come from a household where no one has ever died, where they've never known loss or grief. The bereaved mother is thrilled, sets off on her quest, knocks on one door after another. And soon learns the lesson that Sharon encountered in her Asian philosophy class: Loss is part of life; no household is free of it. The woman buries her son, and becomes a nun and enlightened.

When finally Sharon was ready to leave India, Dipa Ma told her that, upon returning to the United States, it would be her turn to teach. And because old mental habits die hard, Sharon's reaction was: "Who, me? What am I worth, what could I possibly pass on to anyone?"

"You understand suffering," said Dipa Ma. "That's why you should teach."

"And that," Sharon told me, "is the first time in my life I thought that suffering was worth something."

...

Ever since the conflict with my mother, I'd had trouble holding the line against people who were bullying or manipulative. When I finally started to draw proper boundaries, I found that the only way I could protect myself from them was to steel myself with indifference or anger. I didn't like how this felt; I thought there must be a better way. So when a friend told me about loving-kindness meditation and offered to introduce me to Sharon, I jumped at the chance.

I went to see her one day, in her bright, spare studio apartment overlooking lower Fifth Avenue in Greenwich Village. Sharon has a deep, mellow voice, and a calm, embracing presence. She listened quietly as I told her my story, and its emotional aftermath. I felt embarrassed to admit to my bitter side, which seemed the opposite of all she stood for. But she just listened in her unsurprised way. Yes, she said, matter-of-factly, in the manner of one who has heard such things many times before. Yes, you can do better.

I didn't feel judged. I felt in the hands of a maestro.

Which didn't mean I wasn't my normal skeptical self. I was intrigued, but still wondered whether this whole loving-kindness project was actually possible. There's an idea, in the **metta** tradition, that you could love all beings the way a mother loves her only child.

But I don't think I **can** love random people in the same infinite way I love my sons. I'm not even sure I should. Isn't that the point, for your children to know that, in your eyes, they count most? That you'd give your life for them more readily than you would for others? And what about sadists and psychopaths? I should love **them** the way I love my children? That didn't seem right.

But Sharon's response to such questions, like everything about her, was eminently reasonable. You're not going to invite everyone to move in with you, she said. You're still going to protect yourself. Not everyone's going to be your friend. But you can wish everyone love.

She gave the example of a friend who'd cut off contact with her mentally ill, physically violent mother. This friend happened to be studying with the Dalai Lama at the time that her abusive mother begged to see her again. The friend was scared of her mother; she didn't **want** to see her. But she felt guilty: "I'm spending all this time with the Dalai Lama," she thought, "and I don't want to spend time with my own mother."

She asked the Dalai Lama's advice. He suggested that she send her mother loving-kindness . . . from a safe distance. A heart full of love doesn't necessarily require physical presence, he said. If she were the child and you were the parent, he said, the responsibility would be different; you would have to be there. But as the child, the love can be present, even when you're not physically together.

Ever the doubter, I asked Sharon what this actually meant. "Maybe it makes the **daughter** feel good," I said, "because she's the one who gets to sit around thinking about loving-kindness. But her mother's far away, and she has no idea any of this is happening. All she knows is that her daughter refuses to see her. So what good does it really do?"

"Making yourself feel good is not a nothing," Sharon said.

This hadn't occurred to me.

"It also allows the connection to grow," she added. "Maybe she'll write to her mother and tell her that she's thinking of her. Maybe she'll tell her that she wishes her well. Maybe one day she'll be ready to meet her in person, in a public place that feels safe."

For Sharon, the simple act of privately wishing people well has a way of changing the way we relate to them, and to the world. Do you tend to get lost in thought and look through the cashier at the grocery store? Maybe you'll start looking **at** them, ask about their lives. Do you tend to be fearful? Love is the antidote to fear. Fear causes you to shrink and withhold; love opens you up. Do you tend to focus on your mistakes and shortcomings? Maybe you can shift your emphasis from one true place ("I have a lot of flaws and made a lot of mistakes today") to another true place ("I have a lot of flaws and made a lot of mistakes, **and** I'm also worthy, and will try again tomorrow"). Maybe you'll start giving that second true place more airtime.

But it's one thing to accept these ideas intellectually, to **want** to practice **metta.** It's another to actually do it. Even in Sharon's beatific presence, I found myself doing anything I could to procrastinate **actually meditating.** I taped our sessions, and the transcripts are hilarious. Every time we were about to start, I would ask Sharon another theoretical question. Obligingly she explained the Buddhist traditions of sympathetic joy, equanimity, compassion. Never did she rush me.

But even I could intellectualize for only so long. Finally, she taught me what to actually **do.**

When Sharon first studied **metta** in Burma, she was given these phrases to repeat:

May I be free from danger.
May I be free from mental suffering.
May I be free from physical suffering.
May I have ease of well-being.

The idea is to wish these states first to yourself, then to an ever-widening circle of people: loved ones, acquaintances, the difficult people in your life, and then finally to all beings. (Some people feel uncomfortable starting with themselves; you can switch the order until you find the sequence that suits you.)

At first, this might strike you as the practice of all sweet, no bitter. But life's dualities lie at **metta**'s heart. We wish each other freedom from danger, because we understand that ease is elusive. We wish each other love, because we know that love and loss are forever twinned.

When she started teaching in 1985 in New England, Sharon's students were fine with the phrases from Burma. But then she taught a retreat in California, and her students lined up to complain that they didn't want to say negative words like **danger** and **suffering.** They wanted positive words, upbeat words. There's no law of **metta** governing which words to use, and Sharon's a capacious soul. So in California, she switched her phrases to

May I be safe.
May I be happy.
May I be healthy.
May I live with ease.

I understood the Californians' point, but this seemed all wrong to me. It seemed like trying to deny reality. Like trying to forswear the bitter part of bittersweet.

I told Sharon I preferred the Burma version. And, together, we closed our eyes and said the magic words.

. . .

Since then, I've practiced **metta** on and off. Sometimes—okay, often—it feels formulaic, contrived. But whenever I practice for a sustained time, I notice that it's easier to hold boundaries in a calm and friendly way. I'm also less likely to recoil with embarrassment over a stupid thing I said seventeen years ago, more apt to address myself with the same care I'd show a beloved child. And, most of all, I find it easier to see love not only in its particular forms—the love of **my** spouse, **my** children, **my** friends—but also as an eternal essence that takes different forms at different times. It's easier to see that love can show up—that we can conjure it up—in the most unexpected guises.

Franz Kafka was one of the great European novelists of the twentieth century. But there's another story, this one written not **by** Kafka but about him, by the Spanish writer Jordi Sierra i Fabra. This story is based on the memoirs of a woman named Dora Diamant, who lived with Kafka in Berlin, just before his death.

In this story, Kafka takes a walk in the park, where he meets a tearful little girl who just lost her favorite doll. He tries and fails to help find the doll, then tells the girl that the doll must have taken a trip, and he, a doll postman, would send word from her. The next day, he brings the girl a letter, which he'd composed the night before. Don't be sad, says the doll in the letter. "I have gone on a trip to see the world. I will write you of my adventures." After that, Kafka gives the girl many such letters. The doll is going to school, meeting exciting new people. Her new life prevents her from returning, but she loves the girl, and always will.

At their final meeting, Kafka gives the girl a doll, with an attached letter. He knows that this doll looks different from the lost one, so the letter says: "My travels have changed me."

The girl cherishes the gift for the rest of her life. And many decades later, she finds another letter stuffed into an overlooked cranny in the substitute doll. This one says: "Everything that you love, you will eventually lose. But in the end, love will return in a different form."

. . .

This fictional Kafka, in the voice of the doll, was teaching the girl how to draw strength from her own imagination. But he was also showing her how to perceive love in its many forms—including the form that he brought into being—by inventing the role of doll postman.

Maybe this story is apocryphal, maybe it's factual. The record's not quite clear. Either way, it's deeply true. The fact that love sometimes returns in a different form doesn't mean that you won't feel seared and scalded when it goes away, or fails to appear in the first place, that its absence won't rip your life apart. It can also feel impossible to accept that **the love**

you long for will not return in the form you first longed for it. Your parents who divorced when you were seven will not get back together, and even if they did, you're no longer the child you were when they split. If you do return to your birth country, it will be as a stranger, and you may find that the lemon groves whose scent is still so fragrant in your memory have been paved into parking lots. You will never find again the specific places or people or dreams that you've lost.

But you can find something else. You can have momentary glimpses—which may only be glimpses but still they're momentous—of your own perfect and beautiful vision of the perfect and beautiful world.

> If you're interested in practicing my version of loving-kindness meditation, I have a guided version available on my website, at susancain.net.

. . .

At the age of eighty, my mother developed Alzheimer's. It proceeded in all the usual ways of the disease—she stopped eating and combing her hair, became confused about what day it was, started repeating the same questions again and again. But, as I write this, she's still herself in some fundamental way. And in this interregnum period, before she exits the stage, there's also this: She's forgotten—truly forgotten—the dark years of my adolescence, and all the strained decades that followed. She's sweet, and cozy: thrilled to be together, overjoyed to talk on the phone. She wants to hug and be hugged. And she wants to tell me, again and again, what a good daughter I've been, how I've "never given her any aggravation," how much she loves me and always has.

To this I respond by telling her what a good mother she was during my childhood (careful to put in that modification—**during my childhood**—because it seems important to tell the truth, it seems important to suggest to the invisible person who might be witnessing this exchange that I'm carving out from my praise the years of adolescence and sexual awakening). I want her to know that those childhood years when she infused me with so much care and kindness have given me a reserve of love and power that will sustain me for the rest of my life.

But she brushes this aside, impatiently but kindly. "I'm not looking for compliments," she says. And she means it; she isn't. "I just want you to know what a good daughter you've been." She says this urgently. "I just want you to know." During these final years, she has repeated this, every single time I call, every single time I visit. **I won't be able to tell you much longer, so please remember how much I love you. A good daughter, a good daughter, you've been such a good daughter.** I believe she's telling me the words she longed to hear from her own mother.

One time, I try to tell her lightly, jokingly, that she hasn't always felt this way, that she hasn't always considered me a good daughter. But she looks genuinely puzzled. Her failing memory has edited out those years.

Another time, she peers at me through a fog of confusion. "Sometimes I worry that I did something wrong," she says. "I hope I didn't do anything wrong, but if I did, I apologize." And as she speaks, I feel a familiar sensation of love mixed with guilt, except this time the guilt comes from the fact that even as she's apologizing for long-ago crimes she can no longer recall, I know that I'm going to commit the crime of publishing this book, the way I once handed her my diaries. She's a private person, which is another reason I've waited until the end of her lifetime to write our story.

But I also feel a sensation I can't put my finger on. It takes a while to identify it as relief: that my long-ago perceptions were accurate, after all. For all these years, I've suspected that I must have misremembered my childhood, that it must not have been the Eden I thought. But listening to my mother now—not only to her words, but to the boundlessly sweet and loving way she says them, her heart so full and open—it's all so familiar. I know then that it was all true, this mother I remember, that she really did exist. It once was like this, she once was like this, we once were like this. And for this moment in time, before her memory vanishes for good, this is the way we are, again.

Which isn't to say it's perfect; honestly, it was a

relief, when her hearing started to fail, that she could no longer understand what I was saying well enough to interrogate it. I still long for my mother's life to have unfolded differently, still wish that she'd loved herself, or even liked herself just a little. But I can't change her past. And here in the present, I know that whatever wounds we've inflicted on each other, in her way she succeeded spectacularly as a mother: I never felt unworthy, the way she did. Quite the opposite. My mother told me constantly, ever since I was a child, that the days my siblings and I were born were the best days of her life, and I believed her. I still believe her.

Everything is broken, everything is beautiful— everything, including love. And in the end, nothing could take away my mother's love for me, or mine for her.

Untitled, © Safwan Dahoul
(Instagram: @safwan_dahoul)

PART II

Winners and Losers

How can we live and work authentically
in a "tyranny of positivity"?

CHAPTER 5

How did a nation founded on so much
heartache turn into a culture of
normative smiles?

The word "loser" is spoken with such contempt these days, a man might like to forget the losses in his own life that taught him
something about good judgment.

—GARRISON KEILLOR

Now that we've explored the hidden riches of
sorrow and longing, let's step back to ask why our
society should be so afraid of these emotions. In the
next two chapters, we'll examine America's culture
of positivity—its history and its current manifestations, from religion to politics—and how it com-
pares to other societies. We'll trace its roots in the
economic development of the country. Then we'll

see how a culture of enforced positivity shapes the workplace—and how we might transcend it. Along the way, we'll draw on the insights of leading practitioners and scholars—including the groundbreaking work of Susan David, a Harvard Medical School psychologist and leading management thinker.

. . .

Susan was just fifteen when her forty-two-year-old father was diagnosed with colon cancer. Everyone told her: "Just stay positive. Everything will be okay."

So even as the illness ravaged her father's body, even as it turned out to be very much not okay, Susan kept acting as if it were. She watched stoically as her father grew weaker and weaker. Until one Friday morning in May, before she left for school, her mother whispered that she should say goodbye. Susan put down her backpack and walked down the hallway to her father's deathbed. She was sure he could still hear her, so she told him how much she loved him and always would. Then she picked up her satchel and went to school. Math class, history, biology. She took notes, chatted with classmates, ate lunch. When she got home, he was gone.

The family was devastated, not only emotionally but also financially. During his brief illness, Susan's father, normally a prudent and philosophical man, had gotten the idea that if he just stayed positive and had faith in God, he'd be cured. Also, that if he wasn't positive **enough,** if he showed a lack of faith, he would die. He even canceled his life insurance policy, as proof of this positivity. He'd been paying for that policy all his adult life. When he died, twenty weeks later, the family faced a mountain of debt.

But in the months that followed, Susan walked smiling through the world, as she knew everyone wanted. Susan was upbeat. Susan was strong. Above all, Susan was **okay.** Sometimes teachers and friends asked how she was doing, and that's what she always said: okay. She was a constitutionally cheerful person; she was the master of okay. No one asked "How are you **really**?" and Susan didn't tell them, didn't even tell herself. Only through food did she express her grief. She binged, purged, binged again.

She might have continued this way indefinitely, if not for her eighth-grade English teacher, who one day handed out blank notebooks to Susan's class. As it happened, this teacher had also lost a parent at a young age.

"Write. Tell the truth about your life," the teacher told the class, fixing Susan with kind and piercing blue eyes. "Write as if nobody's reading."

Susan understood that her teacher was talking to her. And "just like that," she recalls now, "I was invited to show up authentically to my grief and pain."

She wrote every day, about the enormity of her loss, the agony of it. She gave these journal entries to her teacher, who always wrote back, but in light pencil, as if to say: **I hear you, but this is your story.**

Her teacher didn't deny Susan's feelings, nor did she encourage them. She simply witnessed them.

But for Susan, these love letters—that's what Susan calls them: love letters—were "nothing short of a revolution." A revolution in a blank notebook. A revolution that saved her psyche; made her strong, resilient, and joyful; and shaped her life's work.

But where did this "tyranny of positivity" (as Susan now calls it) come from?* Why did her father believe that he had to "fight" cancer with blind optimism? And why did his bereaved daughter feel so much pressure to smile?

The answers to these questions can be found in American cultural beliefs about the self. We're encouraged to see ourselves, deep down, as winners or losers—and to show, with our sanguine-choleric behavior, that we belong to the former group. These attitudes shape countless aspects of our lives, often without our realizing it.

But Susan's story—from forced positivity to the revolution in her notebook—is **also** the story of our culture. It's the story of what we've been, and what we could be. It's the story of how each of us—especially those with a bittersweet orientation—can learn to

---

* The phrase comes from Susan David's friend who passed away from cancer, "and what she meant by it," Susan told **The Washington Post,** "was if being in remission was just a matter of positive thinking, then all of her friends in her breast cancer support group would be alive today."

live more wholly in a society that denies its own sorrow and longing.

...

Recently, I looked through some photos from my teen years. There I was, smiling broadly at senior prom and college holiday parties. Yet I remember my state of mind at the moment those photos were taken: sometimes as merry as my pose suggested, but often the smile was a façade. And you might think this is just the way adolescents are. But once I had a boyfriend who grew up in Eastern Europe, and he showed me his photo album from **his** teen years. I was shocked to see him, his friends, and his high school girlfriend posing, on page after page, with pouts and frowns. For them, **that** was cool. He was the one who introduced me to Leonard Cohen.

Americans, it turns out, smile more than any other society on earth. In Japan, India, Iran, Argentina, South Korea, and the Maldives, smiling is viewed as dishonest, foolish, or both, according to a study by Polish psychologist Kuba Krys. Many societies believe that expressing happiness invites bad luck and is a sign of selfishness, shallowness, and an uninteresting, even sinister, mind. When McDonald's opened its first franchise in Russia, local workers were bemused by its ethos of employee cheeriness, according to the radio show and podcast **Invisibilia.**

What is this American smile? they asked. "We are all serious about life, because life is struggle," as one employee put it. "We were always a little bit afraid of America's smile."

They were afraid, I think, because they knew that the smile wasn't real, couldn't be real. This has been our great secret, bursting recently into the open: We're less happy than citizens of other countries, and much less happy than we appear. Even before we'd heard of COVID-19, even before our political divisions took center stage, about 30 percent of Americans suffered from anxiety and 20 percent from major depression over their lifetimes, according to the National Institute of Mental Health and the **Journal of the American Medical Association,** and over fifteen million had taken antidepressants for over five years.

But our cultural rituals—the Fourth of July, New Year's Eve, "Happy Birthday to You"—celebrate birth rather than help us live with impermanence and sorrow. We don't honor deceased ancestors, as Mexicans do on the Day of the Dead. We don't turn over our water glasses at night, as Tibetan monks do to remember that they might be dead by morning. We don't write down our wishes and expose them to the elements, as the Japanese do at Mount Inari. We don't weave imperfections into our rugs, as the Navajo do, or bake them into our pottery, as the Japanese practice with the art form of **wabi sabi.** Even the sympathy cards we send deny our right to grieve, according to a study by the psychologists Birgit Koopmann-Holm and Jeanne Tsai. Compared with German cards, which feature black-and-white designs and sayings like "In deep sadness" and "Words will not lighten a heavy heart," American cards are colorful, with cheery proclamations like "Love lives on" and "Memories will bring comfort." Christ dies on the cross, but we focus on the birth and resurrection.

I once read about a remote tribe that required mothers to give up something precious every year, to prepare for their sons' departures at adolescence. My boys, as I write this, are ten and twelve. If we performed that ritual here, what would I renounce as I prepare for my sons to turn thirteen? My smartphone? My favorite dress, the one I wear to all my speaking engagements that requires no ironing? This is no moot question. My sons are marvelous, and I expect to be thrilled when they turn into independent young men. But I don't want to give up my dress and phone. Am I prepared to give up my boys?

After all my years considering these questions, I actually think that the answer is yes. But whatever equanimity I've gained has come despite our cultural practices, not because of them.

. . .

Historically, the United States has seen itself as the land of abundant resources, the frontier of limitless self-invention, the nation whose streets were paved with gold (or so dreamed the immigrants who ventured here).

Yet America has buried its bitter stories under the sweetness of this vision. Our alt-history includes the Declaration of Independence, a document written under penalty of treason and most of whose signatories lost "their lives, loved ones, and fortunes in the war," as Barbara Ehrenreich puts it in her book **Bright-Sided: How the Relentless Promotion of Positive Thinking Has Undermined America.** It includes the obliteration of Native American life and cultures. It's drenched in the blood and cries of slavery, our great national tragedy and sin: oceans of tears whose waves still wash our shores. This alt-history sweeps through the Civil War, which produced a scale of death that the United States hasn't seen before or since, according to Harvard historian Drew Gilpin Faust: The fatality rate was six times that of World War II, or about six million dead, in current population terms. Add to these horrors the multitudes of immigrants fleeing famine and genocide, crossing the seas to make their homes here, often with an unspoken pact never to speak of their pasts.

And all of this the generations carry forward, into their psyches, into their families, into the body politic. If recent advances in epigenetics are any indication (as we'll see in chapter 9), some may have passed down these experiences through the expression of their DNA, too, the cellular memory of ancient traumas encoded confusingly in American-born babies bred for optimism and cheer.

Our tyranny of positivity stems, in part, from underappreciated historical roots. The original dominant American culture, established by the white settlers who arrived in New England, reflected the tenets of Calvinism, a religion in which heaven existed, but only for those predestined for it. Hell was a terrifying place, abundant descriptions of which gave many children chronic nightmares. The doctrine of predestination meant that there wasn't much you could do to escape your assignment of either heaven or hell. But what you **could** do was show, by virtue of your ceaseless labor, that you were destined for the former. To do this, you had to till the land, clean the kitchen, and never seek pleasure for its own sake. There was no place for sorrow **or** joy—there was only the need to show that you were one of the winners, with a one-way ticket to heaven.

Calvinism seemed to loosen its grip on American culture during the nineteenth century, the era of commercial expansion. Instead of an empty frontier that early settlers had viewed as "a hideous and desolate wilderness, full of wild beasts and wild men," as an early settler named William Bradford put it, Americans looked out their windows and began to see roads and railways. "Why should we grope among the dry bones of the past?" Ralph Waldo

Emerson asked in 1849. "The sun shines today also. There is more wool and flax in the field. There are new lands, new men, new thoughts."

But Calvinism was replaced by the new national religion of business, in which you were predestined not for heaven or hell but for earthly success or failure. This was, as the writer Maria Fish put it in a review of Scott Sandage's fascinating book, **Born Losers: A History of Failure in America,** a "reconfiguration of the doctrine of predestination," with success as the holy grail, and the tycoon as high priest and alpha role model. To "be a man" increasingly meant to be a businessman. Farmers "must be extensively engaged in buying or selling," warned the **North American Review** in 1820, and "conversant with many commercial transactions." A man who failed to do this "will be a great loser."

This word—**loser**—had been part of the English language for hundreds of years, but now it carried new meaning. In the sixteenth century, it simply meant "one who suffers loss." But by nineteenth-century America, according to Sandage, the "loser" acquired a stink. It became something you **were,** while others were not. It came to mean, according to the Online Etymology Dictionary, a "hapless person, one who habitually fails to win." Another person's misfortunes **should** elicit compassion—as we saw in chapter 1, the very meaning of the word **compassion** is "to suffer **with**" someone. But the term **loser** now evoked not empathy but contempt.

Loss became a condition to avoid, by relentlessly cultivating the mindset and behaviors of a winner.

One problem with tying inner worth to outer fortune was the elusive nature of commercial success. Even if you were fortunate enough to find the grail of prosperity, could you keep it? This was the century of boom-and-bust capitalism. Each economic expansion minted a new crop of successful businessmen who were ruined overnight during the panics of 1819, 1837, 1857, and 1873. Many despaired; some died by suicide. And through all this, a question started to preoccupy the culture. When someone went bankrupt, whose fault was it? The economic system? A poor business decision? Bad luck? **Or could loss and heartache be traced to some mysterious flaw in the soul of each ruined businessman?**

Increasingly, failure was attributed to such flaws of the soul. Some "have failed, from causes beyond the control of human power," one lawmaker noted in 1822, but "this latter class must be comparatively small." The "loser" became, in Sandage's words, a "national bogeyman." Emerson, in his 1842 journal, recorded the proverb that "nobody fails who ought not to fail. There is always a reason, in the man, for his good or bad fortune, and so in making money." Similarly, "Failures that arise from inevitable misfortune alone are not so numerous as they are generally supposed to be," declared a Boston lecturer in 1846. "In most cases, insolvency is caused by mistakes that originate in personal character."

If the question of who was a winner and who a loser was answered by looking "in the man," then it followed that we'd start to seek the characteristics that would predict wealth and victory. We'd try to acquire the positive and vigorous affect of a winner.

Enter the New Thought movement, which initially focused on the mind's power to cure illness but, later in the century, to generate worldly success. The movement replaced the Calvinistic ethos of the Pilgrims with the belief in a forgiving deity and a universe of goodness in which people could heal and thrive—by adopting a relentlessly positive outlook. Even the great psychologist William James, who had the skepticism of a scientist and regarded the movement as "moonstruck with optimism," still noted its "healthy-mindedness" and exclaimed, in his seminal 1902 book, **The Varieties of Religious Experience,** that because of New Thought, "cheerfulness has been restored to countless homes."

James also observed the movement's banishment of sorrow: "One hears of the 'Gospel of Relaxation,'" he wrote, "of the 'Don't Worry Movement,' of people who repeat to themselves 'Youth, health, vigor!' when dressing in the morning as their motto for the day. Complaints of the weather are getting to be forbidden in many households and more and more people are recognizing it to be bad form to speak of disagreeable sensations, or to make much of the ordinary inconveniences and ailments of life."

Children were also trained in mandatory cheer.

In 1908, the organization that would become the Boy Scouts trained its charges to "look for the bright side of life. Cheerfully do tasks that come your way." Children were warned to disguise sadness: "You should force yourself to smile at once and then whistle a tune, and you will be all right. A scout goes about with a smile on and whistling. It cheers him and cheers other people, especially in time of danger, for he keeps it up then all the same."

But these attitudes applied most urgently to the pursuit of wealth. A 1910 ad for a correspondence self-help course showed a round-shouldered "loser," the copy asking: "Are you a Misfit?" Other ads depicted winners: "The go-ahead man buys Kuppenheimer Clothes." By the 1930s, self-help books such as **Think and Grow Rich** by Napoleon Hill became massive bestsellers, eventually selling millions of copies. In his mega-bestselling **The Power of Positive Thinking,** Norman Vincent Peale advised readers that "whenever a negative thought concerning your personal powers comes to mind, deliberately voice a positive thought to cancel it out."

These notions persisted even through the 1929 stock market crash and the Great Depression. In 1933, unemployment was at 24.9 percent; almost 20,000 businesses had failed and 4,004 banks had closed. And still, the idea that failure came from "in[side] the man" held firm. A 1929 headline: LOSER IN STREET CHOOSES SUICIDE. A 1937 article about a suicide by carbon monoxide–filled car: "Reilly left a note saying he had been 'a failure in life.'" A psychiatrist, recalling his middle-class patients of the era: "Everybody, more or less, blamed himself for his delinquency or lack of talent or bad luck. There was an acceptance that it was your own fault, a kind of shame about your own personal failure."

By 1955, the word **loser** had become a feature of adolescent slang, pop culture, and scholarly study. Losers soon appeared in the form of comic strip characters like Charlie Brown, antiheroes like Willy Loman, and performers like Woody Allen. Sociologists and journalists, from David Riesman to William Whyte, Jr., wrote bestselling books about them. Musicians sang of them in hit songs, from Frank Sinatra's "Here's to the Losers" to the Beatles' "I'm a Loser," and, more recently, Beck's blunt version: "I'm a loser baby, so why don't you kill me?" Charles Schulz once said that his **Peanuts** characters represented different aspects of himself. Philosophical Linus, crabby Lucy, insouciant Snoopy . . . and melancholic Charlie Brown, who was the heart of it all, the center of the strip, yet the one we could never admit to being. "I didn't realize how many Charlie Browns there were in the world," Schulz said. "I thought I was the only one."

Today, the division of society into winners and losers is starker than ever. As the journalist Neal Gabler wrote in **Salon** in 2017, "America is deeply divided between those who are considered (and consider themselves) winners, and those who . . .

are considered by the winners to be losers. Losers are cultural pariahs—the American equivalent of India's untouchables. . . . You have to be a winner to have any respect, including self-respect." The "prosperity gospel," without ever mentioning the word **Calvinism,** holds that wealth is bestowed by God upon the worthy, and withdrawn from the undeserving. This "gospel" was endorsed by 17 percent of Christians surveyed by **Time** magazine in 2006, while 61 percent agreed that God wants people to be prosperous. Conversely, use of the term **loser** has skyrocketed since the 1960s, according to the Google Books Ngram Viewer. Reverence for winners and contempt for losers famously shaped the worldview of former president Donald Trump, as when he recast the war hero John McCain as a loser because he'd been a POW in Vietnam. Many on both sides of the political divide recoiled from this statement, but Trump was instinctually tapping into our cultural legacy.

As these examples suggest, this legacy is reflected in most areas of public life, from religion to politics. In the next chapter, we'll explore how it affects the workplace, too, and how we can transcend its codes of enforced positivity. But it's also endemic on the college campuses whose graduates feed that workplace. Even before the pandemic, rates of anxiety and depression had soared at many universities, according to Dartmouth College researchers and the American Civil Liberties Union of Southern

California, and so had the pressure to appear happy and victorious. Recently, media outlets from PhillyMag.com to ESPN.com reported cases of college students who appeared happy and successful, but were struggling on the inside. At the University of Pennsylvania, a student named Madison Holleran died by suicide soon after posting a cheerful photo on Instagram. Another Penn student came close to suicide because, as **New York** magazine put it, "she was so overwhelmed with the pressure to keep up appearances."

When I read these stories, they struck a chord I'd first heard long ago. I remembered how, when I was a student at Princeton, it had seemed to me that everyone's life was perfect. They didn't have distraught mothers telephonically interrogating them every night; they weren't mourning a lost past or longing for a dimly imagined future. They'd already arrived wherever they were supposed to be; it seemed they'd been there all along. Of course, I knew there were exceptions. Take Back the Night marches were starting then, and I'd heard my classmates' stories. My roommate had grown up on a Native American reservation, and I knew all about her struggles to fit in at Princeton. Other socially acceptable sorrows were sometimes visible, too—bad breakups, a parental divorce.

Still, I'd wondered what really lay beneath Princeton's iconic, glamorous surfaces. How did most of my classmates **really** feel? What were their everyday losses, the kind we feel we have no permission to mourn—the ones that psychologists now call "disenfranchised griefs"? These were little discussed. Did they even exist?

I decided to find out. I couldn't go back in time, but I **could** talk to today's generation of students. With the amazing latitude that showing up with a writer's notebook grants you, what if I just asked them what their lives are really like?

. . .

It's a clear and brisk February morning, almost three decades after the day I graduated, and I'm back on campus: soaring spires and seven-speed bicycles leaning against ivy-draped archways. Except this time, instead of arriving squished in the back seat of my parents' sedan, stuffed with suitcases and stereo equipment, I've driven myself here with a slim overnight bag in the trunk. Instead of the cramped dorm room in Lourie-Love Hall from which I spoke to my mother every night, I check into the Peacock Inn, a few blocks from campus. I felt so lucky to have been a student here, but much, much luckier to be an alum.

During the intervening years, I've married my husband, Ken, and given birth to two sons and the writing life I dreamed of. Life has its challenges, but I really do wake up grateful every morning. Ken, who's not normally the woo-woo type, suggests that

I send a message back to my freshman-year self. Tell her everything worked out, he says. Tell her you have your own family now; tell her you're a published author. I nod, liking the idea.

Princeton seems to have changed in some ways since I graduated, not in others. The village, which hugs the campus, is still composed of high-end boutiques centered around Palmer Square, with none of the scruffiness of a typical college town. There are more students of all colors and nationalities now, more Indian and sushi restaurants; on campus, the nineteenth-century Gothic architecture is punctuated with gleaming new STEM buildings made of glass and steel. But Charlie Brown would still feel out of place here.

I have a meeting on Prospect Avenue—the "millionaire's row" of mansion-like "eating clubs" known, in Princeton lingo, as "The Street." These clubs, where most juniors and seniors take their meals and throw parties, dominate campus life. I'm heading to Cannon Club to meet Luke, a Princeton junior who interned for me during high school, and some of his friends.

Cannon's clubhouse has a collegiate Gothic stone façade and an eponymous cannon sitting on its front lawn; inside, there's dark wood wainscoting, oil paintings of long-gone gentlemen, and the aroma of stale beer. Cannon is known as the club for down-to-earth athletes. Luke, who's thoughtful and intelligent and dressed in pressed chinos and a V-neck

sweater, leads me upstairs to a common room out-
fitted with a boardroom table and a few sofas. A
group of athletes, big and burly and clad in team
jerseys, lounges at the table, feet up. Luke tells them
that he's booked the room. The athletes rise affably,
asking if we wouldn't mind if they hang out on the
outdoor balcony. Sure, says Luke, and they head
outside to smoke cigars.

Luke ushers in his friends: Paige, Heather, and
Nick. Other than Paige, who's a cross-country run-
ner, all identify as NARPs, which means "non-athletic
regular person"—translating to "reasonably socially
adept, even though I'm not an athlete." Nick's an
art history major from South Florida. He's wearing
stylish glasses and multiple lanyard bracelets. I feel
a familiar flicker of apprehension as we sit down—a
bit of social anxiety, but more the worry **What if I
drove all the way to Princeton for nothing?** Maybe
the students won't open up. Maybe they'll think my
questions are weird—after all, the point of this exercise is to talk about things you don't normally say out
loud. Or maybe their inner lives really are as shiny as
my classmates' outer surfaces always seemed.

But then the opposite thing happens, approxi-
mately two and a half minutes into our conversation. Not only do the students not think my project
is strange; not only are they introspective and forth-
coming; but also they proceed to name and decon-
struct the very thing I wondered about during my
years at Princeton. They call this thing "effortless

perfection": the pressure to appear like a winner, with-out needing to try. And it has many manifestations.

Academically, says Nick, "you have to look as if you studied the least. You're the most underprepared and the most successful. You're always talking about how much you have to do, but there's an expectation that no one should see you do it."

Socially, effortless perfection means an easy grace that gets you accepted to the most exclusive eating clubs just by showing up and being—apparently—yourself. "You should drink a lot and be really fun," he explains, "but not enough to look silly. You should be able to carry on an engaging conversation and joke about a number of different things—you can have weird quirks, but not too weird. You have to be unique, but also fit the mold. You're incred-ibly sociable but manage to do very well in all your classes. You should be able to have an intellectual conversation, but also shotgun a beer. It's like there's an algorithm. Whether through nature or nurture, I happen to fit the algorithm," concludes Nick, who was recently accepted at Ivy, Princeton's most pres-tigious club. His tone is matter-of-fact, reportorial, neither boasting nor apologizing.

Effortless perfection is also about masking any signs of loss, failure, or melancholia. "There's always a worry about your reputation," explains Heather, "a concern for how you're being perceived." If, like Nick, you've been fighting with your father recently, you would try your "utmost to not let it be seen.

Like, not have my face betray there's something wrong. I'd try to carry on doing my normal things." If, as in Luke's case, you don't get into your first-choice club, you mustn't let your hurt show. "A lot of heartbreak here comes from the clubs," says Paige. "You know who got in and who didn't. I don't think that people are authentic about how much it hurts. People who were hosed* don't talk about it. It's still not a fully open conversation. This morning, they published the results of how many people got into each club. They just talked about the numbers—not the emotional implications."

These social codes would be difficult for many students—many teens and young adults experience heightened levels of stress, melancholy, and longing. But even if you're in the throes of actual grief, the protocols of silence reign. Anna Braverman, a therapist at Princeton Counseling and Psychological Services whose office I visit later, says that many students who see her are in literal or figurative mourning.

"Some people don't have supportive parents," she tells me. "Or they have parents with severe issues. And they never stop wondering what it would have been like if I grew up with supportive parents, or wishing one day we'll be able to fix this problem, and we'll be a normal family. At vacation time, people say to them, 'Oh, you must be so happy to go home,' and they have to say, 'Yes, I'm so happy.'

---

* Princeton lingo for "rejected."

And they're not. They're mourning what might have been. They're thinking, 'Wouldn't it be awesome if I could have a perfect holiday with my family?' It can be a mourning as intense as bereavement."

But the social code is to keep these things hidden. "You're supposed to say that everything is great," says Braverman.

The fact that so many students struggle heightens the irony that the confidants they choose, in the form of campus therapists, are sworn to secrecy. "Those of us, like myself and my colleagues who have office hours and have students on our sofas all day long," former associate dean Tara Christie Kinsey told the Princeton Perspective Project in a radio interview, "we all get together and we talk about how students who are experiencing anxiety or struggles think that they're the only ones who are experiencing the thing that they're experiencing. And we're all saying, if you were on the sofa ten minutes earlier, you would have heard the exact same thing."

The term **effortless perfection** was coined not at Princeton but at Duke University in 2003, and at first it referred to pressure reserved specifically for young women: to be smart, beautiful, thin, and popular, without seeming to try. But the concept soon expanded, with students at other schools developing their own terms. The University of Pennsylvania has "Penn Face," which means the smiling and confident faces students display, no matter their actual feelings. Stanford calls it "Duck Syndrome," referring to the ability of ducks to glide smoothly across a lake as they paddle madly below the surface. These norms run so strong that students were moved to create a private Facebook group called "Stanford University Places I've Cried." Its home page quips that it's "a tribute to the happiest place on earth," as Stanford is known. The group had 2,500 members, last I looked. The "Stanford University Places I've Smiled" page had forty, before being taken down altogether.

It's no accident that the phrase **effortless perfection** originated at the nation's elite universities, where young winners attempt to hold their gains. Or that it was born during an era of rising rates of anxiety, depression, and suicide on campus. Because the phenomenon is not so much about perfection as it is about victory. It's about being **the kind of person** who wins; about floating so high that you avoid the bitter side of life; it's about **not** being a loser. Effortless perfection may be a buzzword at most of our universities, but it comes from the same cultural pressure under which we've buckled since the beginning of the American republic. Combine this with new realities of growing inequality and social strife, and you get an ever-increasing pressure to feel like a winner in a society that produces relatively few of them.

I wonder, as I sit in conversation with Anna Braverman, the Princeton therapist, if she realizes that she's talking to my past self. Does she sense that I was one of those students wishing I could go home for a "perfect holiday," one of the ones who wouldn't have believed that the classmate sitting on the couch ten minutes ago had similar struggles? Does she know that even if I'd known, I wouldn't have been comforted, that I just would have thought that there was something wrong with that person, too, some problem "in the man"?

And what happens to these students—to all of us—as we reach adulthood and make our way to the workplace, to start families of our own, and beyond? How do we get to the point of seeing our sorrows and longings not as indications of secret unworthiness but as features of humanity? How do we come to realize that embracing our inner loser as well as winner—the bitter and the sweet—is the key to transcending them both, the key to meaning, creativity, and joy?

Susan David, the psychologist and management thinker you met at the start of this chapter, has devoted her career to answering these questions.

CHAPTER 6

How can we transcend enforced positivity in the workplace, and beyond?

I was going to buy a copy of **The Power of Positive Thinking,** and then I thought, "What the hell good would that do?"

—RONNIE SHAKES

Today, Susan David teaches clients, including the United Nations, Google, and Ernst & Young, about "emotional agility," which she defines as a process of "holding difficult emotions and thoughts loosely, facing them courageously and compassionately, and then moving past them to ignite change in your life." But as she observes our global work culture today, she sees many people stuck in the stage she was in right after she lost her father at fifteen, when she was still wearing a public smile and vomiting up ice cream in private. She sees a "tyranny of positivity" in which you should never cry at work but if you can't help it then for goodness' sake do it quietly in a bathroom stall.

For Susan, this is a big problem. Not only because it's just plain better to see life clearly, in all its bittersweetness. But also because if we don't allow ourselves difficult emotions, like sorrow and longing, then these feelings will undermine us at every turn. "Research on emotional suppression shows that when emotions are pushed aside or ignored, they get stronger," Susan told the audience in her popular TED Talk. "Psychologists call this amplification. Like that delicious chocolate cake in the refrigerator—the more you try to ignore it . . . the greater its hold on you. You might think you're in control of unwanted emotions when you ignore them, but in fact they control you. Internal pain always comes out. Always. And who pays the price? We do. Our children, our colleagues, our communities."

She stresses that she's "not anti-happiness," that she **likes** being happy. Susan and I are close friends, and I can attest to this. She's very upbeat by nature, warm and affectionate, with an easy laugh and a dimpled smile. "Hi, gorgeous," her emails often begin, and it feels like a verbal embrace; she has an arms-wide-open, up-for-anything approach to life and love. I think it's because Susan's so obviously joyful that people receive her message so well. They open up to her about all the things they wish they didn't feel. "I don't want my heart to be broken," they say. Or, "I don't want to fail."

"I understand," Susan tells them. "But you have dead people's goals. Only dead people never get stressed, never get broken hearts, never experience the disappointment that comes with failure."

. . .

Susan has dedicated her life's work to helping others to accept and integrate their sorrow, longing, and other "difficult" emotions. And she's not alone. In the very business culture that wrote our national story of winners and losers, a new narrative is struggling to be born. The organizational psychologist Peter Frost, in an influential paper called "Why Compassion Counts!," observed that suffering is at the heart of most religions, yet forbidden to be expressed at work. "If, as the Buddha is reported to have said, suffering is optional but an inevitable part of the human condition, then we ought to find suffering as a significant aspect of organizational life," he wrote. "Our theories ought to reflect this somehow." Inspired by his call, a group of organizational psychologists, led by Frost and University of Michigan organizational psychologist Jane Dutton, founded a consortium dedicated to inspiring "a new vision of organizations as sites for the expression of compassion." They called it the CompassionLab, which is now run by University of Michigan scholar Monica Worline, co-author with Dutton of an important book on compassion at work.

In one fascinating project by two members of the CompassionLab, management professors Jason Kanov and Laura Madden combed through transcripts of employee interviews that Kanov had conducted for a previous study on social disconnection. They found two things: One, the interviews were full of stories of pain and suffering at work: panic attacks, injured relationships, feelings of devaluation. Two, the interview subjects rarely used words such as **pain** or **suffering** to tell their stories. They were anxious but said they were **angry;** they were sad but said they were **frustrated.** "There's an unspectacular mundane suffering that pervades the workplace," Kanov told me. "But we don't feel allowed to acknowledge that we suffer. We endure way more than we should, and can, because we downplay what it's actually doing to us."

Certain kinds of suffering are more socially acceptable to express in the workplace than others, Kanov told me. "If one's suffering is triggered by something acute and widely seen as painful (e.g., the death of a close family member, or being a victim of a calamity outside of their control), it's more likely people will acknowledge and express their pain at work. It's the chronic suffering, and the everyday suffering—triggered by relationship challenges, financial struggles, non-life-threatening afflictions, work stress, office politics, poor management, etc.—that is largely suppressed and/or undiscussable at work. And this is the kind of suffering that is particularly rampant."

Beyond the CompassionLab, this opening up of the emotional landscape is gaining traction in the world of organizational leadership. Concepts such as "bringing your whole self to work" and "the gift of failure"—the title of Jessica Lahey's excellent book—have gone mainstream. **Harvard Business Review** regularly runs articles on the virtues of compassionate leadership. Management scholars have even started to highlight the unique advantages of melancholic leaders.

Researchers have long known that the emotions leaders present affect our perception of how powerful they are. Leaders who behave angrily during challenging situations are often assumed to be more powerful than those who react sadly. Indeed, when I went looking for examples of prominent bittersweet types, it was easy to find creative figures, but much harder to find business leaders. This was not, I suspect, because melancholic managers are in short supply, but rather that they don't identify publicly as such. Yet a 2009 study by management professors Juan Madera and D. Brent Smith found that showing sorrow rather than anger sometimes leads to better outcomes for leaders, including stronger relationships with followers, and a greater perception of effectiveness.

Tanja Schwarzmüller, a researcher at the Technical University of Munich, wondered what could explain these results. Organizational psychologists had long studied the various kinds of power that leaders wield: Some hold "positional" power (including the perception that they can and will bestow rewards and punish transgressors), while others tend to "personal" power (including the ability to inspire others to identify and sympathize with them). Researchers had also shown that angry people are generally considered aggressive and confident, while melancholic types are viewed as more timid and less assured—but also as warmer, and more sympathetic and likable.

Based on this, Schwarzmüller and her team hypothesized that the difference between angry and sad leaders is not their relative amounts of power, but rather the **kind** of power these leaders wield. To test this, they designed a series of studies in which subjects were shown videos of actors dressed as business leaders, delivering a speech about their company's poor financial year. The "angry" actors frowned and shouted, with narrowed eyes and clenched fists. The "sad" leaders stood with arms hanging loosely by their sides, speaking in slow, gloomy tones. The researchers found that the angry leaders were perceived as having the ability to reward or punish followers: In other words, they had more "positional" power than the sad leaders did. But melancholic leaders tended to have more personal power. They inspired more loyalty among their hypothetical followers, who were less likely to want to sabotage them, and more likely to "feel accepted and valued."

Though the study was conducted with actors rather than actual leaders and followers, it has various implications. It shows us the particular kind of power that melancholic leaders might authentically hold. In some situations—for example, an emergency in which an organization faces an outside threat—displays of anger might be more effective. But in other cases, such as the recall of a product shown to harm the company's customers, a bittersweet touch might be more appropriate. (Indeed, the 2009 study by Madera and Smith examined this situation and found that anger mixed with sorrow is sometimes best.) "If followers mess up on an important project," Schwarzmüller told Ozy Media's digital magazine, "it might be good to consider saying, 'I'm sad this happened,' instead of 'I'm angry this happened.'" Personal power "motivates people to work for you toward shared goals, and because they like you."

We're often taught to focus on our strengths, not weaknesses. But we shouldn't confuse a bittersweet temperament, or a "negative" emotional state such as sadness, with weakness. Indeed, some of our most self-aware leaders face their sorrows, limitations, and temperaments head-on—and learn to integrate them into a fuller self.

Tim Chang, for example, is a venture capitalist

who's helped birth some of Silicon Valley's most successful start-ups. Over the years, Tim observed that people build companies and teams that reflect not only their values and strengths but also what he calls their "core wounds." Greatness, he told me, often comes from developing a superpower that adapts to the blow that almost killed you. But people's desire to turn themselves from "losers" into winners can also undermine them. "In Silicon Valley, there's a lot of overcompensation," he explained. "Maybe that's the real engine of human innovation. We're most passionate about that which we're most denied, and these things manifest in the companies and teams we build. If you've been bullied, your whole life is trying to disprove the peers or family members who once tormented you. If you have deep insecurity, you might hire a lot of yes people."

Tim decided to subject himself to his own self-inquiry, through coaching, therapy, and brutally candid 360 reviews from his colleagues. The results were illuminating. He was "the product of tiger parents," he told me, "where the playbook was external validation—get good grades and the world will take care of you. You're always seeking approval. You derive self-worth from getting the maximum score based on scoring systems others have prescribed." Growing up, he knew his parents loved him, but they didn't say so directly and there were "no hugs given freely." They wanted to toughen him up for a hard world. Even when he graduated from Stanford

Business School and became a venture capitalist, he was met with skepticism: **You don't even know how to balance your own checkbook, how could you possibly manage other people's money?** "I remember the day I made it onto the **Forbes** Midas list," Tim says. "Finally, my parents thought, **Maybe this guy knows what he's doing.**"

Tim is a kind, creative, sensitive soul—a bitter-sweet type. (He scores 6.5 out of 10 on the quiz.) He'd been the kid lying on a hill after school, staring at the clouds and pondering the meaning of life. He'd wanted to be a professional actor or musician, but that path was out of the question in his family. For most of his early career, he'd felt like an imposter in the business world.

Combine Tim's temperament and upbringing, and you get someone who's bursting with creativity and compassion, and who's "extremely good at quick connection building through collaboration and brainstorming"—someone with a lot of "personal" power. But you also get a leader hungry for approval and love, who avoids conflict, who seeks harmony at all costs yet doesn't feel understood. Entrepreneurs loved working with Tim not only because he was brilliant but also because he was empathic and driven to help. But he realized that he was gravitating not to the most promising business founders, but to those so desperate for help or enamored of his creativity that they'd give him the appreciation he craved.

Only once he understood these patterns could

he be more authentic and discerning with his investing—by accepting his own nature, integrating his worlds, and allowing himself time and outlets for the creative projects he still loves. Early in his career, Tim had believed that he needed to pursue deals in the fields that **others** deemed to be "hot" sectors. Now he began to explore investments in areas **he** was personally passionate about—especially creative fields such as gaming, entertainment, music, and personal biohacking. He also started to meld his creative interests with his work world. (His band Coverflow became a fixture in the Silicon Valley conference afterparty scene, he says, and a unique way for him to connect with top founders and start-ups.) "I had to do everything wrong by trying to always do things 'right' in the eyes of others," he told me, "before I got a little more peace—by being myself."

Lara Nuer, the co-founder of a firm called Learning as Leadership, is another leader who faced her own personal history and difficult emotions, incorporating them into a richer self. Like Tim, Lara had thought of herself as a thoughtful, empathic leader—the kind she deeply wanted to be. But a few years into her tenure, she realized that she had a problem. When she had to give negative feedback to her employees, she procrastinated, often telling herself that she needed time to collect more data. Sometimes, she'd never get around to sharing the feedback at all. Eventually, though, the truth would come out (as truth always does). Maybe Lara would start acting aloof toward the underperforming employee. Or quietly angry. To her staff, these behaviors seemed to come out of the blue. They felt they didn't know where they stood with their boss; they started to mistrust her. So there was one Lara, who wanted the best for people and a supportive work culture. And there was the other Lara, creating the opposite reality.

As it happens, Lara's firm teaches techniques for resolving just these kinds of issues, helping teams and individuals to resolve their "limiting behaviors" and "ingrained dysfunctions." She subjected herself to her own company's process, beginning by examining her early childhood. Her family had moved from Paris to Montreal when she was four years old, and she was the new kid in school. All she'd wanted was to be liked and accepted. But she had thick frizzy hair and flat feet that required her to wear weird shoes that went up to her ankles. In grade-school hierarchy, she was a second-class citizen.

We're all familiar with the idea that childhood experiences shape our adult lives. But we're not always aware of exactly **how.** Lara had known for a long time that her painful school experiences made her a more empathic leader. But it took her much longer to realize—and to own—the ways in which they also made her unkind. The only way forward was to confront her whole self, including the part that still felt "less than." She realized that the story she'd told herself for years was that she was too "nice" to speak hard truths. But she wasn't only nice—she was also afraid. Afraid of being disliked by those she criticized; afraid of being the weird girl again.

"In the moment of giving feedback, when I tell you only great things," she told me, "I feel liked and accepted. That's a real feeling I get. It doesn't mean that you **do** like me more, but it's what I perceive. But in trying to be liked, I was creating more separation."

Lara had to learn that being a kind leader meant being candid—not only with her employees, but also with herself. But even more, she had to learn that she wasn't a "loser" now, any more than when she had frizzy hair and wore therapeutic shoes.

The business press is full of advice on how best to give employee feedback, and most of it understandably focuses on the state of mind of the feedback's **recipient:** On their behalf, we should be direct; we should criticize constructively. But Lara's story reminds us that, as with all interactions, emotional agility needs to be present on **both** sides. We all have personal histories and emotional triggers that can hijack our reactions during difficult conversations. The more we accept our own makeup, the better chance we have of managing it. A person giving feedback can't be mindful of its recipient's equilibrium—until she's achieved her own.

. . .

Perhaps you're thinking that such approaches might fly in relatively gentle workplaces but not, say, in the rough-and-tumble culture of an offshore oil rig. In which case, I'd like to introduce you to Rick Fox, who for many years was the charismatic leader of a Shell Oil rig in the Gulf of Mexico. This rig, which was described in a fascinating segment on the radio show **Invisibilia,** had a macho culture in which you would **never** talk about your sorrows. You also wouldn't ask questions when you didn't understand something. You would never show weakness, period.

I had the chance to talk with Rick on the phone one day. The first thing that struck me was his deep, hypnotic voice; he sounded like a cross between a country singer and a prophet. But he was as tough and reticent as the rest of the guys on the rig. And as he turned forty, he faced two enormous challenges: one, his staff was about to move to an exponentially bigger, far more deadly deepwater rig, and he didn't know how to keep them safe. And two, his teenage son Roger had stopped speaking to him. Father and son were "at each other's throats," and Rick didn't know why.

He took what he called a "big leap." He hired a consultant named Claire Nuer, who happens to have been Lara Nuer's mother and co-founder of the firm Lara now co-leads. He told Nuer about his problems with drill schedules and numbers of oil barrels produced per day. She told him to forget all that and instead to face his real issue: fear. His work was scary, managing so many people was scary, and keeping them safe was scariest of all. The sooner he'd admit this, said Nuer, the better he could solve his managerial problems.

Rick signed up for an extended program with Nuer. He brought others with him, too: his boss, his staff, even his son Roger. Nuer encouraged the men to talk to each other, in intensive sessions that lasted from nine A.M. to eleven P.M., for nine days straight. They opened up about painful childhoods and troubled marriages and sick children. Sometimes they cried. Some resisted this process. Some resented it. But many were relieved.

Rick, for his part, realized that the more he projected a false vision of himself as an all-knowing, all-powerful leader and father, the more his team—and his son—lost faith in themselves. Since they weren't omniscient and immune from weakness, the way he appeared to be, they concluded that they were "losers" compared to Rick, the "winner." Rick realized how invested he'd been in this false image of himself as a perfect leader, impervious to pain. But really, he'd just been passing his own pain onto his men—and onto his family.

Rick had never known his own father, and he'd been raised by a struggling single mother. But he never talked about his upbringing, and this code of stoic self-denial had trickled down to Roger in unspoken ways. Roger, who'd spent his childhood comparing himself to his seemingly invulnerable father, felt ashamed of everything from his deepest insecurities to his most basic gaps in knowledge. "I remember the first time I heard the word **Phillips-head screwdriver,**" he said on **Invisibilia.** His father "would say, you know, go get me a Phillips-head out of the shop. And I didn't even think to say—'Hey, Dad . . . I don't know what you're talking about.' So I went to the shop to look for something I had no idea what it was and felt stuck 'cause, you know, I didn't want to be vulnerable."

In time, normalizing their sorrows worked. The guys on the rig started developing genuine connections with each other. They grew more comfortable admitting problems at work. They started sharing ideas. They ended up with sky-high productivity levels, and an incredible **84 percent decline** in their accident rate. Their story was so astounding that it became the subject of a well-known case study conducted by Harvard Business School professor Robin Ely and Stanford professor Debra Meyerson.

For Rick, a similarly miraculous thing happened at home. Father and son healed their relationship. He and Roger are close friends now, and Rick told **Invisibilia** that thank goodness Roger, who's now a psychiatrist, didn't have to wait till he was forty to tell the truth of how he really felt. "My son's a beautiful human being," he said. "And I can't get enough of being around him."

. . .

Of course, it's one thing to come to these revelations quietly, and it's another to air them in public, with colleagues, bosses, and direct reports. For some people, the process that Rick Fox went through sounds awful. As an avowed introvert, I'm instinctively wary of this kind of thing. Indeed, a 2018 study called "When Sharing Hurts," by another member of the CompassionLab, Babson College organizational psychologist Kerry Gibson, found that managers who disclose troubles to subordinates can lose status and undermine their influence. When we're challenging the tyranny of positivity, in other words, we should be mindful of our roles, our personal preferences, and the culture of our organizations.

But is there a way to create a work culture that **implicitly** transcends the tyranny of positivity? Can we bake into work culture the idea that human sorrow is inevitable, and instill the value of responding with compassion?

In 2011, a group of scholars from the CompassionLab published a study of a remarkable organization: the billing unit of a community hospital in an impoverished neighborhood in Jackson, Michigan. This department's workers had the dreary job of collecting unpaid bills from sick people. It's hard to imagine a less inspiring task; turnover is endemic in the industry. But this unit, known as Midwest Billing, created a culture in which it was assumed that personal troubles were a normal part of every worker's life. Far from reflecting poorly on a team member's inner worth, these were opportunities for teammates to show each other compassion. Staff members cared for each other when their mothers died and when they went through divorces and were victims of domestic violence. Even if someone just had a cold, the employees of Midwest Billing helped each other out. As one staff member described it, "If you came to work at this place and you weren't as compassionate a person as others, you [would] see how good it makes people feel. You see how people get excited about doing things for people, and I think it just becomes a part of your norm if it wasn't before. If you practice it enough, it becomes the norm." Another staff member recalls:

> My mother passed away completely unexpectedly. I've always lived with my mom. Always. [It] was just the worst time of my whole life. I remember telling my uncle, "I need to go back to work because I need to have my mind off everything that's going on. But I also need to go back to work because I am surrounded by women who open their arms to me." . . . Still to this day, it's so hard for me to look at Latisha, because I remember the look on her face when I came in [after my mother died]. I did not expect any of the compassion and sympathy and the love, the actual love that I got from my co-workers. You don't expect that.

Sharing troubles turned out to be very good not only for mental health, but also for business. During the five years prior to the study, Midwest Billing got its bills collected more than twice as fast as before, beating industry standards. Turnover rate in the unit was only 2 percent, compared with an average of 25 percent across all of Midwest Health System, and a significantly higher rate across the medical billing industry.

For Susan David, the lesson of such studies is clear. "Businesses are often trying to shape themselves to be safe, innovative, collaborative, and inclusive," she told me. "But safety holds hands with fear; innovation holds hands with failure; collaboration holds hands with conflict; and inclusion holds hands with difference. These business outcomes **depend** on an openness to the bittersweet. Indeed, on normalizing bittersweet."

But even if you're not fortunate to work in a culture like the one at Midwest Billing, there are other, more private ways to transcend the tyranny of positivity, and to embrace your full emotional life: sorrows, longings, and all. In 1986, University of Texas social psychologist James Pennebaker launched a series of landmark studies that would echo not only Susan David's work but also the story of her life. Pennebaker had gotten married soon after college graduation. But when he and his wife started fighting, he drank and smoked, got depressed, withdrew from the world. Until one day he wrote some things down. Not an essay or a tract. He just wrote the contents of his heart, as Susan had done in her class-room notebook. And he noticed that the more he wrote, the better he felt. He opened up to his wife again, and to his work. His depression lifted.

Pennebaker decided to study this phenomenon, and he didn't stop for the next forty years. His results have been nothing short of astonishing. In one study, he divided people into two groups. One group was asked to write about their difficulties for twenty minutes a day, for three days; they wrote about sexual abuse, breakups, abandonment by a parent, illness, death. The other group wrote about everyday things, such as what shoes they were wearing.

Pennebaker found that that the people who wrote about their troubles were markedly calmer and happier than those who described their sneakers. Even months later, they were physically healthier, with lower blood pressure and fewer doctor's visits. They had better relationships and more success at work.

In another study, Pennebaker worked with a group of despondent senior engineers who'd been laid off four months earlier by a Dallas computer company. Most were over fifty and had worked at the company their entire adult lives. None had found new work.

Once again, Pennebaker divided the men into two groups. One group wrote down their feelings of rage, humiliation, and fear of the future; the other group described neutral topics. And once again, the results were almost too remarkable to be true. Within months, the men who'd written out their cares were **three times** more likely than the control group to have found work.

I've been struck by Pennebaker's work from the moment I heard of it, probably because it so closely reflects my own experience. Those diaries I kept as a teenager tore my relationship with my mother apart. But they also saved me. They were the place I made sense of myself—not only of who I was then, but also of who I hoped to be, and eventually became.

Throughout college and early adulthood, I kept my diaries in a tattered red backpack, zipped shut with a combination lock. At that stage of life, you move around a lot, from one dorm room or shared apartment to another. Everywhere I went, I dragged that backpack with me. Until one day, during one of the moves, I lost it. Left it behind, in some apartment building closet. Maybe because I'm forgetful by nature. Or maybe because the diaries had already done their work, and I didn't want them anymore.

When Pennebaker started his research, he probably wasn't thinking of Calvinism and its cultural sequelae of viewing ourselves as happy winners or abject losers. But his work implicitly rejects this outlook. "Expressive writing" encourages us to see our misfortunes not as flaws that make us unfit for worldly success (or otherworldly heaven), but as the seeds of our growth. Pennebaker found that the writers who thrived after pouring their hearts onto the page tended to use phrases such as "I've learned," "It struck me that," "I now realize," and "I understand." They didn't come to **enjoy** their misfortunes. But they'd learned to live with insight.

If you're intrigued by the idea of expressive writing, I'd like to suggest a new daily ritual for you: Find a blank notebook. Open it up. And write something down. Draw on your bitter, or on your sweet.

If you're having a great day and don't feel like plumbing your depths, write down something that elevates you. Over my writing desk, I keep a Post-it that reads: "It's urgent to live enchanted." It comes from a poem by the Portuguese author Valter Hugo Mãe, and it reminds me to focus on the wondrous.

If you're having a terrible day, write that down, too. Write exactly what's wrong, and how you feel about it and why; write why you feel disappointed or betrayed, what you're afraid of. If you feel like writing possible solutions to your problem, that's fine. But you don't have to. It doesn't have to be great prose, either. All you have to do is write.

Just the way Susan David learned to do, back when she was fifteen and she lost her father. And the way she teaches people to do today.

• • •

It's October, and Susan and I have come to Lisbon to attend the House of Beautiful Business conference, co-founded by a thinker and dreamer named Tim Leberecht, the German American, Portugal-based author of **The Business Romantic.** The conference is dedicated to the idea that in the age of smart machines and algorithms, "being human is the ultimate differentiator." It's based in a grand nineteenth-century home whose rooms have been given new names for the week, including the Chamber of Deep Emotion, the Bureau of Inquiry, and the Office of Exponential Humanity. Susan's here to give her signature workshop.

The conference, whose agenda includes events such as Twelve Toasts to Madonna, a Funeral March, and a Silent Party, kicks off on a Saturday night with a salon called "Major Desires, Minor Keys: An Evening on Melancholia, Sadness, and Grief as the Ultimate Taboos and Surprisingly Productive Forces in Business." The salon is to open with a performance of fado, the Portuguese music of yearning.

As a frequent keynote speaker on the untapped talents of introverts in the workplace, I've attended a gazillion business conferences, and I've never seen one open with an exploration of melancholia, sadness, and grief. But if you're going to hold a conference showcasing the role of sweet sorrow in human ingenuity, Lisbon is the ideal spot. The streets are lovely and cobble-stoned; the air is salty from the sea and, one imagines, centuries of tears of women yearning for shipwrecked husbands. The icon of a woman gazing longingly at the ocean is at the heart of fado music, which is the musical expression of

saudade, the uniquely Portuguese word meaning (as we saw in chapter 2) an intimate, melancholic longing, laced with joy and sweetness. **Saudade** defines the city; it's the namesake of countless cafés, pastry shops, and music bars; it's the key to the Portuguese soul.

Tim is tall, elegant, and friendly. He says that his default state is "comfortable sadness." "How often are you happy? How often are you sad?" he asks rhetorically. "Most of us are sad much more often."

In the United States, this kind of talk would fall in the category of confession. But in Europe, Tim says, "this view of things is cultivated. The films of Truffaut, of Antonioni. I was in L.A. recently, listening to Bach on the freeway. It was strange to listen to Bach in Los Angeles."

The salon on melancholy opens with Tim passing out "sadness cookies." They look like regular fortune cookies, but on one side they say "House of Beautiful Business," and on the other they offer a sadness fortune.

"Those who let their eyes adjust," my cookie reads, "can see in the darkness."

. . .

Susan has delivered her workshop many times before, to countless people who declare it some of the most valuable time they've ever spent. What happens at the workshops is super-confidential, but I've participated in enough of them to describe their tenor without revealing anyone's secrets.

Imagine one such gathering, of tech titans at a fancy Silicon Valley conference: There's Susan, standing in the center of the room, in her purple silk top with matching plum lipstick. Telling her story and asking us to think about our own lives. Leading us through various exercises, most of them centered around . . . a yellow Post-it.

We're each given our own Post-it, on which we're to write an "I am" statement about ourselves, based on a memory or a self-conception that holds us back:

"I am a fraud," someone writes.

"I am selfish."

"I am needy."

Susan advises us to choose something we'll be comfortable sharing with one other person in the room. But she also invites us to go deep: "You're not saying there's something wrong with you. You're not saying that you have a pathology. You're saying that you're human. Welcome to humanity."

She asks us to take our Post-its and to put them on our chests. "I want to invite you as a group to reflect on how it feels to have this thing that is a difficult struggle on your chest," she explains. "That is not something we typically do. We typically wear our armor: our jewelry, shoes, suit jackets. How does it feel?"

People call out the answers. They shout them out, in a hurry, as if they can't wait:

"It feels uncomfortable," they say.

"It feels exciting."

"Exposed."

"Heavy."

Then, one answer that I'll always remember:

"Real. It feels real. I could talk about this more easily than all the other stuff I've talked about at this conference."

Susan asks us to take off our shoes, to put them neatly in front of our seats, and to place our Post-it notes right next to our shoes. Then we get up and sit in someone else's seat. We're to read this other person's Post-it, to consider the struggles of the human who walks in those shoes: "The meetings they might move into where they feel the need to arm themselves," says Susan. "The conversations they don't have with their loved ones. There you have a pair of shoes in front of you, and a note of something the person might not even share with those closest to them."

"Turn their note over," she instructs. "And now . . . write to that person something you wish they would know."

The room goes quiet as we switch seats, gaze at each other's shoes, read intimate notes scribbled in an unfamiliar hand.

"I am abandoned," the notes say.

"I'm always anxious."

"I'm too restrained and controlled."

"What do you feel when you read these notes?" asks Susan.

"The message I read makes me want to cry," one person says.

"I'm not alone," says another. "We are all struggling."

In this particular workshop, most people in the room are prosperous men with impressive titles. Trust me when I say that if you saw these men striding into a board meeting, it would not occur to you that they feel abandoned, anxious, restrained, or alone.

Susan asks us to think of a person in our lives who encourages or empowers us. It could be a friend, a parent, a partner; it could be someone who's not alive anymore. But if that person could give you advice about what's on your Post-it note, she asks, would they still be able to love you? What would they say?

I scan my memory; my mind alights on an old friend who'd noticed my tendency during conflict to assume that the other person must be right and I must be wrong.

"Just because someone makes a claim against you doesn't mean it's true," this friend had told me. Then, as if anticipating this very workshop that I'd attend years later, he'd suggested that I carry a yellow sticky around with me that says I'M PROBABLY FUCKING RIGHT.

Every time I think of his advice, I laugh. Sometimes, I even think he had a point.

. . .

Toward the end of my time in Lisbon, Susan and I head together to another House of Beautiful Business activity: a tour of the city, focused on the life of its most famous (and infinitely bittersweet) poet, Fernando Pessoa. Poets are a **very big deal** here. The tourist shops stack poetry collections by the cash register the way in other capital cities you'd find maps and key chains. The main squares feature marble statues not of military heroes or heads of state, but of revered poets. And the most celebrated of all is Pessoa, who observed, not unlike Buddha and his mustard seed, that "there are ships sailing to many ports, but not a single one goes where life is not painful."

I'm in the middle of writing this book, so it feels crucial that I take this tour. It's one of the reasons I came to the conference.

Susan isn't especially interested in Pessoa, but she's agreed to come along. We're to meet the group at a far-flung Lisbon address, but our GPS doesn't work properly, and we're chatting so intently that we're distracted. By the time we arrive, we're half an hour late and the tour has left without us. In the meantime, it's started to rain, hard, and neither of us has an umbrella. But it's warm outside and the organizers hand us a map showing the route. **You'll catch up in no time,** they say. **Just look for the group of orange umbrellas! You can duck under one of those.**

Susan and I traipse through the storm, down this alleyway and across that boulevard, but the promised coterie of umbrellas doesn't materialize. We stop to study the map, but the rain instantly reduces it to a pulp. Susan bursts out laughing, and a split second later I see the hilarity, too, and soon we're doubled over on a soaking street corner. We decide to take shelter at the famed café A Brasileira, where Portugal's iconic poets gathered almost a century ago. High ceilings covered with oil paintings. A marble bar. Black-and-white-tiled floors. And just outside the door, a statue of Pessoa himself, sitting at a café table in bowler hat and bowtie. Passersby line up to have their picture taken with him, even in the pouring rain.

We drink steaming cocoa under an outdoor umbrella near the statue. I'm still craning my neck, hoping for the miraculous appearance of the missing tour group. If only we'd left earlier for the tour, I'm thinking; if only we hadn't got lost, and even (I confess) if only I'd gone on my own without the insanely agreeable company of Susan David to distract me, then I would have gotten to take the tour. I'm thinking, **I flew all the way to Lisbon and I'm missing one of the experiences I came for.** And it takes me almost to the end of the afternoon—once it's almost over, in fact—to realize that I may have missed Pessoa, but during this afternoon of deep conversation, Susan and I have crossed the threshold into "friends for life."

Susan is the type of friend who has the perfect airplane carry-on that doubles as an elegant purse, and tells you where to find one like it. She's the type with whom you could share the most embarrassing social gaffes or moral transgressions, and she'd just give you a wry and sympathetic smile and raise her wineglass. She's the type who traipses good-naturedly through a rain-soaked city with you to track down a tour guide who can possibly-maybe-who-knows shed a few grains of insight into the life of a forlorn poet who lived a century ago. I may have lost the tour, but I've found something—someone—much grander.

. . .

So, now that you've virtually attended one of Susan's seminars, let's add on to that the expressive writing ritual we talked about—drawing on the insights we just gained from her work. Can you try writing down an "I am" statement about yourself, something based on a memory or a self-conception that's holding you back? **I can't focus and I'm a bad employee. I'm afraid to stand up for myself. I gossip too much and hurt people.** Ask yourself the questions that Susan would ask, if she were here with you:

Would the people who love you still love you if they knew what you just wrote? Would you still love you? **Do** you still love you?

Hopefully, the answer to these questions is yes. But if you're not sure, or if the answer, for now, is no, remember Susan's advice: You're not saying there's something wrong with you. You're not saying that you have a pathology. You're saying that you're human. Welcome to humanity.

My paternal grandparents,
photographer unknown

PART III

Mortality, Impermanence, and Grief

How should we live, knowing that we and everyone we love will die?

CHAPTER 7

Should we try to live forever?

> Someday when the descendants of human-
> ity have spread from star to star, they won't
> tell the children about the history of Ancient
> Earth until they're old enough to bear it; and
> when they learn they'll weep to hear that
> such a thing as Death had ever once existed.
>
> —ELIEZER YUDKOWSKY,
> FROM **HARRY POTTER AND
> THE METHODS OF RATIONALITY**

My brother, who was an abdominal radiologist at Mount Sinai hospital in New York City, died of complications from COVID-19 in April 2020. In the days that followed, I felt a pit of nausea, both literal and existential. What is this seasickness that comes when a person's gone, even if, as in the case of my brother, they hadn't been part of your daily life for a very long time?

It wasn't the loneliness of my brother's widow, gazing at her husband's empty side of the bed, the books unread on his nightstand, no one to talk to or snuggle with tonight, or the night after that or after that or after that. It wasn't the sorrow of missing my brother's wry humor and willingness to go to three different supermarkets looking for just the right bananas to bring our elderly mother. It wasn't the sound of my normally stoic father, sobbing over the phone when I told him the news. (He would die of COVID, too, before the year was out.)

The nausea is related to these aspects of grief, but its true source, I think, is the realization that made my son cry on the last day of third grade: What once was will never be again. Never again this teacher, never again this particular configuration of classmates, never again will you learn long division for the first time (even if you don't care very much for math).

My brother was sixty-two when he died. He'd met his love, Paula, seven years earlier. They were devoted to each other from the start, married a few months before the pandemic struck. It was his first marriage. At their wedding, he observed that some of the toasts were on the theme of "Better late than never," but the real message was "WORTH THE WAIT."

In the days after his death, his colleagues at the hospital told me stories about him. That he was known to bring a portable ultrasound unit to a patient's room in the middle of the night, to double-check a difficult diagnosis. That time was of no importance to him: "The patient was his only concern." That he'd recently won the award for Outstanding Lecturer, and another for Teacher of the Year, his department's highest honor. He was a modest person; I wasn't surprised that he'd never mentioned these achievements. But I would have liked to say congratulations.

My brother was eleven years my elder. He taught me how to ride a bike, he invented a game in which if I broke this absurd rule or that one, I'd have to go to "Proper School"—I can still see him at the phone in the family kitchen, pretending to talk to the teachers who ran the imaginary school. In the days after his death, all these memories crowded my mind at five in the morning. It all happened so many years ago. What once was will never be again.

You can get used to the idea that everything passes. You can read the Stoic philosophers, who teach us to accept death as inevitable; you can follow their advice to practice "memento mori" (remembering death as a way of appreciating life); you can meditate on impermanence. I do these things regularly. They prepare you to some degree. But the terrible beauty of transience is much greater than we are. In our best moments, especially in the presence of sublime music, art, and nature, we grasp the tragic majesty of it. The rest of the time, we simply have to live it.

The question is: How? How are we supposed to live such an unthinkable thing?

In the next chapters, we're going to explore seemingly contrasting answers to one of life's most pressing questions.

. . .

It's August 2017, at the San Diego Town and Country Hotel and Convention Center, and the second annual RAADfest conference—"the Woodstock of radical life extension"—is about to start. The adherents of this cause go by various names: anti-death activists, radical life extension advocates, transhumanists, super-longevity enthusiasts. I'm going to call them "immortalists."* "Take your place in the revolution against aging and death," the RAADfest home page advertises. "The speakers are world-renowned scientists, thought leaders and visionaries on radical life extension. . . . These people are the stars—the real super heroes of our time."

Immortalism is a growing movement of people who believe that we can and should live forever. Even today's fifty-year-olds have a shot at many extra years of healthy lifespan, if we achieve "longevity escape velocity," says technologist Aubrey de Grey, a

---

* Some have moved away from this term in recent years, given that the movement is focused only on death by "natural" causes and not, say, by tsunamis or getting hit by a bus. "Life extension advocate" might be a more precise term, but it's too unwieldy for this book's purposes.

charismatically eccentric immortalist leader whose Methuselah beard reaches almost to his belly button.* After that, we'll be able to add on another two or three hundred years; eventually, we might not have to die at all. Instead of tackling specific late-life diseases such as Alzheimer's, he says, the aging process itself is the enemy.

I've come to RAADfest to explore the human quest to defy death. What does it tell us about these most bittersweet questions: How should we live, knowing that we'll die? When people wish for immortality, what are they really after? Is it everlasting life they truly want, or is it something else? Does death give meaning to life, as the philosophers say, and, if so, what would it mean to live without it? I'm keen to dig into these questions among people who've thought about them for years.

When I text my friend Dr. Raffaella de Rosa, chair of the Rutgers University–Newark philosophy department, from the San Diego airport, she's skeptical about the conference. "I'm all for not suffering in old age," responds Raffaella, who has short, spiky blond hair and dresses in the unapologetically sensual manner of a woman who embraces life with gusto. "We are all headed there and it's scary! But defying death is unbelievable! Heidegger says death shapes our life!

---

* Incidentally, as this book went to press, de Grey was facing allegations of sexual harassment, which he denies.

Death gives a sense of urgency. Do you think that these people really believe what they are preaching?"

Then, another text: "I wish I could be there with you and listen to the arguments."

But one of the first things I notice, upon arriving at RAADfest, is that there are no such arguments. People here are impatient with doubt; the vibe is more "Thank goodness we're together with like-minded people who know that death is stupid." "Death gives as much meaning to life," someone once wrote on the Stanford Transhumanist Association Facebook page, "as having your stomach ripped out gives meaning to having a stomach."

Instead of pondering philosophy, say the RAADfesters, we should commit to twenty-first-century technology and healthy living. At the coffee machine, someone jokes that any smokers at this conference would steal miles away to take their puffs. I feel suddenly embarrassed by the cookie I'm eating with my latte. I think of my extremely manageable autoimmune problem, a topic that comes up often at RAADfest because of the immune system's connection to longevity, and feel a twinge of guilt. Did my excessive love of chocolate somehow cause my health issue? Was it the stress of my **Quiet** book tour? What about my choice of book topics? As you can see from this book you're reading right now, I don't gravitate to the upbeat. But topics like longing and poignancy, joy and sorrow, would play poorly here. Who needs bittersweet? Life's fragility is not to be cherished; it's not mysteriously beautiful. It's a problem to be solved, with your buoyant spirit and impressive technology.

As I enter the hotel ballroom where we're to gather for the next three days, the theme song from the 1980 movie **Fame** blasts from the speakers:

I'm gonna live forever
I'm gonna learn how to fly (high) . . .

RAADfest has a mixed reputation in the life extension community. I've been told to expect an assortment of groundbreaking scientists, investors, crystal enthusiasts, snake oil salesmen, and elderly people desperate for a few more years. The crowd is majority male, mostly white, with a smattering of aging hippies and twiggy, dewy model-esque types. It's easy to pick out the scientists: some a bit schlumpy, others resolutely business casual in chinos and oxford shirts for the men, smart blouses for the women.

I ask the aging couple seated to my left what brought them here. "We're just trying to stay alive," they say. They heard about the conference from **Life Extension** magazine. "How about you?" the woman asks me. "Do you work in the life extension field?" When I say no, I'm a writer, they lose interest.

A band called Living Proof—three middle-aged guitarists and an elderly keyboard player—takes the stage to perform a song about immortality. "Out of the ashes, we are meant to stay alive!" they belt out, to a standing ovation.

"They did great tonight," a woman sitting behind me tells her seatmate, the way you would about a beloved hometown band. Clearly, they know each other from other such events. They seem glad to be reunited, reflecting the chipper and optimistic mood of the crowd. But then I ask the seventy-something gentleman to my right, a retired English professor, what brings him to RAADfest.

"Fear," he answers grimly.

. . .

The program begins in earnest. We'll be hearing presentations from the likes of a cryobiologist and biogerontologist named Dr. Greg Fahy, who uses human growth hormone to regrow thymus, a key ingredient of our immune systems; a Harvard Medical School geneticist named Dr. Sukhdeep Singh Dhadwar, who's trying to bring the woolly mammoth back from extinction while also searching for the genes that cause Alzheimer's; and Dr. Mike West, a renowned polymath who was one of the first scientists to isolate human embryonic stem cells and whose biotech company aims to cure age-related degenerative diseases.

But first, Bernadeane, a woman with only one name, takes the stage. She and her erstwhile romantic partner, James Strole, are the co-founders of People Unlimited, the Arizona-based producers and sponsors of RAADfest. Bernie, as she's called, wears a long black dress, a black beret, a platinum-white Louise Brooks–style bob, and red lipstick. She's eighty years old, and even by the standards of a young woman you'd describe her as chic, possibly even as a knockout. (The next day, she'll appear onstage in ankle boots and a miniskirt, boasting a sizable thigh gap.)

Bernie was born in 1937, she tells us, but it wasn't until 1960—at age twenty-three—that "I heard an individual speak on the radio, and he said the physical body didn't have to die. And ever since, I've been an activist against aging and death. So I'm not preparing for death. I'm prepared to live like I never have before. I think death stinks. And I don't think anyone should do it. I'm thankful that I have forever. I have a feeling in my body that I don't have to die. I'm not embarrassed. I walk out of death like I'm walking out of prison."

Bernie is part motivational speaker, part agent provocateur. "It's not the end of your life when you experience menopause," she declares, "it's only the beginning, believe me! We've got to claim our rights to live free of death. I'm so excited, because I see no end for us. We have to feel it. We have to create it. I'm enjoying like never before. It's wonderful where you get to a place . . . I'm into my eighty-first year now"—the crowd cheers—"and just to know it's not the end for me. I don't think the eighties are taking me down. I'm rising up in the midst of all of it! I see something for human beings that we've never seen before!"

I've always assumed that my eighties could be pretty bleak, if I make it there at all. But to hear Bernie tell it, that's just a story we tell ourselves. The wrong story.

"A new world is coming into view!" Bernie cries. "I am not stopping! Don't stop! Stay alive!"

"Yeah!" shout the audience members. "Woo!" "Right on, Bernie!" "Viva la revolución!"

Who are these people? Are they quacks? Are they brilliant and far-seeing? Are they in denial? Are they the inevitable products of our culture of winners and losers, determined to "win" the battle with mortality? Do they really expect to cure or vastly delay death? Is this a cult? At least one cult education website has followed the work of James and Bernie, documenting the sums they charge for their seminars. But Bernie and James say that they're making a living selling life, and what's wrong with that?

Certainly, some of the scientists here seem deadly serious in their mission to wake people up from what de Grey, the technologist with the Methuselah beard, calls the "pro-aging trance." "People would like to pretend that something that they don't want to happen—death—won't happen," he says, "and they can get on with their miserably short lives. They need to wake up and be less cowardly. They prefer to say: 'It's a blessing in disguise,' and that they've made their peace with aging. The problem is that when someone has the expectation that some ghastly thing will happen to them in the distant future, they have a choice: either spend their lives preoccupied by it, or find some way to put it out of their minds and make the best of it. And if indeed there is nothing to be done, then it makes perfect sense to trick yourself into thinking it's a blessing in disguise and not stress about it."

I'm struck by this viewpoint. I'd always thought that I wasn't particularly afraid of death—I react much more to the prospect of bereavement than to my own mortality. But recently I had a breast cancer scare. It turned out to be nothing, but awaiting my results, I was more frightened than I'd expected.

So maybe what sets the immortalists apart from the rest of us is not only their techno-optimism; maybe it's also their willingness to look death in the face. Most of us cope with mortality by pretending that it won't happen to us. But the immortalists cannot, will not, do that. They consider impermanence to be the great wound of the world, and they're doing everything in their power to heal it. "Someday when the descendants of humanity have spread from star to star," writes the author and artificial intelligence theorist Eliezer Yudkowsky in a work of Harry Potter fanfiction, "they won't tell the children about the history of Ancient Earth until they're old enough to bear it; and when they learn they'll weep to hear that such a thing as Death had ever once existed." The tenderness of this passage, wrapped in science fiction bravado—it gets me every time I read it.*

Indeed, many of the RAADfest scientists open their lectures with moving images of someone weeping over the dead body of a beloved. They describe their own grief over lost mothers, fathers, children. They issue fervent pleas to "rescue our elders," a phrase they've turned into a rallying cry. They describe conversion moments when they came face-to-face with heartbreak itself—and with the bliss of trying to cure it. For Mike West, the polymath who first isolated human stem cells, the awakening came at age twenty-seven, as he ate a hamburger in his Michigan hometown, across the street from a cemetery. "All of a sudden," he recalls, "it was kind of like the Buddha's experience: I suddenly woke up. I saw the graves of all my friends and loved ones there, with the year and the date that they died. It was like I saw the sun rise on that day. I said, 'That ain't going to happen.' I didn't know how we could ever accomplish such a thing, but I decided to devote the rest of my life to trying to solve this really significant problem of human mortality."

. . .

* That's why it doubles as the epigraph to this chapter!

The first immortalist I met, several months before RAADfest, has his own such story. Keith Comito is a computer programmer, mathematician, technology pioneer—and the president of the Lifespan Extension Advocacy Foundation. He has a narrow, friendly face and crinkly brown eyes; on the day we get together, at his favorite Greenwich Village coffee shop, he's wearing a T-shirt emblazoned with a periodic table of Marvel characters. He awaits me with green tea in hand: He gave up coffee in college, he explains, back when he thought it was bad for you. Staying up until three A.M. to complete his many projects is also bad for longevity, Keith acknowledges with a dimpled grin, but there's too much he wants to accomplish while he's still alive: especially longevity, which, for Keith, is the holy grail.

Keith acts in conscious homage to **The Epic of Gilgamesh,** the world's first great work of literature, about a king longing for immortality. Keith bounces in his seat, literally becomes airborne, as he recounts the famous tale: the seeking, questing king who found the flower of immortality and tried to bring it back to his people, but fell asleep on the way home, allowing a snake to eat the flower. Immortality is the real goal of all heroes' journeys, Keith declares; **Star Wars** and **The Odyssey** are just sublimated versions of the age-old desire to live forever. He sees himself as such a protagonist, but without the sublimation part.

Keith is one of those people who's fully themselves,

with no artifice or desire to posture. "It's giving me chills right now!" he exclaims, referring to the king's quest. During our two hours together, he'll refer three more times to the goosebumps he gets from the very idea of immortality. He says he'd be this inspired to work on extreme longevity even if he knew that he personally was going to die. It's "the feeling of being able to perhaps at last do something truly meaningful and healing for humanity" that energizes him. "How exciting is it to be alive right now that you potentially get to finish the first hero's journey—how exciting that we get to bring the flower back! People are looking for meaning in their lives? This is the first meaning that ever was—since the first stories were carved in stone!" He gesticulates expansively, his hand periodically colliding with my laptop, for which each time he pauses to apologize genuinely. In high school, I think, Keith would have been nerdy but well-liked for his irrepressible enthusiasm. **"You get to bring the flower back!"**

But when you take a closer look at **Gilgamesh** and the other literature of immortality (from **Gulliver's Travels** to the legend of the **Flying Dutchman,** the topic has always captured authors' imaginations), the storytellers are mostly warning us. That it's not only impossible to live forever (the snake will eat the flower) but also unwise. That we'd take up too much space. That after a few hundred years, we'd get bored; life would lose its meaning.

I ask Keith about these objections. Unlike the

RAADfesters, he has a taste for philosophical arguments, and he counters with a thought experiment.

Do you want to die tomorrow? he asks me, and my answer, of course, is no. What about the next day, he asks. Still no? Then how about the next day? The day after that? What about the day after the day after the day after the day after that?

The answer is always no. It turns out to be impossible to imagine the day when I'd say: Yes. Today's the day I'd choose never to see my family again, today's the day when I'd declare it okay never to see another sunset, and no more espresso martinis either, no more randomly sublime moments with old friends, belting out that Journey song we listened to when we were sixteen, no more sunny mornings by café windows.

If the bargain were getting to stay alive but growing increasingly infirm, then sure, many of us would say that it's time to go. But that's not what the immortalists are fighting for. They want a life that's free not only of death, but also of illness and decrepitude. They want to heal us all.

Like the immortalists I met at RAADfest, Keith knows why he's unable to suppress thoughts of death the way the rest of us do. His birth parents met in an asylum; they were plagued by drug addiction and mental illness; from the day Keith was born, he lived with foster parents who eventually adopted him and whom he now describes as his "true parents in every way." But the two sets of parents fought a bitter custody battle. His foster parents won; his biological parents died by the time Keith was in elementary school, his mother by starving to death, his father by suicidal overdose. Keith was devastated, but he didn't know what to do with his grief. He wasn't even sure he was supposed to feel it: Wasn't he lucky to have a good life with a loving family? But he knew that he'd crossed over to a world where his friends couldn't follow him: the world where death is real.

"In **Lord of the Rings,**" he explains, "there's a magic ring. When the characters put it on, they shift into a shadow dimension, where the bad guys' minions can see them. They've crossed over into that plane of reality. That's what happened with me and death. When you're a typical young child, you don't think of death. You think your parents are immortal and by extension you are, too. Your parents buffer you. But when you know as a young child that the beings that created you are dead, the wall is gone. There's a direct line between you and death."

He invented all kinds of ways to handle this situation. At first, he wanted to be a priest. (Even though he now considers himself agnostic, he's "very susceptible to the religious pull," and can still stare at a crucifix for hours.) Then, he became an autodidact, learning everything he could about self-empowerment, science, and fitness. He took up yoga, martial arts, gymnastics, biotech. "But as I'm getting older," he says, looking down at his wiry arms, "Father Time is going to remove this from me.

So why shouldn't I spend all my time working on life extension? If you have tons of interests and one of them is extending healthy life, you might want to work on this one first."

. . .

The most common objection to the immortalist project is that it's delusional—no matter how advanced our technology gets, the snake will always eat Gilgamesh's flower. (Personally, I doubt that we'll cure death, though I'm optimistic that eventually we'll extend our "healthspans" beyond our grandparents' wildest imaginings.)

But the deeper concern is that humans aren't meant to be gods. If we did live forever, some wonder, would we still be human? If our capacity for love and bonding emerges from our impulse to care for tearful infants, as we saw in chapter 1, what happens when we lose our vulnerability? Could we still love and be loved? If, as Plato said, we can't grasp reality without contemplating death, what would it mean to bypass it altogether? And then there are the practical concerns. If we defeat death before we find other habitable planets, will there be room for everyone? Will we usher in a new era of scarcity and conflict?

Some immortalists have ready responses to these quibbles. Not only are they going to cure death; they'll remove loss from the human condition, and elevate love in its place. If we can solve mortality, they reason, then we can figure out how to cure depression, end poverty, stop wars. "I think it is absolutely true," one of the scientists at RAADfest told me, "that when we solve one of the core problems facing humanity [i.e., death], we'll somehow empower ourselves to have more of a shot at the other ones. Especially because this problem of mortality has ground us down since the dawn of civilization. If we could do this, we could do anything."

Part of this utopian vision—at least the part that has to do with world peace—derives from a field in social psychology called terror management theory. According to this theory, the fear of death encourages tribalism, by making us want to affiliate with a group identity that would seem to outlive us. Various studies have shown that when we feel mortally threatened, we become jingoistic, hostile to outsiders, biased against out-groups. In one such experiment, subjects who were reminded of death were more likely than the control group to give their political opponents mouth-burning quantities of hot sauce! In another study, politically conservative students asked to think of what will happen to their bodies when they die were more likely than a control group to advocate extreme military attacks on threatening foreign nations. So if immortality frees us from our fear of death, goes the thinking, we'll grow more harmonious, less nationalistic, and more open to outsiders.

The founders of People Unlimited adopt this view explicitly. "There is a big picture message we feel is vital to deliver," explains their website, "that immortality, rather than being a dehumanizing element as Hollywood vampire stories suggest, in fact brings out the best in our humanity. It doesn't just end death, it ends the separation between people; by neutralizing the inherent fear of death, immortality empowers us to open our hearts to people like never before. The toxicity of contemporary life is a serious threat to our health, and perhaps the greatest toxicity is that which comes from people. This deathless passion creates a whole new level of togetherness in which people are lifted by people, rather than brought down."

It's a nice idea, but solving toxicity and conflict is unlikely to be this simple. Indeed, our true challenge—as this discussion suggests—may not be death at all (or not only death), but rather the sorrows and longings of being alive. We think we long for eternal life, but maybe what we're really longing for is perfect and unconditional love; a world in which lions actually do lay down with lambs; a world free of famines and floods, concentration camps and Gulag archipelagos; a world in which we grow up to love others in the same helplessly exuberant way we once loved our parents; a world in which we're forever adored like a precious baby; a world built on an entirely different logic from our own, one in which life needn't eat life in order to survive. Even if our limbs were metallic and unbreakable, and our souls uploaded to a hard drive in the sky, even if we colonized a galaxy of hospitable planets as glorious as Earth, even then we would face disappointment and heartbreak, strife and separation. And these are conditions for which a deathless existence has no remedy.

Maybe this is why the prize, in Buddhism and Hinduism, is not immortality, but freedom from rebirth. Maybe this is why, in Christianity, the dream is not to cure death but to enter heaven. We're longing, as Llewellyn Vaughan-Lee (the Sufi teacher you met in chapter 2) and other mystics might say, to reunite with the source of love itself. We're yearning for the perfect and beautiful world, for "somewhere over the rainbow," for C. S. Lewis's "place where all the beauty came from." And this longing for Eden, as Lewis's friend J.R.R. Tolkien put it, is "our whole nature at its best and least corrupted, its gentlest and most human." Perhaps the immortalists, in their quest to live forever and to "end the separation between people," are longing for these things, too; they're just doing it in a different language.

But they're also, I think, pointing in a different direction. Sure, I'd love to live long enough to meet my great-great-grandchildren, and if I can't, I hope that my children live to meet theirs. Yet I also hope that this won't cause them—cause us—to deny the bittersweet nature of the human condition. The RAADfesters believe that beating death will reveal the road to peace and harmony. And I believe exactly the opposite: that sorrow, longing, and maybe even mortality itself are a unifying force, a pathway to love; and that our greatest and most difficult task is learning how to walk it.

CHAPTER 8

Should we try to "get over" grief

and impermanence?

. . . and, when the time comes to let it go,
to let it go.

—MARY OLIVER,
"IN BLACKWATER WOODS"

Like my brother, the Japanese Buddhist poet Issa married late, in 1814, when he was fifty-one. He'd had a hard life. His mother died when he was two; his stepmother whipped him, he said, a hundred times a day. Later, Issa took care of his father, who suffered from typhoid fever, until he passed away, too. Issa's wife gave birth to two sons, each of whom died after a month. But then the couple had a daughter—a healthy, beautiful daughter named Sato. Happiness, finally! But Sato contracted smallpox, and died before her second birthday.

Issa was one of Japan's "Great Four" haiku masters. The heartbroken poet wrote of his inability to accept impermanence: "I concede that water can never return to its source, nor scattered blossoms to their branch, but even so the bonds of affection are hard to break." He considered the subject again in this haiku:

It is true
That this world of dew
Is a world of dew.
But even so . . .

It's a curious poem: so mild-mannered that you hardly notice the depth of protest it contains. It appears to be about the essential Buddhist idea that our lives are as ephemeral as a dewdrop. The Buddhist (and Hindu and Jain) answer to the question of how to live, knowing that we'll die, is to practice non-attachment: We should love, but we shouldn't cling to our desires (in Issa's case, for a daughter to live) or our aversions (here, her death by smallpox). Our difficulty accepting impermanence is the heart of human suffering. For this reason, many of the great contemplatives constantly reminded themselves of death, for example by putting out their fires at bedtime without keeping the embers lit for morning. Who knew if they'd be alive by then?

But there's a big difference between awareness and acceptance. Which is why "this world of dew / Is a world of dew" isn't the heart of Issa's poem. Its true, thrumming center is those three unassuming words: But even so.

But even so, says Issa, I'll long for my daughter forever. But even so, I'll never be whole again. But even so, I cannot accept, will not accept, **do you hear me as I whisper that I do not accept** the brutal terms of life and death on this beautiful planet. But even so, but even so, but even so.

. . .

How are we supposed to live, knowing that we and everyone we love will die? Issa offers his own bittersweet answer. You don't have to **accept** impermanence, I believe he's telling us. It's enough to be **aware** of it, and to feel its sting.

Because this, in the end, is what connects us all.

Think about the state of mind in which Issa writes. Does he believe that he, and he alone, has trouble with nonattachment? No; he knows that we all feel this way; he's writing to all his fellow humans who say **I get it about the dewdrops and I don't care, I want my daughter back.** Why did he bother writing haiku in the first place, and why do we still read them two hundred years later? It's because we know exactly how Issa feels, and **he knows that we'll know,** and we know that the people who read them two hundred years hence will also know (unless the immortalists succeed in their project). By turning his experience into poetry, Issa invites us to the shared sorrow of being mortal, the communal longing of being human; he guides us to the love that I've always felt to be the unseen power source of all those sad songs with which we've inexplicably filled our playlists. This is the ultimate paradox: We transcend grief only when we realize that we're connected with all the other humans who can't transcend grief because they will always say, because we will always say: But even so, but even so.

Have you gone through life quietly registering your own protest against mortality; do you feel keenly the pain of separation? Perhaps you keep such musings to yourself, feel vaguely embarrassed by them: notwithstanding the immortalists' adventures, they run so counter to our cultural programming. We have certain phrases that we use for everyday situations—**Get over it; Move on**—and we put a gentler sheen on them when it comes to bereavement: **Let it go,** we say, a phrase that has increased astronomically in usage during the past twenty years, according to the Google Books Ngram Viewer. And don't get me wrong: It's a wise precept, a liberating idea. I keep Mary Oliver's poem (the one in this chapter's epigraph) taped over my writing desk. During the past few years, I've gotten pretty good at letting go.

But in contemporary culture, the phrase implies a certain forced compliance. We once had, in the West, a tradition called **ars moriendi**—the art of dying. These guides to death, often in the form of printed pamphlets, were so popular that one version written in Latin in 1415 was reprinted in more than one hundred editions throughout Europe. But by the 1930s, the deathbed had moved from the family home, where people once expired in their bedrooms of childbirth, flu, and cancer, to hospitals, where they died safely out of view. Thus began the century-long collusion, with which we still live, to pretend that death happens only to other people.

Death became "shameful and forbidden," as Philippe Ariès wrote in his account **Western Attitudes Toward Death.** "A single person is missing for you, and the whole world is empty. But one no longer has the right to say so aloud." Mourners began to shoulder an "ethical duty to enjoy oneself," observed the anthropologist Geoffrey Gorer in his work **Death, Grief, and Mourning,** and an "imperative to do nothing which might diminish the enjoyment of others." They must "treat mourning as morbid self-indulgence," and the rest of us "give social admiration to the bereaved who hide their grief so fully that no one would guess anything had happened."

In this chapter, I'd like to propose a different view. I hope to show you how living in a bittersweet state, with an intense awareness of life's fragility and the pain of separation, is an underappreciated strength and an unexpected path to wisdom, joy, and especially communion.

. . .

When our sons were six and eight years old, we rented a summer house in the countryside for ten days. The boys swam, played outside, went for ice cream. They also fell in love with a pair of donkeys named Lucky and Norman, who lived in a fenced-off field next door. Every day the boys brought the donkeys apples and carrots. At first, the animals were too shy to accept these gifts. But after a few days, they hurried across the field at the sight of the children, who watched raptly as the donkeys ground their offerings into fruit juice spraying from their mouths.

It was a tender summer romance. But like all such romances, it had to end. Two nights before we went home, our usually happy boys started crying themselves to sleep, sad about leaving the donkeys. We told them that Lucky and Norman would be fine without us, that other families would feed them, too. We said that who knows, we might return to the same house next summer; maybe they'd see Lucky and Norman again.

But the only thing that consoled them was when we said that the pain of goodbye is part of life; that everyone feels it; that they would feel it again. This would seem a depressing reminder, but it had the opposite effect. When children (especially those growing up in relative comfort) grieve a loss, they're crying in part because we've unwittingly taught them a delusion—that things are supposed to be whole; that real life is when things are going well; that disappointment, illness, and flies at the picnic are detours from the main road. In "Spring and Fall," the poet Gerard Manley Hopkins writes to a young girl who's upset that the leaves are falling from the trees in "Goldengrove":

> Margaret, are you grieving
> Over Goldengrove unleaving?

He doesn't tell her to stop crying, he doesn't say that winter is beautiful, too (even though it is). He tells her the truth about mortality:

> It is the blight man was born for,
> It is Margaret you mourn for.

This doesn't mean that the kids shouldn't go back to their games and their innocence and their glee. It means that the news of transience comes to children, as well as to adults, as a relief, as the end of the gaslighting. The sorrow they see on the glorious horizon is real; they're not alone in perceiving it.

But even so: For kids as well as for grown-ups, three words that unite us with everyone who's ever lived.

. . .

The outlook embedded in these three words does more than connect us in some ineffable fashion. According to Dr. Laura Carstensen, an influential psychology professor who runs the Stanford Lifespan Development Laboratory and Stanford Center on Longevity, it also has the power to help us to live in the present, forgive more easily, love more deeply, and experience more gratitude and contentment, and less stress and anger.

Carstensen is sixty-ish, with salt-and-pepper bobbed hair, tortoiseshell glasses, and a demeanor that manages to be simultaneously modest and commanding. In 2012, she gave a popular TED Talk called "Older People Are Happier," describing her surprising findings that older people tend to enjoy the attributes I just described. Of course, folk intuition has always held that age confers wisdom. But Carstensen upended generations of assumptions about **why** this might be so. As Atul Gawande describes in his insightful book **Being Mortal,** Carstensen found that the key isn't age, per se, or the experience that comes with it, but rather the awareness of impermanence. It's the knowledge that time is limited. It's the sense of "but even so."

In one study, Carstensen and her colleagues followed a group, ages eighteen to ninety-four, for ten years. Using the "experience sampling" method, she had her subjects carry pagers and report their emotional states at random times of day and night. She found that the older people reported less stress, anger, worry, and distress than the young and middle-aged. She also discovered what she and her colleagues call a "positivity effect" as we age. While younger adults

tend to have a "negativity bias," predisposing them
to focus on unpleasant or threatening cues, older
people, Carstensen found, are more likely to notice
and remember the positive. They focus on smiling
faces; they tend to ignore the frowning and angry.

At first, other social scientists viewed these findings
as a "paradox of aging." After all, no matter how wise
you might be, it's still no fun to inhabit a weakening
body, or to fill your calendar with funerals as your
friends and family die. So why should older people
be happier? Were they better at stoicism, matter-of-
factly smiling through their depressing realities? Was
the cohort that Carstensen studied—members of
the so-called Greatest Generation—culturally con-
ditioned to a stiff upper lip? But the data turned out
to apply to members of all generations, whether they
were World War II vets or baby boomers: The older
they got, the calmer and more contented they grew.

Carstensen had a hunch about what was really
going on. She thought that the real answer was the
state of poignancy, which the elderly visit much more
than the young (and which, as we know, is the heart of
bittersweetness). Poignancy, she told me, is the richest
feeling humans experience, one that gives meaning
to life—and it happens when you feel happy and sad
at the same time. It's the state you enter when you
cry tears of joy—which tend to come during precious
moments **suffused with their imminent ending.**
When we tear up at that beloved child splashing in

a rain puddle, she explains, we aren't simply happy: "We're also appreciating, even if it's not explicit, that this time of life will end; that good times pass as well as bad ones; that we're all going to die in the end. I think that being comfortable with this is adaptive. That's emotional development."

We can all enter this state, but it happens more frequently for our elders, Carstensen hypothesized, because of their numbered days. The young delude themselves that the music will never stop playing. So it makes sense for them to explore rather than savor; to meet new people rather than to devote time to their nearest and dearest; to learn new skills and soak up information, rather than to ponder the meaning of it all; to focus on the future rather than to remain in the present. Poignancy, for the young, may be touching, but it can feel irrelevant to the daily act of living.

All these youthful activities are wonderful, of course, in an expansive, life-building way. But when you know, really know, that you won't live much longer, your perspective narrows—and deepens. You start to focus on what matters most, stop caring so much about ambition, status, and getting ahead. You want the time you have left to be charged with love and meaning. You think about your legacy, savor the simple act of being alive.

Once Carstensen puts it this way, the contentment of our elders makes perfect sense—as it always has to sages and philosophers, who have come up with all kinds of ways (such as keeping skulls on their writing tables) to remind themselves of death.

Still, here in twenty-first-century Western society, Carstensen's fellow scientists were initially skeptical of her ideas. But Carstensen could see things that other researchers could not. Not because she was a mystic, or a monk; but because, at the age of twenty-one, she herself had come close to death.

After a devastating car accident, she'd been placed on the orthopedic ward, where she shared a room with a succession of octogenarians with broken hips. And during those dark weeks when she hovered between life and death, she started to notice that she was developing the same priorities as her aged roommates. Like them, her social focus narrowed, and her thirst for meaning deepened. She found herself longing to spend time with the people she loved best.

While recovering, she spent the next four months in the hospital, bored and immobile, looking like a figure in one of those cartoons where the patient lies flat on their back with one leg strapped to the ceiling. Her father visited every day and suggested that she take a course at the University of Rochester, where he was a professor. He told her to pick any field she wanted, and he'd attend class on her behalf, taping the lectures. Laura chose psychology. Back then, she had no particular interest in the aging process. But later in her career, when she read that older people have smaller social networks, that they're unlikely to show up at senior centers for lunch and other social programs that are thought to be good for them, it made sense to her. She remembered how she'd felt back in the hospital. Why spend time making new friends when your days are numbered? Wouldn't it be better to seek meaning in the moments and relationships you already have?

At the time, as Gawande recounts, the prevailing theory was that, as we approach the end of our lives, we start to disengage. But Carstensen suspected that this was all wrong. We may not want to talk to random people at a senior citizen center, but that doesn't mean we want to stop connecting. On the contrary, she thought: As we come to the end, we forgo expansion in favor of communion and meaning.

After that first decade-long study following subjects aged eighteen to ninety-four, Carstensen conducted more and more groundbreaking research, testing her hypothesis that the awareness of impermanence, rather than age itself, causes us to make the life choices of an older and wiser person. She continued to find that older people tend to value time with close friends and family over meeting new people. But when she asked them to imagine that medical progress would grant them another twenty years to live, she found that the old made the same choices as the young. Conversely, young people who were terminally ill with AIDS made the same choices as octogenarians—and so did perfectly healthy young people who were primed for impermanence by, say, imagining that they were about to move far away from their loved ones.

Carstensen even found these patterns among healthy people facing social unrest. Young and strong Hong Kong residents who were worried about Chinese rule in 1997, and later about the SARS epidemic, made the same social choices as older people. But when life appeared to settle down after the political transition, when the threat of SARS subsided, these young people started acting "like themselves" again. Again and again, Carstensen's studies showed that the important variable is not how many years since you were born—but how few good years you feel you have left.

All this is great news if you're eighty. But it has huge implications for the rest of us, too. If Carstensen is right that wisdom comes not only from experience but also from priming "life's fragility," as she puts it, then there should be many ways to achieve this state. After all, we can't (and probably don't want to) make ourselves thirty or fifty years older—but we can always change our perspectives.

. . .

If you're a naturally bittersweet type, you have a head start; you're constitutionally primed to feel the tug of impermanence. Another way to get there is simply to wait for middle age, which seems to carry some of the psychological benefits of aging without the downsides of your body falling apart. Carstensen has developed a short quiz called the "Future Time Perspective" scale, which you can find on her website lifespan.stanford.edu, and which measures two categories: how great a sense of possibility you have, and how aware you are that you'll die one day.

When I took the quiz, at age fifty, I found that I answered the first set of questions (which measures your expectation of a future filled with promise) like a young person, and the second set (which measures your sense that time is running out) like an octogenarian. Just like a twenty-one-year-old, I'm still full of plans and ideas and excitement. But I have an acute consciousness, which I lacked fifteen years ago, that time is limited. This gives me no anxiety, at least not yet; but it does make me feel as if I should soak everything up while I still can. Carstensen told me that this was typical of midlife.

But even if you're twenty-two, or you're not temperamentally bittersweet, Carstensen believes that there are other ways to access the wisdom of the aged. She advises—surprise!—listening to bittersweet, minor key music (I have a playlist for you, along with my curated collection of bittersweet poetry and art, at www.susancain.net).

She also recommends meditating on death. Notice impermanence in nature—the splendor of autumn, the baby sparrow fallen on your driveway. Spend time with older people in your family; ask if you can record their life stories. It's hard to believe that they won't always be there to tell them. Realize that one day those stories will live only in digitized form.

We can also follow the religious traditions we've grown up with—Ash Wednesday in Christianity, for example; Yom Kippur in Judaism; meditations on impermanence in Buddhism; all remind us of mortality. In **The Imitation of Christ,** an influential Christian devotional book, the medieval scholar Thomas à Kempis encourages Christians to live as if they might die at any time. This is similar to the wisdom of the Stoic philosophers, who advised us to remember death at exactly the moments we feel most invincible.

When the Romans triumphed, writes Ryan Holiday, an influential author on Stoicism, the victorious commander would be stationed at a place of honor, where the adoring crowds could see him best. But instead of immersing himself in glory, he was followed by an aide whispering in his ear, "Remember, thou art mortal." Marcus Aurelius, too, wrote in his **Meditations,** "You could leave life right now. Let that determine what you do and say and think." Seneca suggested that each night we tell ourselves that "You may not wake up tomorrow," and that we greet every morning with the reminder that "You may not sleep again." All of these practices are meant to help us treat our lives, and each other, as the precious gifts they are.

As I mentioned, I've tried these practices, and I know how helpful they can be. When I kiss my children good night, sometimes I remind myself that they could disappear tomorrow, or I could. Maybe this strikes you as morbid, but these thoughts cause me to put down my cellphone immediately, or better still, to leave it in another room.

But sometimes "memento mori" happens inadvertently. My father introduced me to the music of the great Belgian songwriter Jacques Brel when I was a teenager. We both adored his songs—the brilliance and pathos of them. A love of Brel, and of music in general, was one of the many gifts my father gave me. During the weeks when he was in the hospital with COVID and I waited for news of him, I started listening to Brel again. Decades had passed since I'd last heard those songs, and now, as an adult well into midlife, I realized that his great theme had been the passage of time. This could have made me sad, I suppose, but instead I felt loved: Brel had predicted this moment; my father had known it was coming when he played the music for me all those years ago; and now, I knew it, too. Jacques Brel, my father, me. And you.

. . .

Reflecting on Carstensen's work, I've started to envision her as a religious figure dressed up as a scientist. She laughs when I tell her this, but acknowledges her fondness for a well-known rabbinic story. It goes like this:

A rabbi walks with a little boy down a path, and they come across a dead bird. The boy asks why the bird had to die.

"All living things die," explains the rabbi.

"Will you die?" asks the boy.

"Yes," answers the rabbi.

"Will I?"

"Yes."

The boy looks distressed.

"Why?" he asks urgently.

"Because that's what makes life precious," says the rabbi.

I ask Carstensen why she likes this story so much. "Because," she says, her voice choked with emotion, "my research tells the same story with data."

. . .

If Carstensen's work focuses on how we react to our **own** mortality, there's still the question of how to respond to bereavement. It's no accident that Issa's poem is about the death of a child—for many, the most trying of all heartaches.

Issa was wrestling with the ideal of nonattachment, which seems to operate in stark contrast to Western attitudes toward mourning. Freud, for example, advised not preemptive nonattachment but rather the breaking of attachment after death: the gradual withdrawal of investment in the person we had loved, the painful, laborious process of breaking emotional ties. He called this "grief work."

A more updated view, espoused by contemporary Western scholars of grief, such as Columbia professor of clinical psychology George Bonanno, author of an influential book called **The Other Side of Sadness,** focuses not on "letting go" but on our natural capacity for resilience. When we lose our beloveds, says Bonanno, we may fall to our knees, we may curse the heavens. But we humans are wired to withstand grief; we've lost our loves for as long as we've drunk our mothers' milk. Some bereaved people do suffer from chronic grief—or from moderate distress—for a prolonged time. But many of us are more resilient than we think.

We assume that the standard trajectory following bereavement is a long period of agony followed by a painstakingly slow recovery, but the reality, says Bonanno, is more complex. We may laugh at a joke the day after our daughter dies; we may sob at her memory fifty years later.

In the immediate aftermath of a bereavement, it's common to move back and forth between intense emotions of happiness and sorrow. As the author Chimamanda Ngozi Adichie described it in **The New Yorker,** soon after her father died: "Another revelation: how much laughter is a part of grief. Laughter is tightly braided into our family argot, and now we laugh, remembering my father, but somewhere in the background of the laughter there is a haze of disbelief. The laughter trails off."

"The dominant experience is sadness," explains Bonanno, in a podcast interview with Dr. David Van Nuys, "and there are also some other emotions. . . . There's anger, sometimes contempt, or shame, where people are having all kinds of memories and difficult experiences. . . . So rather than this elaborate, steady state of months of deep sadness, it's really much more of an in and out kind of an oscillatory state, and this sadness is punctuated at times by positive states and smiling, laughter and connection to other people." For many people, says Bonanno, these "periods of sadness . . . gradually get less intense."

This doesn't mean that even the most resilient move on completely. "They may not resolve the loss," he says. "They may not fully put aside the pain. But they're able to continue functioning." We're built to live simultaneously in love and loss, bitter and sweet.

The Eastern emphasis on nonattachment presents a different view of bereavement. It doesn't deny grief—even the Dalai Lama is said to have mourned when his mother died. And it certainly doesn't deny love. "Nonattachment is not against love, as is commonly conceived," says the Hindu spiritual leader Sri Sri Ravi Shankar. "It is a higher form of love." Rather, it advises loving in a nonattached way.

I find great wisdom in this view . . . and still I've wondered whether the principle of nonattachment can apply, should apply, to a bereaved parent—to Issa. Or is it swept away by the tidal wave of misery that explodes over any such mother or father?

I decided to conduct an informal survey, starting with Sri Sri, whom I was fortunate to interview one day at a Yale University forum. He answered without hesitation: Yes, it still applies. A parent will mourn, of course. But "your grief of someone's death or disease is only because they are yours. Even the overwhelming love you feel for your child comes in an attached or nonattached version. Loving your child for what he is, is one thing. And loving your child because he is yours, is another. Love without attachment is your love for your son because of what he is. Loving your son because he is yours is love with attachment."

Of course, he says, a parent needs time to adjust to their new reality. "One can grow into it," he says. "For a mother, it may not be possible immediately."

Next, I went to visit a colleague named Stephen Haff. As the mother of young boys, I'd been advised by Sri Sri, in an echo of the loving-kindness tradition I'd learned from Sharon Salzberg, to loosen the bonds of attachment by expanding the scope of my maternal love. "You should love many more children as your own," he'd said, "just as you love your sons. When you expand your attachment, then detachment happens. A broader sense of wisdom comes into your life."

As it happens, Stephen lives exactly the life that Sri Sri prescribes. Sandy-haired, scruffy, and intense, a brilliant drama school grad, he's devoted his career to teaching underprivileged children in a cheerful one-room schoolhouse that he operates on a shoestring budget out of a storefront in Bushwick, Brooklyn. It's called Still Waters in a Storm, and it's a reading and writing after-school sanctuary where kids and teens, most of them Mexican immigrants, can immerse themselves in literature and drama. The kids write poetry, fiction, and memoir, then take turns reading their work aloud as the others listen in what Stephen calls "a sacred hush." He spends sixty hours a week at the school, barely able to pay his own family's rent. He told me that others confess that they don't understand the depth of his "love for random children." But "every kid who comes in the room," he says, "I'm in love. I do whatever I can for all of them. I want to hear all of their voices."

Yet when I asked Stephen about Sri Sri's advice, he pulled from his pocket a folded-up piece of paper that he carries around with him, containing a quote from George Orwell. "In this yogi-ridden age," Orwell had written (all the way back in 1949, before there was a yoga studio on every corner), "it is too readily assumed that 'non-attachment' is not only better . . . but that the ordinary man only rejects it because it is too difficult. . . . If one could follow it to its psychological roots, one would, I believe, find that the main motive for 'non-attachment' is a desire to escape from the pain of living, and above all from love, which, sexual or non-sexual, is hard work."

Stephen turned and looked me in the eye. "Loving someone means nothing if it doesn't mean loving some people more than others," he said. "And understanding that makes me better able to love. I understand there's a hierarchy. I love my students, but I absolutely love my own children more, and I have no interest in training myself away from that. It's too strong. It's too far away from the heart of nature. And I want to feel that feeling utterly. I've often admired Buddhist ideas, but at the same time wondered what they really meant. Is it really, ultimately, a cold-hearted thing? When I first read that Orwell quote, it was like permission to be a person."

What would happen, I asked Stephen, as gently as I could, if something happened to your "own" kids, the kids you and your wife are raising?

"If I were to lose my children," he answered without hesitation, "I would be destroyed. I would be terribly destroyed about the others as well. But with my own children, I would be ruined."

Finally, I talked to another friend, Dr. Ami Vaidya, who's the co-chief of gynecologic oncology at HMH Hackensack University Medical Center. Ami started her training by bringing children into the world; now her work often involves treating mothers with terminal ovarian cancer, as skillfully and empathetically as she possibly can. Ami happens to be Hindu, and believes in reincarnation, in what she describes as a "circular pattern between life and death." When she was small, her grandmother made a thumbs-up sign and explained to her that there was a little Ami, the size of her thumb, who lived in her heart. "She told me that our bodies can't live forever, and when they die, that soul moves on and finds a new body to live in. And that soul goes on and on. It never dies. Eventually that soul breaks the cycle of birth and death and can be one with the universe. That's the idea of OM."

For Ami, this belief system makes death easier to bear. It also influences the way she thinks about medical treatment. "The body means nothing," she explains. "We cremate the body and we don't even keep the ashes. It's really a transient thing, all of it, that allows folks to accept loss, and to look at this life as very, very limited."

Ami is committed to giving her patients the full range of treatment options, so they can chart their own course, with dignity. Western cancer patients, she says, tend to want to try everything, "even if there's a three percent chance of any efficacy of stabilizing the disease—not even curing it! And for many unfortunate patients with advanced or recurrent disease, the symptoms can be harsh. Their quality of life can be severely impaired—no energy to get out of bed, limited ability to eat or drink. For them, stable disease isn't much of a life. But we grasp and cling at any opportunity because we just don't want to face the loss. My Hindu patients are less likely to do the last-ditch three percent treatment. This is a generalization—there are absolutely exceptions. But they're more likely to say: 'This is our time.'"

"I'm not saying that Hindus are happy about death," Ami hastens to explain. "They feel just as much loss. But there's more of a sense that death is part of life. There's a fatalism, a sense that we don't have an ability to change it, that there's a power that's greater than ourselves, even greater than science's ability to find treatments and cures. Things happen for a reason. If this is our time, this is our time."

It's a powerful point of view. And yet. When I ask Ami about Issa's case—the death of a child—she stops short. Ami is terrifically energetic, fiercely intelligent, a gifted physician. To talk with her is to find yourself borne aloft on a river of effortless words and ideas. But now she speaks more haltingly. "I think it's the hardest with children," she says slowly. "I think asking for that acceptance is too hard. Thank God I'm not a pediatric oncologist. That's one thing I could never do. Especially not after having my own children. Day to day, I hold on to my kids with everything that I have. I don't really know how we can turn to those families and provide them with comfort for that loss. Losing a child is the deepest, most profound loss that exists. When it comes to the loss of a child—I don't have a good way to describe or talk about that. To me, that's just a suffering that some are forced to endure."

At first, I'm confused. If you truly believe that

the soul lives on, that it's all a near-infinite cycle of rebirth, shouldn't this belief ease even the most grievous losses?

But the doctrine of reincarnation doesn't solve the pain of separation between two attached souls, Ami explains. "It's unlikely those two souls will meet again. And who knows where one will land and where the other will land. And that is a true loss."

And there it is again: the oldest problem, the deepest dream—the pain of separation, the desire for reunion. That's the nub of human heartache and desire, regardless of your religion, birth country, personality. That's what Issa was trying to tell us; that's what we've all known, all along.

Both Buddhism and Hinduism teach that, once our attachments are gone, we reach nirvana, which is not up in the sky or in some distant and fantastical place, but rather an enlightened state that anyone can access here on earth—a state in which we meet pain and loss, as well as comfort and togetherness, with equanimity and compassion.

So maybe none of the people I've just described is enlightened: not Stephen, not Ami—not even Issa. Definitely not Issa. Maybe once you're fully enlightened, bittersweetness is beside the point. I wouldn't know. (And if you think you do, consider the spiritual teacher Ram Dass's observation that if you think you're enlightened, you should go spend a week with your family at Thanksgiving.)

But there are different pathways to the peace we

all seek. "Let it go" is one such pathway, and it takes us a certain distance. "Know how resilient you are" is another route, and it lends us comfort and courage. Nonattachment is a third way, and it helps us aspire to an expansive love that exists apart from possession. Others take comfort in the faith that they'll reunite with their loved ones in heaven.

But Issa's way—"but even so"—carries a different wisdom: one that expresses the longing that many of us sense is the force that will carry us home. "But even so" opens up the arms that seem to fold tightly across the chest of the world when our loved ones leave us. "But even so" connects us with everyone who's ever grieved, which is to say: everyone.

. . .

When Lois Schnipper's only daughter, Wendy, was diagnosed with ovarian cancer at the age of thirty-eight, the oncologists said they would treat it as a chronic disease. So, during the ten years of Wendy's illness, despite the grim prognosis for ovarian cancer at the time, Lois believed that Wendy would live. Lois is a constitutional optimist, and so was Wendy, who went on living her life as normally as possible with her husband and daughters: school plays and soccer games and family vacations. In the photos from those years, Wendy's hairstyle changes—sometimes a bandanna wrapped around her head, sometimes her pin-straight brown hair grown back curly from the chemo—but her smile is always bright. There was one medical crisis after another—frequent trips to the hospital, the family gathered in yet another waiting room as Wendy endured her latest harrowing procedure—but each time the crisis resolved, each time Lois continued to believe that Wendy would outlive her.

In contrast, Lois's husband, Murray, who has a less optimistic nature and who lost his own father at age sixteen, prepared for the worst. He savored those ten years with his daughter, but he also spent them in a defensive crouch. Which meant that when Wendy finally died, Murray was ready (as ready as you can ever be), while Lois was flattened. For two years she rarely emerged from her house, she woke up every day in tears, gained ten pounds. She hung photographs of Wendy in a crazy quilt all across the walls of the house in which she and Murray had raised her. Her sunny, capable self was gone for good, or so it seemed.

Eventually, with Murray's support, and his gentle suggestion that making a shrine to Wendy was helping no one, Lois found her way back. She realized that she had other children and grandchildren who needed her, too; that to stay mired in grief was to exclude them, to tell them they didn't matter—and to signal that they should spend the rest of their lives sequestered, too. She realized that she still had Murray, whom she adores. And she still loved life. "I like being with people, going places," she says. "It's still exciting to me."

Looking back now, she's glad that she didn't diminish the joy of those final ten years with Wendy with a more realistic outlook of her prognosis. She wouldn't trade those good times for an easier acceptance of her death.

Lois is a close friend—my sister's mother-in-law—and she tells me all this calmly, over brunch at a cozy restaurant on the Upper West Side of Manhattan, Murray by her side. She's eighty-two years old at the time of our conversation. Listening to her recount her experience, I love her, I admire her, I take mental notes of what to do when disaster strikes—yet also I feel that, in her breathtaking optimism, she's utterly alien to me. I'm more like Murray: I would have seen the diagnosis clearly; I would have braced for disaster. This is who I am, for better and for worse. Psychologists even have a name for it: "defensive pessimism." How remarkable, I think, for the gazillionth time, that humans come in so many varieties.

But then Lois says something that makes me realize that she's not alien at all; suddenly we're joined back together in the strange beautiful unity of humans, doing our best with our painfully imperfect source codes. "It's like a cracked mirror now," Lois says. "Something is always missing. The mirror doesn't get put back the way it was, but if you work, you can get a piece of it back."*

---

* Lois read about the image of a mirror in a book whose name she can't recall; I'm sorry we can't credit the author!

Pause.

"But it takes a certain amount of will," Lois adds quietly.

She says the words so faintly, almost as an afterthought: "But it takes a certain amount of will."

Lois, in the year 2016, two hundred years after Issa wrote his haiku, had looked at me across a cheerful table setting, a spinach omelette and a strawberry smoothie, and she had said to me the words that humans must always say: But even so. But even so. But even so.

· · ·

Two hundred years ago, Issa taught that we should be aware of impermanence—we should notice how ephemeral the dewdrops are—but we shouldn't pretend that grief disappears. No matter how much your culture tells you to smile, it's not human to simply move on.

But this doesn't mean that we can't move forward.

This distinction—between moving on and moving forward—is the heart of a TED Talk given by author Nora McInerny, and it's the most powerful framework I've found for embracing the bittersweet nature of existence that unites us all. After losing her husband Aaron to brain cancer, McInerny asked other bereaved partners what advice about grief they'd hated most. The most common reply: the exhortation to "move on."

She herself had since remarried. She and her new husband had four kids in a blended family, a house in the suburbs, a rescue dog. Life was good. But it was also, she said, still with Aaron. Not "in the way that he was before, which was much better. . . . It's just that he's indelible, and so he is present." He's present in her work, in the child they had together, in the person she's become—the person her second husband fell in love with. She hasn't moved on from Aaron, she says. She's "moved forward with him."

McInerny's observations carry on Issa's legacy—and also show us how to live it.

"What can we do other than try to remind one another that some things can't be fixed, and not all wounds are meant to heal?" she continues. "We need each other to remember, to help each other remember, that grief is this multitasking emotion. That you can and will be sad, and happy; you'll be grieving, and able to love in the same year or week, the same breath. We need to remember that a grieving person is going to laugh again and smile again. . . . They're going to move forward. But that doesn't mean that they've moved on."

CHAPTER 9

Do we inherit the pain of our parents and ancestors? And, if so, can we transform it generations later?

What is silenced in the first generation, the second generation carries in the body.

—FRANÇOISE DOLTO

I started writing this book to solve the mystery of bittersweet music—why we listen to it at all, why so many of us find it so soaring and sublime. But there was also that other question I told you about in chapter 4: why I couldn't speak of my mother without tears, and how I could get this to stop. My solution had been never to speak of her at all—until one October morning at the Open Center in midtown Manhattan.

In my quest to understand mortality, I'd signed

up for a workshop for social workers, chaplains, and psychologists who work with the dying and bereaved. I was no such professional, but I **was** writing this book, which I hoped qualified me to attend. So there I was: feeling composed, and a little detached, not unlike the way I'd felt before the Leonard Cohen memorial concert. I had no idea that I was about to answer my decades-long question about my mother—but also to explore a much larger question of bittersweetness: how to transform the sorrows and longings we inherit from the generations who came before us.

...

We meet in a bright, airy room that doubles as a yoga studio—folded blankets and foam blocks fill the shelves—but today a full-body skeleton stands propped at the front, alongside a small wooden table holding a votive candle and a whiteboard that says: "To understand death is to understand life!"

Dr. Simcha Raphael, a psychotherapist, a "death awareness educator," and the founding director of the Da'at Institute for Death Awareness, Advocacy and Training, sits expectantly by the skeleton. Simcha, who invites us to call him by his first name, seems a cross between an Orthodox rabbi and an old-school California hippie, with a salt-and-pepper beard, navy blue suit, and skullcap, but also a stud earring, silver pendant, and cowboy boots. His speech is a mix of

Talmudic cadence and the quick-witted patter of a Borscht Belt comedian. He was "pickled in the brine of grief," he tells us, having weathered the deaths of many close friends and family members when he was young. But he believes that between this world and the next is a window, not a wall, and that our "death-phobic" society stops us from seeing this.

There are eight of us in the workshop, our chairs arranged in a circle, and Simcha invites us to share our personal experiences with death. One of the first to speak is Maureen, who describes herself as "tough Irish." Maureen comes across as competent, sensible, and cheery. She speaks glowingly of her daughter and husband, with whom she's celebrating a fifteenth wedding anniversary tonight. She has short, straight hair, and she's wearing glasses, running shoes, and a name tag with a smiley face. In a clear, assertive voice, hands resting at her sides, Maureen tells her story.

"I always start out with what I do, because that's the safest place for me to go. I'm a medical social worker. I'm comfortable helping people face their own deaths, and **to the core,**" she says with grim emphasis, "I'm afraid of my own. My father died when I was fourteen, and my mother didn't allow us to grieve. When I started to cry at the funeral, my mother gave me a furious look." Maureen reproduces the look with what I guess is perfect mimicry, the corners of her mouth turned down in stern disapproval.

"My sister lost her hair from the grief," she

continues. "I cried a lot, but never dealt with it. I found a friend who was a father figure, and then that friend committed suicide. Later, I became an alcoholic, and had relationships with abusive men. I've had several abortions, and believe I'm going to hell. I've been sober for fourteen years. I've poured myself into my work, so that I can make restitution for the lives I've taken. So I could somehow lend support to others, where support was not to be had for myself.

"I want to grieve my own terrible mistakes," Maureen adds quietly. "I want to learn to heal that pain, and to ask for forgiveness. How can I forgive myself? If I can do that, it would set me free to help other people."

Simcha listens intently throughout. "I see two things," he says gently. "One, your mother taught you very well to shove your feelings under the rug. Your story is very painful, but if I replayed a video clip of what you just told us, with the sound off, you could be talking about a trip to the Caribbean or a meal you just ate. So, thank you, Mom, but you can have that one back. Two, I see a yearning for healing, and to remove the judgment of yourself. We have to get rid of those three words: **my terrible mistakes.**"

He asks the rest of us to pay attention to what happens when we hear someone's painful story. Do we take it on as our own? Yes. My detachment is crumbling; I feel something coming undone as I listen to Maureen.

Then Simcha asks whether we're judging ourselves:

"Are you thinking that 'she had a four-tissue story and I only have a two-tissue story'?" Yes, that, too. I'm relieved to see others laughing with relief at Simcha's question. I wish that I didn't have to tell my story at all; it feels so thin compared with Maureen's.

But refusing to speak feels wrong, ungenerous. When my turn comes, I talk about my mother—of our great rift when I was a teenager, of feeling, back then, that I'd killed her spirit. I describe how my mother grew up in the shadow of her own mother, and a father whose entire family was being slaughtered, in real time, across the ocean.

And as I speak, the old tears come; I should have known they would. I'm crying like it's a four-tissue story, a seven-tissue story, I'm crying like it's a story of a thousand tissues and still there wouldn't be enough tears. Here's Maureen, whose father **actually** died when she was a teenager, and whose life unraveled as a result, and I'm crying more than she did. I'm sure that Simcha wouldn't want us to compare griefs, but I feel ridiculous.

Simcha isn't judging me, though, and as far as I can tell, neither is the group. "I hear that there's not been a full and healthy individuation," he tells me. "So, part of you is still stuck at sixteen, where you're still wanting to stay bonded to your mother. Where you had to say, I can either be an individual, or feel loved, but I can't be both."

He's right, of course; I've known this for a long time. But then Simcha says something else: that I'm carrying not only my own grief; I'm carrying my mother's grief, too, and the grief of her mother and father, and their mothers and fathers. I'm carrying the grief of the generations.

He asks me my sign. I'm not an astrology type, but I go with it, tell him I'm a Pisces. "You're permeable," he says, nodding. "It's hard for you to know what's yours, and what belongs to other people. To the people who came before you.

"But you can keep the connection to the generations alive," he adds, "without holding on to their pain."

I have a shock of recognition, as I realize—these strange tears, the ones that appear out of nowhere, like a mugger at a street corner—**I've had these tears all my life, had them long before the troubles with my mother.** They came at farewell moments, such as the last day of summer camp at age ten, even though I was ambivalent about camp and glad to go home; I remember feeling mystified by them even then. The tears didn't seem to match the circumstances, except in some cosmic way I couldn't put my finger on.

We have almost no aunts, uncles, cousins in my family of origin; most everyone on both my mother's and father's side was killed in the Holocaust, in their place a century-old sepia photo of vanished relatives I've wondered about since I was a child—a group of men, women, elders, children staring somberly into the camera. Their unsmiling expressions were the fashion in European photography of the 1920s, when the picture was taken, but it had always seemed to me that they were anticipating their fate—as, indeed, some of them had.

In 1926, when my grandfather was a promising seventeen-year-old rabbinical student, he and his father spent all the money they had for train tickets from Bczuch, their small Polish village, to a city called Stanislav, to hear a lecture by a leading thinker who predicted what was to come. "Polish Jews," the speaker had prophesied, "there are two giants: Russia, and Germany. These two giants are competing for hegemony, for mastering the world. They keep on heating the furnaces where they burn and prepare ammunition and bullets and all kinds of vessels for destruction, and they will eventually collide with one another. And you, Polish Jews, will be in the middle of it. You are condemned to be ground to ashes. May I offer you one word of advice: Escape. Run as fast as you can. I am urging you, I am urging you, with all the power in my voice and in my mind: Escape. Run away from here, because otherwise you will be turned into ashes."

The following year, my grandfather left for America on his own, sponsored by the parents of a bride he'd never met—my maternal grandmother. He intended to bring his family as soon as he could. But he lived in poverty, in a tiny Brooklyn apartment, had nothing to give them, nowhere to house them. The Stanislav prophecy was always in his mind, but who knew how real or imminent the threat really was? He waited a little longer, a little longer, and in the meantime, his family was ground to ash. Just as the speaker had predicted.

To the congregation he served for fifty years, my grandfather was the twinkly-eyed rabbi with the lilting voice, sympathetic presence, philosophical bent, and delighted laugh. He knew the Talmud by heart; he was the leader of prayers, the shepherd of souls. To my mother, he was all these things, and a deeply devoted father besides. To me, he seemed in this world but not of it, like a character in a magic-realist tale. He carried the scent of an ancient library, as if he'd emerged, genie-like, from the stacks of old books that filled his small apartment. He was one of my favorite people in the world.

But he was also the man who never forgave himself for his family's destruction, who sighed his way through the afternoons, who almost a century after the trip to Stanislav wept on his deathbed for the parents he left behind. My grandfather commanded the respect of the dominant types of his community, but his heart was with the lost souls. They gathered in his living room and walked with him to synagogue. **"Oy, nebach,"** he would often say, in Yiddish, with a great big sigh, as he recounted to my mother the misfortunes of this or that member of his congregation. **Oy, nebach** means "that poor soul." It's one of the few Yiddish expressions I know, conveyed when I was a little girl playing in the kitchen as he talked to my mother, and I heard him say it in every conversation. **Oy, nebach,** the caption of my childhood.

. . .

Did these historical events somehow transmit to me, did they contribute to my mystery tears, as Simcha now suggests? And if so, by what mechanism—was the transmission cultural, familial, genetic, was it all three? We'll explore these questions in this chapter. But we'll also ask another question. If our task, as the bittersweet tradition teaches, is to transform pain into beauty, **can we do this not only with the pain of the present, and of our own personal pasts, but also with the pain of the ages?**

You may not have a dramatic story of inherited sorrow; your family's history may not be written into the better-known catastrophes of the past few centuries. But chances are that some of your ancestors were serfs or slaves; even if they were kings and queens, the pain of separation likely came for them, too, in the form of war or famine or plague or alcoholism or abuse or any of the other forces of chaos that evict us all from the garden, eventually. We all know, deep in our bones, the bitter side of bittersweet.

Not long after Simcha's seminar, I listened to Krista Tippett, the host of the podcast **On Being,** interview Dr. Rachel Yehuda, a professor of psychiatry and neuroscience and the director of the Traumatic Stress Studies Division at the Mount

Sinai School of Medicine. It was late at night, and I was about to drift off to sleep when Yehuda said something that made me sit bolt upright.

Yehuda works in the emerging field of epigenetics: the study of how genes turn on and off in response to environmental changes, including adversity. The hypothesis she's tested throughout her career is that distress can affect our bodies at a cellular level that passes from one generation to the next. As she told Tippett: "People say, when something cataclysmic happens to them, 'I'm not the same person. I've been changed. I am not the same person that I was.' And we have to start asking ourselves, 'Well, what do they mean by that? Of course, they're the same person. They have the same DNA, don't they?' They do. And what I think it means is that the environmental influence has been so overwhelming that it has forced a major constitutional change, an enduring transformation. And epigenetics gives us the language and the science to be able to start unpacking that."

Early in her career, when Yehuda was studying post-traumatic stress disorder, she and her colleagues set up a clinic for Holocaust survivors at Mount Sinai hospital in New York City. Their intention was to serve the survivors themselves, but that's not what happened. The survivors, who tended to feel that no clinician could understand their experiences, stayed home. It was their **children** who showed up.

The lives of these children—most of whom were now middle-aged—turned out to have a unique pattern. They still felt troubled, decades later, by having witnessed their parents' grief. They felt an overwhelming pressure to live for those who had perished. And they had difficulty with separation—especially from their parents. Most people in their forties and fifties identify as someone's partner or parent. But this group still described themselves as so-and-so's son or daughter. They lived in the shadow of their mothers and fathers.

There were other, more tangible markers, too. The survivors' children were three times more likely to suffer from PTSD, if they'd been exposed to traumatic events, compared with demographically similar Jews whose parents weren't survivors. They were more vulnerable to clinical depression and anxiety. And their blood tests showed the same neuroendocrine and hormonal abnormalities as the survivors themselves.

Clearly this population had a particular emotional inheritance—but how had it been transmitted? Did it have mostly to do with the way they'd been raised, with their relationships with their parents? Or was it also written somehow into their DNA?

To answer this latter question, Yehuda and her colleagues studied a particular gene, associated with stress, in a group of thirty-two Holocaust survivors and twenty-two of their children. They found that this gene, in both parents and offspring, showed a type of epigenetic change called methylation. It was remarkable evidence that "preconception parental trauma" might be passed from one generation to the next.

In 2015, they published these findings in the journal **Biological Psychiatry.** The study was quickly sensationalized in mainstream articles on Yehuda's work and on the dazzling promise of epigenetics in general. Just as quickly, Yehuda's study was criticized within the field for its small sample size, and for failing to include the grandchildren and great-grandchildren of the survivors. Yehuda herself warned, in a 2018 paper in the journal **Environmental Epigenetics,** against "reductionist biological determinism." The science was young, she said, the findings still modest. As it happened, Yehuda's findings were later replicated in a 2020 study using a larger sample and reported in **The American Journal of Psychiatry.**

But lost in this discussion was the question of **why** the press was so quick to report on such a small study, **why** this line of scientific inquiry feels so exciting to us. I believe the answer is simple. It's because it validates one of our deepest intuitions, the one that Simcha shared with me that day at the bereavement seminar: that not only can pain last a lifetime; it can last many lifetimes.

We've had the evidence for a while now that the effects of trauma sometimes endure, physiologically as well as psychologically, throughout a single lifetime. This was the basis of the PTSD diagnosis, which was added to the **Diagnostic and Statistical**

Manual of Mental Disorders (DSM-III) in 1980. At the time, the diagnosis was controversial. Stress often produces short-term "fight-or-flight" responses; when the threat passes, the body tends to return to equilibrium. But evidence started to accumulate that trauma could cause long-lasting bodily change, including to brain neurocircuitry, the sympathetic nervous system, the immune system, and the hypothalamic-pituitary-adrenal axis.

But now we're starting to see evidence that such physiological effects can also endure **across** lifetimes. Beyond Yehuda's preliminary findings is a growing body of animal research. One study showed that water fleas subjected to the odor of a predator produce baby fleas with spiky, armored heads. In another study, mice exposed to a harmless scent, paired with a painful electric shock, gave birth to children **and** grandchildren who feared the same odor—absent any such shock. The University of Zurich epigenetics professor Isabelle Mansuy conducted a fascinating (and very sad) study in which she exposed mouse pups to various ordeals, including separation from their mothers. When these mice grew up, they behaved erratically—both more reckless and more depressed than a control group of mice. For example, if dropped in water, they would react helplessly, and stop swimming. The offspring of these mice showed the same irregular behavior.

Perhaps this wasn't surprising, given that these

pups had been raised by compromised parents. But Mansuy started to breed traumatized male mice with untraumatized females, then removed the males from the mothers' cage before the pups were born, so that the fathers' abnormal behavior couldn't influence their offspring. After the pups were weaned, Mansuy took the further step of raising these mice in separate groups, so the litter mates couldn't influence each other. She did this for up to **six** generations of mice. And her protocol, she says, "worked immediately." The descendants of the traumatized mice showed the same erratic behavior as their forefathers.

Further epidemiological evidence has emerged among humans, too. The sons of released POWs from the U.S. Civil War tended to die earlier in life than the sons of other veterans. The children of Dutch women pregnant during a World War II famine had unusually high rates of obesity, diabetes, and schizophrenia later in life. And a 2018 study of African American women, led by Dr. Veronica Barcelona di Mendoza, a professor at Yale School of Nursing, suggested that racial discrimination can cause epigenetic changes to genes affecting schizophrenia, bipolar disorder, and asthma.

These transgenerational effects—in the children of Holocaust survivors, U.S. Civil War POWs, starving Dutch women, African American women—could, of course, be the product of many and varied causes. They may have little or nothing to do with the scientifically dazzling idea that suffering alters our very DNA. ("Answering that objection," says a **Science** magazine article, "is where mouse models come in.")

But mice or no mice, hidden in these epidemiological examples is a second explanation of the allure of this branch of epigenetics. I believe it's because we intuit that, if pain endures transgenerationally, **then so, too, could healing.** As Tufts University biologist Larry Feig puts it, "If it's epigenetic, it's responsive to the environment. That means negative environmental effects are likely reversible." In other words: Maybe there really is a way, even generations later, to transform sorrow into beauty—to turn bitter into sweet.

Yehuda has understood this from the start. "I'm very challenged by thinking how this information can be empowering and not disempowering," she says of her work. "Research may unintentionally be received as supporting a narrative of permanent and significant damage in offspring," she wrote in **Environmental Epigenetics,** "rather than contributing to discussions of potential resilience, adaptability, and mutability in biological systems affected by stress."

. . .

Transgenerational healing takes many forms, all of them involving the creation of healthy connections with our ancestors. One approach is psychotherapy, which, as Yehuda found in a 2013 study published in **Frontiers in Psychiatry,** seems to produce measurable epigenetic changes. Similarly, Isabelle Mansuy's mouse models show that raising traumatized mice in therapeutic conditions may heal them enough to free their offspring of emotional scars. In a 2016 study, she found that traumatized mice raised in cages enriched with running wheels and mazes didn't pass the symptoms of distress to their descendants.

Therapy comes in many varieties, of course, and it's beyond our scope to explore them all here. But one of its purposes is to help us to notice our own patterns—and to make space for them. In the **On Being** interview, Yehuda described a group therapy session in which a daughter of Holocaust survivors recounted an upsetting incident at work. "And then I remembered," said the woman, "that Dr. Yehuda said I have poor shock absorbers, and I should just let it pass, because my biology is going to have extreme responses before it calms down. And then I did, and it really worked." Yet Yehuda had never offered the metaphor of shock absorbers; supported by the therapy, her client had created that for herself.

We can also undertake—whether through psychotherapy or our own truth-finding mission—to see our ancestors: to really see them, and love them, and thereby to love ourselves. Consider the singer-songwriter Dar Williams's masterpiece "After All," which describes how facing the pain of her forebears healed her from a suicidal depression. "I knew my family had more truth to tell," Williams sings about her journey back in time, researching her parents' difficult childhoods so she could "know [her]self through them."

But sometimes we travel back in time, not only through research, not only through conversation with our families; sometimes it helps to take a physical journey back to the place where the pain originated. Consider the trauma of slavery, as it manifests in its descendants. As I was writing this chapter, I received an email from my friend Jeri Bingham, the creator and host of **Hush Loudly,** a podcast dedicated to introverts. Jeri lives in Chicago, but was writing from Senegal, where she'd taken an unexpected business trip. While there, she'd visited Gorée Island—"the last place our ancestors were held before being brought to America," wrote Jeri, who is African American. "The tour guide talked about how the Portuguese, Dutch, and British took over the island and used it as its last port to cross the Atlantic Ocean. They piled men and women in these rooms, only feeding them once a day to keep them alive. For those souls who died, their bodies were thrown in the ocean."

Her email included haunting photos: A dark, dank-looking room with a narrow sliver of a window, facing the sea that would take the enslaved away forever. Jeri standing in what was called the "Door of

No Return." And two separate holding areas, one marked "Femmes," and another "Enfants": stomach-churning reminders of all the mothers separated from their children, the children from their mothers. The terrible pain of separation.

But Jeri added something surprising. "It felt like sacred ground to me," she said.

Her description of this place of so much pain and sorrow as "sacred" struck me. I thought about how the word **sacrifice** comes from the Latin term that means "to make sacred," and sensed that Jeri was tapping into this etymology. I asked if she wouldn't mind explaining what she meant. And her answer echoed Yehuda's emphasis on the transformation of past injury into present healing, of bitter into sweet.

"It felt sacred," she wrote, "because I was standing on the same ground where maybe millions of slaves, my ancestors, were standing not that very long ago.

I felt their souls. I felt their spirits. When I walked in, I felt fear, anxiety, hurt, heartbreak, anger, terror, and the unknown. Those feelings weren't mine. They were theirs. I felt their sadness, depression and loneliness, even though they were shackled with others; they weren't at home and with their families. They had been taken away from all that they knew and forced into slavery while others profited by making themselves their "owners." I pictured them there, chained together, sitting and lying in their own feces, naked or probably mostly naked, and not knowing what was going to happen next.

As I stood there and processed what I believe were my ancestors' feelings, I also processed my feelings that were of joy, pride, strength and empowerment. All I could think about is . . . look at how far my people have come. I hate what happened to them. I hate how their lives turned out, but I bet they are proud at what we've become. I feel even more responsible now to be the best person I can be, and to not take anything I've been given for granted. I'm blessed to be born into the life that I have and to be given everything I needed and raised by parents who put me first and gave me the world. I left there thinking about my responsibility to my race and culture. It's mind blowing to see where we came from, how we were treated and how we've survived and thrived generations later. I am grateful and humbled to be the manifestation of my ancestors' tragedy and grief.

When Jeri sent me those photos from Senegal, she'd had no idea that I was writing about inherited grief. But when I shared the concept with her, she was stunned. She felt that it touched her soul, and explained so much. "Black people sometimes keep it all inside," she said, "to be strong, unwavering, or unbothered, all of which can sometimes appear to non-Blacks as anger or apathy." But the enslaved, Jeri's ancestors, had never had a chance to grieve. "Stripped from their country, dropped into a foreign land with a way of life and culture that were the diametric opposites of all they knew, they weren't given the time or opportunity to mourn. Instead, they persevered. They raised children and played the cards they were dealt. But the grief never left them."

. . .

Another way to heal generational pain, says Yehuda, is to help **others** currently facing similar trouble.

After I gave my TED Talk on longing and transcendence, a young woman named Farah Khatib approached me outside the auditorium. She had long dark hair, deep brown eyes, and a way of cocking her head to the side that felt like a hug in the form of an unconscious mannerism. "Longing," she said. "I just have it. I don't know why. I'm longing to be whole." But as she told me her story, it was clear that she **did** know why. And it wasn't just Farah's story. It was her sister's story, her mother's story, it was the story of her female ancestors.

Farah was born and raised in Jordan, in a family that considers itself progressive—"but we're not." Growing up female, she was taught "to shrink, to be weak, to please." Her sister died when they were little girls—an event so traumatic that she can't remember how it happened or how old she was at the time. Her parents didn't grieve, at least not openly; they simply never mentioned their daughter again, kept no pictures of her. Then they divorced. Her mother, who struggled with her own pain and grief, and was desperate to escape the family, left Farah with a nanny who was meant to be her surrogate mother, but instead abused her. To survive, Farah became as passive and as invisible as possible. By the time she reached young adulthood, she felt dead inside.

She found work in Singapore, marketing hair care for a multinational company. It was just a job; she didn't expect it to do much for her numbness. But she worked in the consumer research group, which conducted deep interviews with women customers. As Farah listened to them, she felt a stirring. The women's stories, of shame and invisibility, felt oddly familiar. She wanted to hear more. She quit her job, went back to Jordan. But not back home; she started working with previously incarcerated women. She didn't know exactly why she was doing this; she just knew that she wanted to listen to the women. And they, it turned out, wanted to talk. They told her about themselves, but also about their mothers, grandmothers, great-grandmothers: "Women's experiences are very different from men's," Farah told me. "A man who was imprisoned goes back to the village, and it's like a rite of passage. A woman can't find work. Her family would be ashamed. Maybe she was given as a child in marriage—she had no choice, her husband was the age of her father, he raped her.

But we learn not to talk about it. We don't talk about their experiences as a society, we are ashamed—the way my mom won't cry in front of us. We have no pictures of my sister—we don't talk about her. We have to teach grief to our children. The grief of previous generations. The grief of what you could be, but you're not, because you're told who you are."

That was in 2009. In 2013, Farah started a nonprofit to train Syrian women refugees in life skills, finance, and healing. The work didn't make Farah's longing disappear. But it filled her with what she describes (unprompted by me!) as a "bittersweet feeling, connected to a love of life." "For the first time, I'm starting to feel whole," she says. "People tell me I'm too serious and I should let go and have fun. But I don't care about fun. I care about feeling."

She also started to understand why she'd been so drawn to this work. She wanted to untie the ribbon of grief that wrapped the women of her family together with the women of the refugee camps. "I feel I carry so much from previous generations," Farah says. "I carry the grief of my mother. I carry it in my body. I need to carry my sister. I'm carrying so much on their behalf, their generation and previous generations. We don't talk about their experiences as a society; we're ashamed. But we have to talk about who we are. Everything I do in my work is about who you **are.** And it comes from the generations."

. . .

In Farah's case, the sorrows she seeks to transform in others, via her organization, are similar to those that afflicted her ancestors. But sometimes we're drawn to heal wounds that—at least on the surface—appear quite different from those of our forebears.

Dr. William Breitbart is the chair of the Department of Psychiatry and Behavioral Sciences at Memorial Sloan Kettering Cancer Center in New York. He works with dying cancer patients: not to cure them; not to extend their lives; not even to ease their physical pain. His mission is to give his patients a sense of meaning in the time they have left, through a program he developed called meaning-centered psychotherapy. His results have been inspiring: compared with a control group, Breitbart's patients have significantly higher levels of "spiritual well-being and quality of life," and significantly lower physical distress and symptoms.

When he started out as a young psychiatrist working with AIDS and later with advanced cancer patients, Breitbart noticed something consistent: They **wanted** to die. They had three months left, six months left. But they wanted it over with now. "You want to know how you can help me?" one of his earliest patients, a sixty-five-year-old chemist, greeted him at their first appointment. "I have three months to live. I see no value in those three months. If you want to help me, kill me."

At the time, most clinicians weren't surprised by this kind of sentiment. After all, patients like the chemist were in terrible pain, or depressed, or both. When these patients were treated for depression, the desire for death eased for about half of them. Painkillers helped another 10 percent. But the remaining 40 percent still wanted to die.

The problem, Breitbart thought, was that they'd lost their sense of meaning—and there was no medication for that. He had to find another way. For Breitbart, this was no philosophical trifle. Meaning making, he believed, is the heart of humanity; it gives us the power to transcend suffering. He'd read Nietzsche, who wrote that "he who has a why to live for can bear almost any how." If he could help his patients find their "whys," Breitbart thought, even after cancer had taken so much else away, maybe he could save them.

"Do me a favor," he told his chemist patient. "Give me three sessions. And after that, if you still feel that way, let's see what we can do."

I visited Breitbart one May afternoon, in his corner office at the Counseling Center on the seventh floor of Memorial Sloan Kettering hospital. The shelves overflowed with textbooks and medical journals, Buddha statues and Levantine hamsa amulets; the walls were covered with too many diplomas to count; a giant screensaver burst with a field of red tulips. We sat together at the window, Breitbart tall and bearish, with a white beard and rumpled tweed jacket, navy tie slightly askew. It was raining outside.

I wanted to know what made Breitbart go all the

way through medical school and residency, the exhaustive, decade-long training in the finer points of selective serotonin reuptake inhibitors, cancer cells, and chemotherapy, to take a professorship at one of the world's leading cancer centers—and then to become a physician of meaning.

But for Breitbart, as is often the case for people whose healing careers emanate from their deepest being, there was no other possible destination.

"If you were telling my story," he says, "you might be tempted to begin with this fact: When I was twenty-eight, I had thyroid cancer. It was cured. But for the rest of my life, that sense of invulnerability was gone."

But that's not the real answer, he says softly. The real story happened before he was born. Breitbart's mother was fourteen, his father seventeen, when the Nazis came to Poland hunting down Jews. His mother hid in a hole under a stove in a farmhouse owned by a Catholic woman who saved her life. At night, she came out from under the stove and ate potato peels. Breitbart's father had deserted the Russian army and joined a group of partisans fighting in the forest. One night, starving and looking for food, he broke into the farmhouse where Breitbart's mother was hiding. He convinced her to join his brigade of resistance fighters. They spent the rest of the war battling in the woods; they survived; when it was over, they went back to their respective towns, but no one was left. They made their way to New York and found work, he as a night clerk, she sewing ties; they had a son. A son whose life course was determined by these events that happened before he was born.

Breitbart grew up in a community of Holocaust survivors of the kind Yehuda first studied, in a "home in which loss, death, and suffering were very real." His childhood was infused with survivor's guilt. His mother would ask why she and her husband survived when so many others hadn't. It seemed like the ultimate rhetorical question, but there actually was an answer. Even though his parents never spoke this answer aloud, Breitbart knew exactly what it was: They'd survived in order to have a son who would go out into the world to reduce pain. "I'm not someone who's here to gain power," says Breitbart. "I'm not here to accumulate material wealth. I'm here to ease suffering."

We're all given legacies, he explains. "We don't have a choice. Legacies can be profoundly joyful and wonderful. I was given a legacy of suffering and death, but also of survival and existential guilt. I grew up lonely. Everyone had died, so many of our relatives never had a chance to create a life. We were left alive, and we didn't know why."

His voice, as he relates all this, is muted, in a way that I recognize from my own grandfather. It's as if there's a larger, more powerful voice in there, of the grandson of partisans who fought bravely in the Polish forests. It's as if he's keeping that voice safely hidden in the hole under the stove.

"One could view it as a burden, be crushed by it," he continues, looking away from me, at the rain outside the window. "But it's a matter of choosing your attitude to the legacy you're given. There has to be a reason—a meaning for why we survived, and others didn't."

This, of course, is the heart of meaning-centered psychotherapy, or meaning-centered anything. The death sentence has come (it was always here, from the moment we were born). And what do you live for then?

"I love everything about life," Breitbart says, his voice growing louder now. "Familial love, parental love, spousal love, lust. I love beauty, I love fashion, I love art, I love music, I love food, I love plays, I love drama, I love poetry, I love movies. There are very few things I don't have an interest in. I love being alive." He's gesturing widely, at the window, at the pouring, driving rain.

"But even with all these loves," he says, "you're born with a set of limitations: your genetic legacy, your time, your place, your family. I could have been born a Rockefeller, but I wasn't. I could have been born into a family living in a remote tribe where I thought God was a blue elephant, but I wasn't. You're born into this reality: that life is full of dangers, it's an uncertain place. Events occur—you have an accident, someone shoots you, you develop an illness. All sorts of things happen. You have to respond.

"And the big event that I now deal with every

day is the diagnosis of life-threatening cancer. That really knocks you off your life trajectory. The challenge is—how do you transcend this new trajectory? Your responsibility is to create a life of meaning. Of growth, and transformation. It so happens that very few people grow from success. People grow from failure. They grow from adversity. They grow from pain."

After that fateful meeting with his first patient— the chemist who saw no reason to live—Breitbart sat down with one of his postdoc fellows, Mindy Greenstein, and they cobbled together the first version of meaning-centered psychotherapy. The protocol they developed was based on the idea that we all have two existential obligations. The first is simply to survive. But the second is to create a life worth living. If on your deathbed you look back and see a life lived fully, you feel peace. People who believe that they didn't do enough with their lives too often feel shame. But the key to fulfillment, says Breitbart, is learning to love who you **are** (which is unconditional and unceasing) rather than what you've **done.**

One of the most important aspects of the therapy they developed focuses on core being: on the things that make you you. When you're diagnosed with cancer, you can feel robbed of your identity. But the job of the meaning-centered therapist is to listen for the essence of the person that's still there. Maybe all your life you were a care**giver,** and now you find yourself in the uncomfortable position of having to **receive** care. But the therapist might notice that you're still going out of your way to make him or her feel comfortable. You're still asking "How are **you**?" **You're still a caregiver.** The idea is not to paper over your loss, which might be of cataclysmic proportions. The idea is smaller than that, yet also grander: that after all the grief and loss and disruption, you are still—you always will be—exactly who you are.

. . .

Soon after Simcha's bereavement seminar, I talked with him on the phone. I was wrestling with a practical question. I still felt embarrassed by the way I'd cried at his workshop, especially compared to Maureen and her four-tissue loss. And I was concerned that I might do it in public next time, on the publicity tour for this book. "I don't usually go around weeping, the way I did that day," I told him. "I'm a pretty happy person—I think of myself as a happy melancholic. But I'm writing about my relationship with my mother. Maybe someone will ask me about her on national radio, and what if I lose it in front of ten thousand people?"

"I don't know if you ever fully empty the well," Simcha said thoughtfully. "But ask me this question after you finish the book. Because writing the manuscript is part of the process of working it through. By the time you're done writing, the grief may subside."

And this is exactly what happened. For me, writing this book was yet another act of transforming the sorrow and longing of the past into the wholeness of the present. And I'm not worried about my book tour anymore.

But what about you? Do you feel the tug of an ancient grief, and if so, what connection could you make with your forebears that might help put it to rest? You don't have to write a whole book. Maybe you could ask your parents to tell you their stories, as Dar Williams described in her song "After All." Maybe you'll send a paper lantern down a river, as some Japanese do to honor their dead, or set out favorite foods on designated days, as some Mexicans do to celebrate theirs. Maybe, via therapy, you'll start to notice and make space for the transgenerational patterns you've inherited, as Yehuda's client did with her shock absorber metaphor. Maybe you'll travel across the world to the place where your ancestors' pain began, as Jeri Bingham did at Gorée Island in Senegal. Maybe you'll find ingenious new ways to help those who suffer today from pains that remind you of the ones that troubled your parents or ancestors, as Farah Khatib does with her refugee work and Breitbart with his meaning-centered therapy for cancer patients. And maybe, as Simcha said, you won't ever fully empty the well; and this is all right, too.

But there's one more thing we can all do, even as we seek out and honor our parents' stories, our ancestors' stories. **We can set ourselves free from the**

pain: We can see that our forebears' stories are our stories, but they're also not our stories. We may have inherited an echo of our ancestors' torment, but it was not our flesh burned in the ovens; we may have inherited their grief, but it was not us torn naked from our children. The tears they shed ran down their cheeks, not ours, just as their accomplishments were earned by them, even if we may have inherited some of their stature.

It's easier to see this when we look forward. Our stories will inevitably become our children's stories, but our children will have their own stories to tell; we **want** our children to tell their own stories; we wish them that freedom. We can wish the same for ourselves. "Live as though all your ancestors were living again through you," said the ancient Greeks. And this didn't mean literally to reenact their lives; it meant to give them a new life, fresh and clean.

How many times have you heard, from someone whose parent died young: I am now the age my mother was when she got the diagnosis. My father was an alcoholic: I don't want to be like him. Such declarations echo the ancient proverb quoted in Ezekiel: "The fathers ate sour grapes, and the children's teeth were set on edge." **But the Bible quotes this proverb in order to reject it:** We aren't responsible for the sins of our parents, it says. And neither must we bear their pain. This doesn't mean turning our backs on our forebears. We can send our love back to them, across the centuries. But on their behalf and ours, we can follow the bittersweet tradition, and transform their troubles into something better.

When I think now of Simcha's bereavement seminar, I can see that both Maureen and I were just trying, in a confused way, to pay homage to our respective mothers: she, with her stoicism, me with my tears. I cried too much because it seemed that this connected me to my mother. Maureen held her tears back, as a way of bonding with hers.

I visit my mother often now. She's eighty-nine as I write this. Her Alzheimer's is advancing, but she still knows who I am. Dementia has taken so much from her, but it's returned her loving soul, uncompromised by the challenges of everyday life. Every nurse, every doctor who treats her, comments unprompted on how sweet she is, and funny, too; they also bask in this unvarnished version of her spirit. "I won't be able to say it for much longer," she tells me urgently, every time we speak, "so I want you to remember how much I love you."

I sit by my mother's wheelchair, hold her hand. She's thinner than she's ever been in her adult life, having mostly stopped eating, but her face is its normal width because her jowls hang down. Her eyes are small and blue, encased in folds and bags. One day I will have those jowls, those bags. We look into each other's eyes with what feels like infinite mutual understanding. All the trials of our life together, all the pushing and pulling and constrictions and impossible positioning of our mother-daughter love, all the hugs and laughter and conversations, and it comes down to this, this connection. She is my mother, there is no other. I know now that the tears I couldn't stop all these years came not because I separated from her at age seventeen; they came because I **didn't** separate. The problem wasn't that I gave her my diaries in what seemed an unconscious act of emancipation and emotional matricide; it was that I held on to my guilt as a way of holding on to her, to my grandfather, to the generations. But now, as Simcha taught: **I can keep the connection alive without keeping the pain.**

We all think what we think, feel what we feel, are who we are, because of the lives of the people who came before us, and the way our souls have interacted with theirs. Yet these are also our own, singular lives. We have to hold both these truths at the same time.

And if this isn't fully possible—because nothing is fully possible, and life is bittersweet—if I'm still inclined to feel guilty; if you still have whatever tendency you wish you could extinguish; and if we all still have an insatiable longing for the perfect and beautiful world—we should embrace this, too. Because, as the poet Rumi put it in that glorious poem "Love Dogs," the one I shared with you in chapter 2: Your pure sadness that wants help really is the secret cup, the longing we express really is the return message, and the grief we cry out from does, in fact, draw us toward union.

January Day: Lower Manhattan, © Thomas Schaller
(thomaswschaller.com)

CODA

How to Go Home

And did you get what
you wanted from this life, even so?
I did.
And what did you want?
To call myself beloved, to feel myself
beloved on the earth.

—RAYMOND CARVER,
"LATE FRAGMENT"

Ever since that day in the law school dorm, when
my friend asked why I was listening to funeral music,
I'd wondered about the strange magnetism of the
bittersweet. But it took another ten years before I
started learning how to tap its powers.

I was thirty-three years old, a seventh-year associate at a corporate law firm, with an office overlooking the Statue of Liberty on the forty-second floor of a Wall Street skyscraper; I'd been working sixteen-hour days for seven years straight. And even though, ever since I was four, I'd had the impossible dream of becoming an author, I was also a highly ambitious lawyer and about to make partner. Or so I thought.

One morning, a senior partner named Steve Shalen knocked on my office door. Steve was tall and distinguished and decent. He sat down and reached for the squishy stress ball on my desk and said that I wasn't making partner after all. I remember wishing that I had a stress ball, too, but Steve Shalen was using mine. I remember feeling sorry that it had fallen to Steve, who meant well, to tell me this news. I remember the sensation of an edifice collapsing around me, of a dream never coming true.

I'd been working like a maniac all those years in devotion to this dream, which had replaced my childhood fantasy of becoming a writer. The dream was about a type of house—specifically, a redbrick townhouse in Greenwich Village that I'd coveted since my first week of work, when another senior partner had invited the new associates for dinner and I beheld the loveliness of the home he lived in with his family, the tree-lined streets he and his wife and children walked each morning on their way to work and school.

All along the dappled streets of that neighborhood of cafés and curiosity shops, ornate plaques adorned the houses, announcing the poets and novelists who'd been moved to flights of inspiration in those very homes. If it was ironic that they were owned now not by artists but by lawyers, if the price of entry was no longer publishing a chapbook of poems but making partner in an organization devoted to asset-backed securitizations and reverse triangular mergers, I didn't dwell on this. I understood that making partner and acquiring such a home would not cause me to publish heralded volumes of nineteenth-century poetry. But I dreamed of life in a Greenwich Village illuminated by yesterday's writers, and if, in the service of this dream, I must learn about yield curves and debt service coverage ratios and carry dictionaries called **Wall Street Words** home for the weekend, studying them by candlelight in my one-bedroom apartment, this struck me as a price worth paying.

But deep down, I knew that Steve Shalen had just handed me a Get Out of Jail Free card.

A few hours later, I left the law firm for good. And a few weeks after that, I ended a seven-year relationship that had always felt wrong. My parents, children of immigrants and the Great Depression, had raised me to be practical. My father had suggested law school so I could always pay the rent; my mother had warned me to have kids before my biological clock stopped. Now I was thirty-three, with no career, no love, no place to live.

I fell into a relationship with a handsome musician named Raul. He was an expansive, lit-up kind of person who composed lyrics by day and stood around a piano singing with friends at night. He wasn't fully available, but we had an electric connection, and my feelings for him turned into an obsession the likes of which (thankfully) I've never experienced before or since. This was the era before smartphones, and I spent my days dodging into Internet cafés to see if there was an email from him. I can still call up the dopamine rush of excitement at the sight of his name, bolded in dark blue letters in my Yahoo in-box. Between dates, he sent me music recommendations.

I lived alone now, in a nondescript Manhattan neighborhood in a small rental without much furniture, just a fluffy white rug where I lay, looking up at the ceiling and listening to the music Raul had sent. Across the street was a nineteenth-century church and garden, tiny and miraculous, sandwiched between the skyscrapers. I sat for hours in its pews, breathing in its air of hushed mystery. Sometimes, I would meet my friend Naomi for coffee and tell her all the fascinating things that Raul had said during our last visit. It must have been trying for her, listening to all those stories on constant repeat. One day she said, with loving exasperation: **If you're this obsessed, it's because he represents something you long for.**

Naomi has enormous, piercing blue eyes, and she fixed them on me.

What are you longing for? she asked me with sudden intensity.

And the answer came, just like that. Raul was the writing life I'd longed for since I was four. He was an emissary from the perfect and beautiful world. That's what the Greenwich Village townhouse had been, too: a signpost to that other place. All those years at the law firm, I'd misinterpreted the direction the sign was pointing. I thought it was about real estate. But it was really about home.

And just like that, the obsession fell away. I still loved Raul, but in the way you love a favorite cousin; there was no more eroticism in it, no more urgency. I still loved those Greenwich Village townhouses. But I didn't need to own one.

I started writing for real.

. . .

So. What if I asked you this same question:

What are you longing for?

You may not have asked yourself this question before. You may not have identified the important symbols in your life story, you may not have examined what they mean.

You've likely asked other questions: What are my career goals? Do I want marriage and children? Is so-and-so the right partner? How can I be a "good" and moral person? What work should I do? To what extent should my work define me? When should I retire?

But have you asked yourself these questions in

the deepest terms? Have you asked what is the thing you long for most, your unique imprint, singular mission, wordless calling? Have you asked where on earth is your closest approximation of home? Literally, if you sat down and wrote "Home" at the top of a piece of paper and waited a while, what would you write next?

And if you have a bittersweet temperament, or you've come to it via life experience, have you asked how to hold the melancholy within you? Have you realized that you're part of a long and storied tradition that can help you transform your pain into beauty, your longing into belonging?

Have you asked: Who is the artist or musician or athlete or entrepreneur or scientist or spiritual leader you love, and why do you love them, what do they represent to you? And have you asked, What is the ache you can't get rid of—and could you make it **your** creative offering? Could you find a way to help heal others who suffer a similar trouble? Could your ache be, as Leonard Cohen said, the way you embrace the sun and the moon?

And do you know the lessons of your own particular sorrows and longings?

Maybe you experience a chasm between who you are and what you do for a living, and this tells you that you work too much, or too little, or that you want fulfilling work, or an organizational culture in which you fit; or that the work you need has little to do with your official job or income source; or countless other messages your yearning might be sending you: Listen to them, follow them, pay attention.*

Or maybe you're thrilled when your children laugh, but suffer too vicariously when they cry, which tells you that you haven't truly accepted that tears are part of life—and that your kids can handle them.

Or maybe you carry the griefs of your parents or grandparents or great-great-great-grandparents; maybe your body pays the price of their trouble; maybe your relationship with the world is compromised by hypervigilance or hair-trigger anger or a dogged dark cloud, and you must find a way to transform the pain of the ages, even as you find the freedom to write your own story.

Or maybe you mourn your breakups, or your dead, which tells you that separation is the most fundamental of heartaches, but also that attachment is our deepest desire, and that you might transcend your grief when you perceive how connected you are with all the other humans who struggle to transcend theirs, and who emerge in fits and starts, bit by rocky bit, just like you.

And maybe you crave perfect and unconditional love, the kind that's depicted in all those iconic advertisements of a glamorous couple driving their convertible 'round a bend to nowhere; but maybe

---

* This is not to say that you should abandon your paycheck in favor of a dream (I still have my parents' pragmatism!), only that you make space for the dream, too.

you're also starting to realize that the heart of those ads is not the dazzling couple, but rather the invisible place to which their shiny car is driving: that just around that curve, the perfect and beautiful world awaits them; that in the meantime a flame of it is lit inside them. And that glimpses of this elusive place are everywhere, not only in our love affairs but also when we kiss our children good night, when we shiver with delight at the strum of a guitar, when we read a golden truth expressed by an author who died a thousand years before we were born.

And maybe you see that the couple will never arrive, and if they do, they won't get to stay: a situation that has the power to drive us mad with desire (which the advertisers hope we'll attempt to satiate by purchasing their wristwatch or cologne). The world the couple is driving to is forever around the bend. And what should we do with this tantalizing truth?

· · ·

A while after I left the law firm and ended my relationship with Raul, I met Ken, who became my husband. He was a writer, too, and he'd spent the past seven years doing U.N. peacekeeping negotiations in some of the bloodiest war zones of the 1990s: Cambodia, Somalia, Rwanda, Haiti, Liberia.

He did that work because underneath his exuberant personality, Ken was filled with his own longing for a different world. He'd grown up wrestling with the legacy of the Holocaust. He'd lie awake when he was ten, wondering whether he would've had the courage to hide Anne Frank in his attic. And it turned out that he did; in the 1990s, he lived seven years in the eye of humanity's storm, a world of child soldiers, gang rapes, cannibalism, and genocide. He waited helplessly outside a mobile field hospital as a young friend died on an operating table in Somalia, following an ambush. In Rwanda, where eight hundred thousand were slaughtered by machete in ninety days, a rate of killing that surpassed the Nazi concentration camps, his job was to collect evidence for the U.N. war crimes tribunal. He walked the fields of bones—jaws, clavicles, and skulls, baby skeletons cradled in the arms of mama skeletons—trying not to retch from the stench, and from the knowledge that, once again, no one had stopped the killing.

After all those years in the field, he started to feel that his work was futile: There were always more bad actors, more mutilated bodies, more indifferent onlookers. Despite good intentions, no heroic organizations, no noble countries, no individuals with pure motives; things could turn brutal anywhere, anytime. He came home. But "home" meant something different now. Home was friends and family, it was the pleasant shock of on-demand air-conditioning, water running from the kitchen faucet, hot or cold, whenever you pleased. But home was also the Garden of Eden after Eve ate the apple.

Never forget, we say. But forgetting wasn't Ken's issue: He **couldn't** forget what he'd seen; it rarely left his mind. The only choice was to write it all down, to record what he'd witnessed. As he wrote, he kept a framed photo on his desk, a vast field of Rwandan bones. That photo's still there, all these years later.

When we met, Ken and two of his dearest friends from the United Nations were about to publish a book on their experiences, which even if I weren't his wife I would say is brilliant and searing. (And I'm not alone! The rights were purchased by Russell Crowe for a miniseries.)

In contrast, I had my failed legal career and some poems I'd written. (At the time we met, I was writing a memoir, in sonnet form, because why not.) But I brought my sonnets to our second date and handed them to Ken. And later that night, he sent me this email:

HOLY SHIT.
HOLY. SHIT.

Keep writing.
Drop Everything.
Write.

WRITE
WOMAN
WRITE

Ken's faith in me helped make my longing to write a reality. As I watch him now—tying double knots at the crack of dawn on our sons' soccer cleats; planting a literal thousand wildflowers in the garden outside my office; playing fetch with our puppy for minutes that turn into hours—it dawns on me that we share something more. These small moments of quotidian devotion are a form of artistic expression for him: quiet, ritualistic, bittersweet celebrations of a small peace. Though our young adult lives were lived continents and emotional worlds apart, he must have seen in my inchoate writing, and me in his, a shared longing for the art of peaceful repair.

...

But as for the larger promise he'd believed in—a world forever free of mass graves—he's still waiting, we're all still waiting. And what should we do with the eternal elusiveness of our most precious dreams?

I come back, always, to the metaphoric response of the Kabbalah—the mystical branch of Judaism that inspired Leonard Cohen's broken "Hallelujah." That, in the beginning, all of creation was a vessel filled with divine light. That it broke apart, and now the shards of holiness are strewn all around us. Sometimes it's too dark to see them, sometimes we're too distracted by pain or conflict. But our task is simple—to bend down, dig them out, pick them up.

And in so doing, to perceive that light can emerge from darkness, death gives way to rebirth, the soul descends to this riven world for the sake of learning how to ascend. And to realize that we all notice different shards; I might see a lump of coal, but you spot the gold glimmering beneath.

Note the modesty of this vision. Note that it doesn't promise Utopia. On the contrary, it teaches the impossibility of utopias, and by implication that we should cherish what we have, we shouldn't cast it aside in favor of an unobtainable perfection. But we **can** bring the bittersweet tradition to our respective domains, to the corners of the world over which we have some small influence.

Maybe you're a teenager, trying to make sense of your alternately soaring and plummeting emotions, and you're realizing that your life tasks include not only finding love and work, but also transforming your sorrows and longings into a constructive force of your choosing.

Maybe you're a teacher who wants to make space for your students to express the bitter and sweet of their personal lives, as Susan David's English teacher did when she handed her a notebook and invited her to write the truth.

Maybe you're a manager who realizes that sadness is the last great taboo in the workplace, and you want to create a healthy culture, one that's positive and loving yet acknowledges the dark along with the light, and understands the creative energy contained in this bittersweet fusion.

Maybe you're an architect of social media who sees that your industry's algorithms cause its users to transform pain into vitriol and abuse, but you wonder if it's not too late to channel it instead into beauty and healing.

Maybe you're an artist, would-be or working, and you've started to absorb this dictum: Whatever pain you can't get rid of, whatever joy you can't contain, make it your creative offering.

Maybe you're a psychologist who wants to make room in your field for what the mythologist Jean Houston calls a "sacred psychology," which recognizes that, as she puts it, "the deepest yearning in every human soul is to return to its spiritual source, there to experience communion and even union with the Beloved."

Maybe you're a theologian, grappling with our culture's diminishing interest in religion, while knowing that spiritual longing is a human constant that shows up in different guises at different times; in our time, for many it takes the form of a fervently divisive politics, but it also has the power to move us toward unity.

Maybe you're in mourning, and it's dawning on you that you can (as Nora McInerny said) move forward without moving on (if not today, then one day).

Maybe you've reached midlife, or your twilight

years, and you're realizing that the lengthening shad-ows needn't be depressing, but rather a chance to stop and notice the everyday glories you've been too distracted to see.

And for all of us, no matter our domain, there's the simple exhortation to turn in the direction of beauty. You don't have to follow any particular faith or wisdom tradition to realize that the sacred and miraculous are everywhere—literally they are all over the place—even though we moderns tend to walk around not noticing them. I used to puzzle over the nineteenth-century dictum that "beauty is truth, truth beauty." I wondered how you could as-sociate something as superficial as a pretty face or a pleasing picture with the moral grandeur of **veritas.** It took me decades to understand that the dictum was referring to beauty as a state we can access, for brief and transformative visits, through various por-tals: a midnight Mass, a **Mona Lisa,** a small gesture of kindness, a grand act of heroism.

Which brings us back to where we began—the cellist of Sarajevo, and the old man in the forest who refused to identify himself as Muslim or Croat—but only as a musician.

...

When my father died of COVID, we held a tiny graveside service. The twenty-five-year-old junior rabbi delivering the eulogy, who hadn't known him personally but agreed to preside over a stranger's pandemic funeral, praised my father's love of God. I smiled, thinking: "He didn't know Dad." My father was proudly Jewish, but he was impatient with formal religion. But even as I rolled my eyes, I realized that this was an outworn reflex; the way I saw it now, the rabbi's remark no longer seemed incongruous. My father did love God, but by another name—by many other names.

I see now that my father spent a good portion of his life gathering the shards of the Kabbalah's broken vessel. Like all of us, he was far from perfect. But he was constantly doing beautiful things, just for the sake of them. He loved orchids, so he built a greenhouse full of them in the basement. He loved the sound of French, so he learned to speak it fluently, though he rarely had time to visit France. He loved organic chemistry, so he spent his Sundays reading "orgo" textbooks. He showed me, by example, that if you want to live a quiet life, you should just live a quiet life; that if you're a humble person who has no use for the spotlight, to just be a humble person who has no use for the spotlight. No big deal. (These latter lessons later became the basis of my book **Quiet.**)

I watched, too, how he fulfilled his roles as a doctor, a father. How he studied medical journals after dinner, spent the extra hour to sit at the bedside of every last one of his patients in the hospital, kept training the next generation of gastroenterologists until he was well into his eighties. How he shared with his kids the things he loved, like music and bird-watching and poetry, so that one day we would love them too. One of my earliest memories is asking him, over and over again, to play the "Chair Record" (Beethoven's "Emperor" concerto, whose name I was too young to pronounce).

We're drawn to the sublime domains, like music, art, and medicine, not only because they're beautiful and healing, but also because they're a manifestation of love, or divinity, or whatever you want to call it. The night my father died, I listened to music, not because I would find him there—I didn't find him there—but because loving a parent and loving song or sport, nature or literature, math or science, are just different manifestations of the perfect and beautiful world, of the people we long to be with, the place we want to be. Your loved one may not be here anymore, but the manifestations live forever.

My father and I talked on the phone, just before he died. He was in the hospital, trying to breathe.

"Be well, kid," he said, as he hung up the phone.

And I intend to. And so, I hope, will you.

ACKNOWLEDGMENTS

Meeting my literary agent, Richard Pine, back in 2005, was one of the luckiest breaks of my life. What does it mean for a writer to have an extraordinary professional partner like Richard? It means someone who keeps the faith even when you're taking a really, really long time to figure out how to write your book. It means someone whose integrity and literary judgment you can always rely on, and who tells you the truth about your first (and second, third, and fourth) drafts, in a way you can hear it. It means a lifelong friendship. I'm so grateful to Richard and to his most excellent colleagues: Lyndsey Blessing (who is so good at her job that everyone should just do whatever she says), Alexis Hurley, Nathaniel Jacks, and all the team at InkWell—with special thanks to Eliza Rothstein and William Callahan for reading my drafts and providing suggestions that transformed the manuscript.

My editor, Gillian Blake, had a near-miraculous instinct for giving me just the right feedback at just the right time. She is brilliant and perspicacious. She was always there at just the moment I needed her. If you liked this book, then you love Gillian's work as much as I do. It has been such a blessing to work with all the wonderful team at Crown over the years: Julie Cepler, Markus Dohle, David Drake, Christine Johnston, Rachel Klayman, Amy Li, Madeline McIntosh, Rachel Rokicki "Superstar," Annsley Rosner, and Chantelle Walker. I can't thank them enough.

I've loved every moment of my yearslong partnership with the team at Viking/Penguin UK, including Daniel Crewe (who provided deep-seeing edits on this manuscript), Julia Murday, and Poppy North, and, of course, Venetia Butterfield and Joel Rickett.

If you love the cover of this book as much as I do, we have to thank the glorious Jackie Phillips for art direction, and Evan Gaffney for layout.

Renee Wood and I have worked together for almost ten years now, and I really have no idea how I ever managed without her diplomacy, capability, insight, attention to detail, readiness to go the extra mile, and unique sense of humor. I'm daily inspired by her ability to shine a light into the world in the face of chronic illness. Over the years, she and her husband, Prince Leon Wood, have become family.

Great thanks, too, to Joseph Hinson, Joshua Kennedy, Emma Larson, and Ronen Stern. And such deep appreciation for Laurie Flynn and Stacey Kalish, who swooped in, with great cheer and competence, to fact-check this manuscript, provide extra research, and generally bring this book to the finish line. I hope we'll be colleagues for life.

My great thanks to the TED conference, including Chris Anderson, Juliet Blake, Oliver Friedman, Bruno Giusanni, and Kelly Stoetzel, for giving the ideas in this book a platform, almost three years before the publication date (!), and for sharing the ideas of so many, many others.

I'm also so grateful for the friendship and support of my exceptional team at Speaker's Office: Tracey Bloom, Jennifer Canzoneri, Jessica Case, Holli Catchpole, Crystal Davidson, Carrie Glasgow, and Michele Wallace; and at WME: Ben Davis and Marissa Hurwitz.

I met Jeri Bingham just as I was starting this bittersweet project, and ever since she has made life better simply by sharing her loving, "goofball," reflective nature, and her thoughts on bittersweetness, inherited grief, and life itself. Coach Brendan Cahill blew into our family life one day and opened up his seemingly limitless store of wisdom, heart, and inspiration. A particular shout-out to Amy Cuddy, who has understood and nurtured this project from its inception, who regularly dazzles me with her social perceptions and effortless way of articulating them, who is always texting me great bittersweet music, who turns her own bitter experiences into sweetness, and who has been a true-blue friend and Telluride writing partner throughout. I will always be grateful to "QC" Carla Davis and Mytzi Stewart for taking such good and honorable care of my parents for the past five years, even (and especially) when it hasn't been easy. Emily Esfahani Smith has been a great friend, kindred spirit, and spiritual companion through these years of research and writing. Christy Fletcher has been a treasured friend, adviser, and business genius through all these bittersweet years, and I consider myself so lucky to know her. Maritza "Big Hug" Flores was an endlessly nurturing presence in our family during the years I wrote this book and before, and I will always love her. My friendship with Mitch Joel started with breakfasts at TED and has continued over these bittersweet years, not to mention that he may possibly love Leonard Cohen as much as I do. I'm so grateful to Scott Barry Kaufman and David Yaden for collaborating with me to test and validate the Bittersweet Quiz, consulting on various Bittersweet topics, and especially for their friendship, decency, and shared view of life. Emily Klein and I raised our kids together, kept each other sane, and continue to share the joyous bittersweetness of our lives. Cathy Lankenau-Weeks has been such a deep and constant friend ever since Freshman Week, and she has taught me so much about what it means to share life's joys and sorrows (and also laughs). Les Snead has inspired me through these years with his thoughtful, effective leadership and his great generosity with our family, and Kara Henderson has become a friend whose messages on minor key music and everything else have become a regular treat. Emma Seppala is a tender spirit and one of the very first people I interviewed for this book, and she has taught me so much over the years about Buddhism, Hinduism, and loving-kindness meditation. Marisol Simard consulted with great insight and generosity on the book cover, and she and Ben Falchuk have been great and loyal friends since the day we were lucky enough to move in across the street. Andrew Thomson and his wife, Suzie, are among our dearest family friends, and I thank him for drawing on his hard-earned knowledge to patiently answer my endless questions about Sarajevo during the time of the siege. Thank you to "my Judita" van der Reis, my almost-lifelong friend and conversation partner, for being your witty, hilarious, and decidedly nonbittersweet self. If there is such a thing as nostalgia for an experience that one has never actually had, this captures what I feel for Rebecca Wallace-Segall, who was surely my best friend when we were kids, even though we didn't meet until our thirties, but as I've learned through this bittersweet project, it is never too late. Cali Yost has generously shared with me her family stories of bittersweetness, her friendship, and her expansive and ebullient self.

I'm in debt to all those I've quoted, studied, or interviewed for this book: Maya Angelou, George

Bonanno, Alain de Botton, Anna Braverman, William Breitbart, Laura Carstensen, Tim Chang, Leonard Cohen, Keith Comito, Charles Darwin, Susan David, Aubrey de Grey, Raffaella de Rosa, Rene Denfeld, Pete Docter, Jane Dutton, Barbara Ehrenreich, Paul Ekman, Rick Fox, Neal Gabler, Drew Gilpin Faust, Stephen Haff, Stephen Hayes, Kobayashi Issa, Hooria Jazaieri, Jason Kanov, Dacher Keltner, Min Kym, Tim Leberecht, C. S. Lewis, Mariana Lin, Laura Madden, Maureen, Nora McInerny, Lara Nuer, James Pennebaker, Simcha Raphael, Jalal al-Din Rumi, Sharon Salzberg, Scott Sandage, Lois Schnipper, Tanja Schwarzmüller, Vedran Smailović, Sri Sri, Ami Vaidya, Llewellyn Vaughan-Lee, Owe Wikström, Dar Williams, Monica Worline, and Rachel Yehuda.

There are so many others who aren't mentioned by name in **Bittersweet** but who dramatically informed my thinking, whether through formal interviews, reading, or friendship, including but not limited to: Lera Auerbach, Kate Augustus, Andrew Ayre, John Bacon, Barbara Becker, Martin Beitler, Anna Beltran, Ons Ben Zakour, the Berger family, Jen Berger, Lisa Bergqvist, Spiros Blackburn, Brené Brown, Brendan Cahill, Lindsay Cameron, Sensei Chodo Robert Campbell, Paul Coster, Jonah Cuddy, Catherine Cunningham, Geshe Dadul, Rich Day, Lia Buffa de Feo, Michael de Feo, Regina Dugan, Sensei Koshin Paley Ellison, Robin Ely, Oscar Eustis, Aaron Fedor, Tim Ferriss, Jonathan Fields, Sheri

Fink, Erick Flores, Nicoll Flores, Jim Fyfe, Rashmi Ganguly, Dana Gharemani, Panio Gianopoulos, Kerry Gibson, Hillary Hazan-Glass, Michael Glass, Robert Gluck, Seth Godin, Ashley Goodall, Adam Grant, Seth Greene, Rufus Griscom, Jonathan Haidt, Ashley Hardin, Annaka Harris, Sam Harris, Jim Holohan, Maureen Holohan, Zoltan Istvan, Jason Kanov, Jeff Kaplan, Heidi Kasevich, the Keum family, Ariel Kim, Charlie Kim, Emily Klein, Peter Klose, Hitomi Komatsu, Samantha Koppelman, Heesun Lee, Lori Lesser, Salima Lihanda, Mariana Lin, Reut Livne-Tarandach, Laura Madden, Farah Maher, Sally Maitlis, Nathalie Man, Fran Marton, Jodi Massoud, Meghan Messenger, Lisa Miller, Mandy O'Neill, Shlomit Oren, Amanda Palmer, Neil Pasricha, Annie Murphy Paul, Daniella Phillips, Sesil Pir, Josh Prager, John Ratliff, Jayne Riew, JillEllyn Riley, Gretchen Rubin, Matthew Sachs, Raed Salman, Aviva Saphier, Matthew Schaefer, Jonathan Sichel, Nancy Siegel, Peter Sims, Tim Smith, Brande and David Stellings, Daphy Stern, the Sugerman family, Tom Sugiura, Steve Thurman, Tim Urban, Fataneh Vazvaei-Smith, Jean Voutsinas, Sam Walker, Jeremy Wallace, Harriet Washington, Allen Weinberg, Ari Weinzweig, Kristina Workman, and my fellow members of the Invisible Institute, the Next Big Idea Club, and Silicon Guild.

I thank my family for everything: my beloved mother, father, brother, sister, grandparents, and Paula Yeghiayan; the wonderful Schnippers—Barbara,

Steve, Jonathan, Emily, Lois, and Murray; my cherished Romer and Weinstein cousins; my honorary family member, Heidi Postelwait; and Bobbi, Al, and Steve Cain, whose company is always delightful, whose Ann Arbor house is our second home, and whose love, support, and kinship have been among the great joys of my life.

Most of all, I'm grateful for my beloved "pack"— Ken, Sam, Eli, and Sophie. To Sophie: who takes us for walks, hands us her paw, and seems to have arrived in our household straight from the Perfect and Beautiful World. To Eli: One day, you noticed me tearing my hair out over how to structure a chapter, and you handed me a Post-it on which you'd written, "I know it's hard, but just say to yourself 'I can do it.'" That advice, coming from an ace who holds himself to the highest standards, touched me deeply. No one's ever seen an eleven-year-old high-powered field-goal kicker as dedicated to his craft as you. And we burst with pride as we watch you devote the same fierce care to your stellar academics. But most of all, your words reached me because you wrote them, as you live your life, with the empathy of a born mensch. To Sam: I'll never forget a particular look on your face, when you were a baby, an expression of such warmth and sagacity. I thought, who will this boy be at age fourteen? Well, during the time I wrote this book, you've turned into the man you were always destined to be: a scholar-athlete whose smile lights up so many rooms, whose hat tricks have electrified so many soccer pitches, and whose wry humor, brilliant mind, and sheer decency have earned you so many close friends. One day soon, you'll share these gifts with the world. And your father and I will think, for the thousandth time, how lucky we are that you shared them with us from the start. To Gonzo, a.k.a. Ken, who took the boys motor-boating, ball-throwing, ice-skating, and many other action verbs, while I was home writing; who twice stayed up all night editing this manuscript; who brought me coffee from the pastry shop and flowers from the garden; and who delights us daily with his enthusiasm, presence, uniquely Gonzo sense of humor, and dedication to his colleagues and businesses: **juntos somos mas.**

NOTES

PRELUDE:

The Cellist of Sarajevo

xv **The cellist of Sarajevo** Details of this story
are from the novel **The Cellist of Sarajevo** by
Steven Galloway (New York: Riverhead Books,
2009); Vedran Smailović's playing was also reported in many news articles, including **The
New York Times** on June 6, 1992, twelve days
after the death of twenty-two people in line
for bread, https://www.nytimes.com/1992/06
/08/world/death-city-elegy-for-sarajevo-special
-report-people-under-artillery-fire-manage.html.

xvi **This work is commonly attributed** Adagio
in G Minor, Britannica online, https://www
.britannica.com/topic/Adagio-in-G-Minor.

xviii **"I am," said the old man** Allan Little, "Siege
of Sarajevo: The Orchestra That Played in the
Midst of War," BBC **Newshour,** Dec. 21, 2018,
https://www.bbc.co.uk/programmes/p06w9dv2.

INTRODUCTION:
The Power of Bittersweet

xxiii   **"Homesick we are"** A handwritten copy of the poem can be seen on the Garden Museum website, https://gardenmuseum.org.uk/collection/the-garden/.

xxv   **Aristotle wondered why** The Aristotelian **Problema** XXX.1 describes the connection between melancholy and genius. See Heidi Northwood, "The Melancholic Mean: The Aristotelian **Problema** XXX.1," Paideia Archive, https://www.bu.edu/wcp/Papers/Anci/AnciNort.htm.

xxv   **harmonious balance** U.S. National Library of Medicine, "Emotions and Disease," **History of Medicine,** https://www.nlm.nih.gov/exhibition/emotions/balance.html.

xxv   **which I call the "bittersweet"** My conception of bittersweetness, and specifically the idea of "piercing joy," is inspired by C. S. Lewis's writings on **Sehnsucht.**

xxvi   **"has relinquished the ordinary life"** Marsilio Ficino, letter to Giovanni Cavalcanti, **Letters** 2, no. 24 (1978): 33–34, in Angela Voss, "The Power of a Melancholy Humour," **Seeing with Different Eyes: Essays in Astrology and Divination,** ed. P. Curry and A. Voss (Newcastle, UK: Cambridge Scholars, 2007).

xxvi   **Dürer famously depicted** Albrecht Dürer,

"**Melencolia I,** 1514," https://www.metmuseum
.org/art/collection/search/336228.

xxvi "**scarcely conceive of**" Charles Baudelaire, **Les
Fleurs du mal.** Kevin Godbout, "Saturnine
Constellations: Melancholy in Literary History
and in the Works of Baudelaire and Benjamin"
(quoting Baudelaire's "Fusées") (Ph.D. diss.,
University of Western Ontario, 2016).

xxvi **The influential psychologist Julia Kristeva**
Julia Kristeva, **The Black Sun: Depression and
Melancholy,** trans. Leon S. Roudiez (New York:
Columbia University Press, 1989), 10. See also
Emily Brady and Arto Haapala, "Melancholy
as an Aesthetic Emotion," **Contemporary
Aesthetics,** vol. 1, 2003.

xxix "**We do this**" Susan David, "The Gift and
Power of Emotional Courage," TED Talk,
2017, https://www.ted.com/talks/susan_david
_the_gift_and_power_of_emotional_courage
/transcript?language=en.

xxx **in Homer's** <u>Odyssey</u> This is alluded to in Book
I and explored in Book V; see http://classics.mit
.edu/Homer/odyssey.5.v.html.

xxx **longing is the great gateway to belonging** We
have the idea that the great human narrative
is the "Hero's Journey," in which a protagonist
has an adventure, confronts a great challenge,
and emerges transformed. Much of Hollywood
storytelling is based on this progression. But
we've forgotten our other great narrative, which
we might call the "Soul's Journey"—in which

we realize that we've come into this world with
a sense of exile from our true home, that we feel
the pain of separation from the state in which
we loved and were loved beyond measure, and
that the sweet pain of longing helps us return
there. We crave beauty because it reminds us of
that home; it calls us to that journey.

xxx   **"Your whole life"** Llewellyn Vaughan-Lee,
      "Love and Longing: The Feminine Mysteries of
      Love," Golden Sufi Center, https://goldensufi
      .org/love-and-longing-the-feminine-mysteries
      -of-love/.

xxx   **"Those who constantly"** Thom Rock, **Time,
      Twilight, and Eternity: Finding the Sacred in
      the Everyday** (Eugene, Ore: Wipf and Stock,
      2017), 90.

xxx   **"God is the sigh"** Vaughan-Lee, "Love
      and Longing."

xxx   **"Our heart is restless"** Saint Augustine of
      Hippo, **Confessions,** https://www.vatican.va
      /spirit/documents/spirit_20020821_agostino
      _en.html.

xxxii **Beloved of the Soul** Jean Houston, **The Search
      for the Beloved: Journeys in Mythology and
      Sacred Psychology** (New York: J. P. Tarcher,
      1987), 228.

xxxii **"the shore from which"** Mark Merlis, **An
      Arrow's Flight** (New York: Macmillan,
      1998), 13.

xxxii **"the place where all the beauty"** C. S. Lewis,
      Till We Have Faces (New York: HarperOne,
      2017), 86.

xxxii **"Hallelujah," a ballad** "13 Praise-Worthy
Talent Show Performances of Leonard
Cohen's 'Hallelujah,'" Yahoo! Entertainment,
November 11, 2016, https://www.yahoo
.com/news/13-praise-worthy-talent-show
-performances-of-leonard-cohens-hallelujah
-081551820.html.

xxxiii **"to participate joyfully"** This idea can be
found, among other places, in Joseph Campbell,
**A Joseph Campbell Companion: Reflections
on the Art of Living,** ed. Diana K. Osbon (New
York: HarperCollins, 1991); see also https://
www.jcf.org/works/quote/participate-joyfully/.

xxxiv **"I feel an intense longing"** Janet S. Belcove-
Shalin, **New World Hasidim** (Albany: State
University of New York Press, 2012), 99.

xxxvii **According to recent research** D. B. Yaden and
A. B. Newberg, **The Varieties of Spiritual
Experience: A Twenty-First Century Update**
(New York: Oxford University Press, forth-
coming); D. B. Yaden et al., "The Varieties
of Self-Transcendent Experience," **Review of
General Psychology** 21, no. 2 (June 2017):
143–60, https://doi.org/10.1037/gpr0000102.

xxxviii **what Aristotle called** Northwood op. cit.

CHAPTER 1:

What is sadness good for?

3 **"Before you know"** Naomi Shihab Nye,
"Kindness," in **Words Under the Words:**

Selected Poems (Portland, Ore: Eighth
Mountain Press, 1995), 42.

3   **Pixar director Pete Docter** Dacher Keltner and
Paul Ekman, "The Science of **Inside Out**," The
New York Times, July 3, 2015, https://www
.nytimes.com/2015/07/05/opinion/sunday/the
-science-of-inside-out.html.

4   **up to twenty-seven different emotions**
Alan S. Cowen and Dacher Keltner, "Self-
report Captures 27 Distinct Categories of
Emotion Bridged by Continuous Gradients,"
**Proceedings of the National Academy of
Sciences** 114, no. 38 (September 2017); https://
www.pnas.org/content/114/38/E7900.abstract.
See also Wes Judd, "A Conversation with the
Psychologist Behind 'Inside Out,' " **Pacific
Standard,** July 8, 2015; https://psmag.com
/social-justice/a-conversation-with-psychologist
-behind-inside-out.

4   **Fear is funny** Author interview with Pete
Docter, November 30, 2016. See also "It's
All in Your Head: Director Pete Docter Gets
Emotional in **Inside Out**," **Fresh Air,** NPR,
July 3, 2015, https://www.npr.org/2015/07/03
/419497086/its-all-in-your-head-director-pete
-docter-gets-emotional-in-inside-out.

4   **"The idea that you'd cry"** Author interview
with Pete Docter, November 30, 2016.

5   **"I suddenly had an idea"** "It's All in
Your Head."

7   **highest grossing original film** "Inside Out
Sets Record for Biggest Original Box Office

Debut," **Business Insider,** June 2015, https://
www.businessinsider.com/box-office-inside-out
-sets-record-for-biggest-original-jurassic-world
-fastest-to-1-billion-2015-6.

7 **Sadness in the starring role** Keltner and
Ekman, "Science of **Inside Out.**"

8 **"Sadness is at the core"** Series of author interviews with Dacher Keltner, including one in
November 2018.

11 **in his book** Dacher Keltner, **Born to Be Good:
The Science of a Meaningful Life** (New York:
W. W. Norton, 2009).

11 **The word <u>compassion</u>** "What Is Compassion?,"
Greater Good Magazine, https://greatergood
.berkeley.edu/topic/compassion/definition.

11 **"the universal unifying force"** Technically Nick
Cave was referring to "suffering" rather than
"sadness." See his Red Hand Files, https://www
.theredhandfiles.com/utility-of-suffering/.

11 **The compassionate instinct** Neuroscientist
Giacomo Rizzolatti, M.D., first discovered "mirror neurons" in the early 1990s with his colleagues at the University of Parma, when the
team of researchers found individual neurons in
the brains of macaque monkeys that fired both
when the monkeys grabbed an object and when
the monkeys watched another primate grab the
same object. See Lea Winerman, "The Mind's
Mirror," **Monitor on Psychology** 36, no. 9
(October 2005), https://www.apa.org/monitor
/oct05/mirror.

11 **anterior cingulate region** C. Lamm, J. Decety,

and T. Singer, "Meta-Analytic Evidence for Common and Distinct Neural Networks Associated with Directly Experienced Pain and Empathy for Pain," **NeuroImage** 54, no. 3 (February 2011): 2492–502, https://doi.org/10.1016/j.neuroimage.2010.10.014.

12   **the vagus nerve** Jennifer E. Stellar and Dacher Keltner, "Compassion in the Autonomic Nervous System: The Role of the Vagus Nerve," in **Compassion: Concepts, Research, and Applications,** ed. P. Gilbert (Oxfordshire, UK: Routledge, 2017), 120–34. See also Brian DiSalvo and Dacher Keltner, "Forget Survival of the Fittest: It Is Kindness That Counts," **Scientific American,** February 26, 2009.

12   **vagus nerve makes us care** Dacher Keltner, "The Compassionate Species," **Greater Good Magazine,** July 31, 2012, https://greatergood.berkeley.edu/article/item/the_compassionate_species.

12   **people asked to consider** J. D. Greene et al., "The Neural Bases of Cognitive Conflict and Control in Moral Judgment," **Neuron** 44, no. 2 (October 2004): 389–400, https://doi.org/10.1016/j.neuron.2004.09.027.

13   **mothers gazing at pictures** J. B. Nitschke et al., "Orbitofrontal Cortex Tracks Positive Mood in Others Viewing Pictures of Their Newborn Infants," **NeuroImage** 21, no. 2 (February 2004): 583–92, http://dx.doi.org/10.1016/j.neuroimage.2003.10.005.

13   **helping people in need** James K. Rilling

et al., "A Neural Basis for Social Cooperation," **Neuron** 35 (July 2002): 395–405, http://ccnl .emory.edu/greg/PD%20Final.pdf.

13 **We also know that depressed** Yuan Cao et al., "Low Mood Leads to Increased Empathic Distress at Seeing Others' Pain," **Frontiers in Psychology** 8 (November 2017), https://dx.doi .org/10.3389%2Ffpsyg.2017.02024.

13 **conversely, high-empathy people** J. K. Vuoskoski et al., "Being Moved by Unfamiliar Sad Music Is Associated with High Empathy," **Frontiers in Psychology** (September 2016), https://doi.org /10.3389/fpsyg.2016.01176.

13 **"Depression deepens our natural empathy"** Nassir Ghaemi, **A First-Rate Madness: Uncovering the Links Between Leadership and Mental Illness** (New York: Penguin Books, 2012), 85.

13 **experience Keltner's findings viscerally** Michael Brenner, "How Empathic Content Took Cleveland Clinic from Zero to 60 Million Sessions in One Year," Marketing Insider Group, August 29, 2019, https://marketinginsidergroup .com/content-marketing/how-empathetic -content-took-cleveland-clinic-from-zero-to-60 -million-sessions-in-6-years/.

14 **"the happiness of melancholy"** Gretchen Rubin, "Everyone Shines, Given the Right Lighting," January 26, 2012, https:// gretchenrubin.com/2012/01/everyone-shines -given-the-right-lighting.

15 **"union between souls"** https://

embodimentchronicle.wordpress.com/2012/01
/28/the-happiness-of-melancholy-appreciating
-the-fragile-beauty-of-life-and-love/.

17   **"the most vulnerable offspring"** Keltner,
"Compassionate Species."

17   **Orca whales will circle** Center for Whale
Research, "J35 Update," August 11, 2018,
https://www.whaleresearch.com/j35.

17   **Elephants soothe each other** Virginia Morell,
"Elephants Console Each Other," **Science
Magazine,** February 2014, https://www
.sciencemag.org/news/2014/02/elephants
-console-each-other.

18   **"nature, red in tooth"** Alfred, Lord Tennyson,
"In Memoriam."

18   **fellow "social Darwinists"** Dan Falk, "The
Complicated Legacy of Herbert Spencer, the
Man Who Coined 'Survival of the Fittest,'"
Smithsonian Magazine, April 29, 2020,
https://www.smithsonianmag.com/science
-nature/herbert-spencer-survival-of-the-fittest
-180974756/.

18   **For Darwin, says Keltner** Dacher Keltner,
"Darwin's Touch: Survival of the Kindest,"
Greater Good Magazine, February 12, 2009,
https://greatergood.berkeley.edu/article/item
/darwins_touch_survival_of_the_kindest.

18   **Darwin was a gentle** Deborah Heiligman, "The
Darwins' Marriage of Science and Religion,"
Los Angeles Times, January 29, 2009, https://
www.latimes.com/la-oe-heiligman29-2009jan29
-story.html.

19 **witnessed his first surgery** Kerry Lotzof, "Charles Darwin: History's Most Famous Biologist," Natural History Museum, https://www.nhm.ac.uk/discover/charles-darwin-most -famous-biologist.html.

19 **"a chaos of delight" Charles Darwin's Beagle Diary** (Cambridge: Cambridge University Press, 1988), 42.

19 **he lost his beloved** Adam Gopnik, **Angels and Ages: A Short Book About Darwin, Lincoln, and Modern Life** (New York: Alfred A. Knopf, 2009); Deborah Heiligman, **Charles and Emma: The Darwins' Leap of Faith** (New York: Henry Holt, 2009).

19 **"Oh Mamma, what should we do"** Adrian J. Desmond, James Richard Moore, and James Moore, **Darwin** (New York: W. W. Norton, 1994), 386.

19 **"We have lost the joy"** "The Death of Anne Elizabeth Darwin," Darwin Correspondence Project, University of Cambridge, https://www .darwinproject.ac.uk/people/about-darwin /family-life/death-anne-elizabeth-darwin.

19 **"The social instincts"** Charles Darwin, **The Descent of Man, and Selection in Relation to Sex** (1872; repr., London: D. Appleton, 2007), 69, 84.

20 **The dog who took care** Ibid., 74–75.

20 **"relieve the sufferings"** Ibid., 78.

20 **Darwin also intuited** See Paul Ekman's lecture "Darwin and the Dalai Lama, United by Compassion," June 17, 2010, https://

www.youtube.com/watch?v=1Qo64
DkQsRQ.

21 **"he felt the world's pain"** Algis Valiunas,
"Darwin's World of Pain and Wonder," **New
Atlantis** (Fall 2009–Winter 2010), https://www
.thenewatlantis.com/publications/darwins-world
-of-pain-and-wonder.

21 **other species as "fellow creatures"** Darwin,
Descent of Man, 96.

21 **"one of the noblest"** Ibid., 97.

21 **"I will now call myself"** Paul Ekman, "The
Dalai Lama Is a Darwinian," **Greater Good
Magazine,** June 2010, https://greatergood
.berkeley.edu/video/item/the_dalai_lama_is_a
_darwinian.

21 **"In the human mind"** Dalai Lama, **Emotional
Awareness: Overcoming the Obstacles to
Psychological Balance and Compassion** (New
York: Henry Holt, 2008), 197. As described by
Paul Ekman in his talk "Darwin and the Dalai
Lama, United by Compassion," June 17, 2010,
Greater Good Science Center, University of
California, Berkeley, https://www.youtube.com
/watch?v=1Qo64DkQsRQ.

21 **this "amazing coincidence"** Ekman, "Darwin
and the Dalai Lama"; "The Origins of Darwin's
Theory: It May Have Evolved in Tibet,"
Independent, February 16, 2009, https://www
.independent.co.uk/news/science/the-origins-of
-darwin-s-theory-it-may-have-evolved-in-tibet
-1623001.html.

22 **Darwin was exposed** "Origins of Darwin's Theory."

22 **field of "positive psychology"** J. J. Froh, "The History of Positive Psychology: Truth Be Told," **NYS Psychologist** (May–June 2004), https://scottbarrykaufman.com/wp-content/uploads/2015/01/Froh-2004.pdf.

22 **field has also drawn criticism** Barbara Held, "The Negative Side of Positive Psychology," **Journal of Humanistic Psychology** 44, no. 1 (January 2004): 9–46, http://dx.doi.org/10.1177/0022167803259645.

23 **"the comic rather than"** Nancy McWilliams, "Psychoanalytic Reflections on Limitation: Aging, Dying, Generativity, and Renewal," **Psychoanalytic Psychology** 34, no. 1 (2017): 50–57, http://dx.doi.org/10.1037/pap0000107.

23 **the psychiatrist Amy Iversen** "The Upside of Being Neurotic," **Management Today,** May 10, 2018, https://www.managementtoday.co.uk/upside-neurotic/personal-development/article/1464282.

24 **"second wave" that** Tim Lomas, "Positive Psychology: The Second Wave," **Psychologist** 29 (July 2016), https://thepsychologist.bps.org.uk/volume-29/july/positive-psychology-second-wave.

24 **Maslow called "transcenders"** Scott Barry Kaufman, **Transcend: The New Science of Self-Actualization** (New York: Penguin Books, 2020), 223.

25 **"Your vagus nerve"** Dacher Keltner, "What Science Taught Me About Compassion, Gratitude and Awe," November 4, 2016, https://www.dailygood.org/story/1321/what -science-taught-me-about-compassion-gratitude -and-awe/.

25 **high-ranking people** P. K. Piff et al., "Higher Social Class Predicts Increased Unethical Behavior," **Proceedings of the National Academy of Sciences** 109, no. 11 (February 2012): 4086–91, http://dx.doi.org/10.1073 /pnas.1118373109.

25 **less helpful to their colleagues** Kathleen D. Vohs et al., "The Psychological Consequences of Money," **Science** 314, no. 5802 (November 2006): 1154–56, https://doi.org/10.1126 /science.1132491.

25 **less likely to experience physical and emo- tional pain** Lisa Miller, "The Money-Empathy Gap," **New York,** June 29, 2012, https://nymag .com/news/features/money-brain-2012-7/.

26 **witnessing the suffering of others** J. E. Stellar, V. M. Manzo, M. W. Kraus, and D. Keltner, "Class and Compassion: Socioeconomic Factors Predict Responses to Suffering," **Emotion** 12, no. 3 (2012): 449–59, https://doi.org/10.1037 /a0026508.

26 **"People are starting"** Keltner, "What Science Taught Me About Compassion."

26 **"Collect your own data"** Hooria Jazaieri, "Six Habits of Highly Compassionate People," **Greater Good Magazine,** April 24, 2018,

https://greatergood.berkeley.edu/article/item/six
_habits_of_highly_compassionate_people.

27 **"There's no empirical evidence"** Jazaieri, "Six
Habits of Highly Compassionate People."

CHAPTER 2:

Why do we long for "perfect"
and unconditional love?

32 **"The sweetest thing"** Lewis, **Till We Have
Faces,** 86.

33 <u>**The Bridges of Madison County**</u> Robert James
Waller, **The Bridges of Madison County**
(New York: Warner Books, 1992); "**Bridges
of Madison County** Author Robert James
Waller Dies, 77," BBC News, March 10, 2017,
https://www.bbc.com/news/world-us-canada
-39226686.

34 **yearning for our missing half** Plato,
Symposium, 12 (of the MIT Symposium document), http://classics.mit.edu/Plato/symposium
.html. See also Jean Houston, **The Hero and
the Goddess: "The Odyssey" as Mystery and
Initiation** (Wheaton, Ill.: Quest, 2009), 202.

35 **writer-philosopher Alain de Botton**
De Botton, "Why You Will Marry the Wrong
Person," **The New York Times,** May 28, 2016,
https://www.nytimes.com/2016/05/29/opinion
/sunday/why-you-will-marry-the-wrong
-person.html.

36 **"one of the gravest errors"** Alain de Botton,

" 'Romantic Realism': The Seven Rules to Help
You Avoid Divorce," **The Guardian,** January 10,
2017, https://www.theguardian.com/lifeandstyle
/2017/jan/10/romantic-realism-the-seven-rules
-to-help-you-avoid-divorce.

40   **My favorite YouTube video** "Baby Reacts
to Moonlight Sonata," November 19, 2016,
https://www.youtube.com/watch?v=
DHUnLY1_PvM.

41   **known as "chills"** Jaak Panksepp, "The
Emotional Sources of 'Chills' Induced by
Music," **Music Perception** 13 no. 2 (1995):
171–207, https://doi.org/10.2307/40285693;
see also Rémi de Fleurian and Marcus T. Pearce,
"The Relationship Between Valence and Chills
in Music: A Corpus Analysis," **I-Perception** 12,
no. 4 (July 2021), https://doi.org/10.1177
%2F20416695211024680.

41   **a "deeper connection"** Fred Conrad et al.,
"Extreme re-Listening: Songs People Love . . .
and Continue to Love," **Psychology of
Music** 47, no. 1 (January 2018), http://dx.doi
.org/10.1177/0305735617751050.

42   **Even pop music** Helen Lee Lin, "Pop Music
Became More Moody in Past 50 Years,"
Scientific American, November 13, 2012,
https://www.scientificamerican.com/article
/scientists-discover-trends-in-pop-music/.

42   **keys of "joyous melancholy"** Shoba Narayan,
"Why Do Arabic Rhythms Sound So Sweet
to Indian Ears?," **National News,** January 17,

2011, https://www.thenationalnews.com/arts
-culture/comment/why-do-arabic-rhythms
-sound-so-sweet-to-indian-ears-1.375824.

42 **Spain uses its "saddest melodies"** Federico García
Lorca, "On Lullabies," trans. A. S. Kline, Poetry
in Translation, https://www.poetryintranslation
.com/PITBR/Spanish/Lullabies.php.

42 **A musicologist in 1806** "Affective Musical Key
Characteristics," https://wmich.edu./mus-theo
/courses/keys.html.

43 **"the pathos of things"** David Landis Barnhill,
"Aesthetics and Nature in Japan," **The
Encyclopedia of Religion and Nature,** ed. Bron
Taylor (London: Thoemmes Continuum, 2005),
17–18, https://www.uwosh.edu/facstaff/barnhill
/244/Barnhill%20-%20Aesthetics%20and
%20Nature%20in%20Japan%20-%20ERN.pdf.

43 **researchers at the University of Jyväskylä**
Vuoskoski et al., "Being Moved by Unfamiliar
Sad Music Is Associated with High Empathy."

44 **Another longstanding explanation** Mahash
Ananth, "A Cognitive Interpretation of
Aristotle's Concepts of Catharsis and Tragic
Pleasure," **International Journal of Art and Art
History** 2, no. 2 (December 2014), http://dx
.doi.org/10.15640/ijaah.v2n2a1.

44 **yearning melodies help our bodies** Matthew
Sachs, Antonio Damasio, and Assal Habibi,
"The Pleasures of Sad Music," **Frontiers in
Human Neuroscience** (July 24, 2015), https://
doi.org/10.3389/fnhum.2015.00404.

44   **babies in intensive care** Joanne Loewy et al., "The Effects of Music Therapy on Vital Signs, Feeding, and Sleep in Premature Infants," **Pediatrics** 131, no. 5 (May 2013): 902–18, https://doi.org/10.1542/peds.2012-1367.

44   **Even happy music** Sachs, Damasio, and Habibi, "Pleasures of Sad Music."

45   **the "mysterious power"** Federico García Lorca, **In Search of Duende** (New York: New Directions, 1998), 57.

45   **Plato defined as a yearning desire** Ray Baker, **Beyond Narnia: The Theology and Apologetics of C. S. Lewis** (Cambridge, Ohio: Christian Publishing House, 2021), 67–68.

45   **But because pothos** "Pothos," Livius.org, https://www.livius.org/articles/concept/pothos/.

46   **"seized by pothos"** Houston, **Search for the Beloved,** 124.

46   **pothos that set Homer's Odyssey** Ibid.

46   **the "inconsolable longing"** C. S. Lewis, **Surprised by Joy: The Shape of My Early Life** (New York: HarperOne, 1955).

46   **"that unnameable something"** C. S. Lewis, **The Pilgrim's Regress** (Grand Rapids, Mich.: William B. Eerdmans, 1992).

46   **"stabs of joy"** Lewis, **Surprised by Joy.**

47   **"achingly beautiful promise"** Peter Lucia, "Saudade and Sehnsucht," Noweverthen.com, https://noweverthen.com/many/saudade.html.

47   **"this aching creature"** Michael Posner, **Leonard Cohen, Untold Stories: The Early Years** (New York: Simon & Schuster, 2020), 28.

47   **"Do you know"** Merlis, **Arrow's Flight,** 13.

48   **"My artistic life"** Nick Cave, "Love Is the
　　 Drug," **The Guardian,** April 21, 2001, https://
　　 www.theguardian.com/books/2001/apr/21
　　 /extract.

48   <u>**saudade,**</u> **a sweetly piercing nostalgia**
　　 The Welsh have the word **hiraeth** for a
　　 similar concept.

48   **Hindu legend says** Sandeep Mishra, "Valmiki—
　　 The First Poet," Pearls from the Ramayana,
　　 August 14, 2020, https://www.amarchitrakatha
　　 .com/mythologies/valmiki-the-first-poet/.

48   **"Longing itself is divine"** Sri Sri Ravi
　　 Shankar, "Longing Is Divine," https://wisdom
　　 .srisriravishankar.org/longing-is-divine/.

49   **Italian painters used to paint the Madonna**
　　 Siddhartha Mukherjee, "Same But Different,"
　　 The New Yorker, April 25, 2016, https://
　　 www.newyorker.com/magazine/2016/05/02
　　 /breakthroughs-in-epigenetics.

51   **"Listen to the story"** Rumi, **The Essential
　　 Rumi** (Harper One, 2004), p. 17.

53   **"The Pain of Separation"** "The Pain of
　　 Separation (The Longing)," July 29, 2014,
　　 https://www.youtube.com/watch?v=
　　 Za1me4NuqxA.

54   **Islamic State has killed** Rukmini Callimachi,
　　 "To the World, They Are Muslims. To ISIS,
　　 Sufis Are Heretics," **The New York Times,**
　　 November 25, 2017, https://www.nytimes.com
　　 /2017/11/25/world/middleeast/sufi-muslims
　　 -isis-sinai.html.

54   **Here he was, telling Oprah** "Llewellyn
      Vaughan-Lee and Oprah Winfrey Interview,"
      March 4, 2012, Golden Sufi Center, https://
      goldensufi.org/video/llewellyn-vaughan-lee-and
      -oprah-winfrey-interview/.

54   **"Longing is the sweet pain"** Llewellyn
      Vaughan-Lee, "Feminine Mysteries of Love,"
      Personal Transformation, https://www
      .personaltransformation.com/llewellyn_vaughan
      _lee.html.

55   **who left behind reams of ecstatic poetry**
      Shahram Shiva, **Rumi's Untold Story** (n.p.:
      Rumi Network, 2018).

55   **bestselling poet** Jane Ciabattari, "Why Is
      Rumi the Best-Selling Poet in the US?," BBC,
      October 21, 2014, https://www.bbc.com
      /culture/article/20140414-americas-best-selling
      -poet.

55   **Saint Teresa of Avila Teresa of Avila: The
      Book of My Life,** trans. Mirabai Starr (Boston:
      Shambhala Publications, Inc., 2008), 224.

56   **"Longing is the core"** Rumi, **The Book of Love**
      (San Francisco: HarperCollins, 2005), 98.

55   **Mirabai wrote poetry** Mirabai, "I Send Letters,"
      Allpoetry.com, https://allpoetry.com/I-Send
      -Letters.

56   **"I have heard you"** Ibid., 146.

57   **Freedom (or nirvana)** Joseph Goldstein,
      "Mindfulness, Compassion & Wisdom: Three
      Means to Peace," PBS.org, https://www.pbs.org
      /thebuddha/blog/2010/May/11/mindfulness
      -compassion-wisdom-three-means-peace-jo/.

57   **"After a lot of training"** The quote is from **Buddha's Advice,** the blog of a practicing Buddhist, lynnjkelly, https://buddhasadvice .wordpress.com/2012/04/19/longing/.

60   **"the greatest power"** Llewellyn Vaughan-Lee, **In the Company of Friends** (Point Reyes Station, Calif.: Golden Sufi Center, 1994).

60   **"the disciple has to become"** Llewellyn Vaughan-Lee, "The Ancient Path of the Mystic: An Interview with Llewellyn Vaughan-Lee," Golden Sufi Center, https://goldensufi.org/the -ancient-path-of-the-mystic-an-interview-with -llewellyn-vaughan-lee/.

65   **Western tradition of love songs** Llewellyn Vaughan-Lee, "A Dangerous Love," Omega Institute for Holistic Studies, April 26, 2007, https://www.youtube.com/watch?v=Q7pe _GLp_6o.

66   **"Our commonest expedient"** C. S. Lewis, **The Weight of Glory** (New York: Macmillan, 1966), 4–5.

CHAPTER 3:

Is creativity associated with sorrow, longing—and transcendence?

70   **a "boudoir poet"** David Remnick, "Leonard Cohen Makes It Darker," **The New Yorker,** October 17, 2016, https://www.newyorker.com /magazine/2016/10/17/leonard-cohen-makes -it-darker.

70   he **"existed best"** Sylvie Simmons,
     "Remembering Leonard Cohen," CBC Radio,
     November 11, 2017, https://www.cbc.ca/radio
     /writersandcompany/remembering-leonard
     -cohen-biographer-sylvie-simmons-on-montreal
     -s-beloved-poet-1.4394764.

70   **"It was as if"** Andrew Anthony, "Leonard
     Cohen and Marianne Ihlen: The Love Affair
     of a Lifetime," **The Guardian,** June 30, 2019,
     https://www.theguardian.com/film/2019/jun/30
     /leonard-cohen-marianne-ihlen-love-affair-of-a
     -lifetime-nick-broomfield-documentary-words
     -of-love.

71   **"There are some people"** Simmons,
     "Remembering Leonard Cohen."

71   **According to a famous early study** Marvin
     Eisenstadt, **Parental Loss and Achievement**
     (New York: Simon & Schuster, 1993).

72   **People who work in the arts** Kay Redfield
     Jamison, **Touched with Fire** (New York: Simon
     & Schuster, 1993).

72   **study of the artistic psyche** Christopher
     Zara, **Tortured Artists** (Avon, Mass.: Adams
     Media, 2012).

72   **an economist named** Karol Jan Borowiecki,
     "How Are You, My Dearest Mozart? Well-Being
     and Creativity of Three Famous Composers
     Based on Their Letters," **The Review of
     Economics and Statistics** 99, no. 4 (October
     2017): 591–605, https://doi.org/10.1162
     /REST_a_00616.

73   **measured their blood for DHEAS** Modupe

Akinola and Wendy Berry Mendes, "The Dark Side of Creativity: Biological Vulnerability and Negative Emotions Lead to Greater Artistic Creativity," **Personality and Social Psychology Bulletin** 34, no. 12 (December 2008), https://dx.doi.org/10.1177%2F0146167208323933.

73 **sad moods tend to sharpen** Joseph P. Forgas, "Four Ways Sadness May Be Good for You," **Greater Good Magazine,** June 4, 2014, https://greatergood.berkeley.edu/article/item/four_ways_sadness_may_be_good_for_you.

74 **adversity causes a tendency to withdraw** Tom Jacobs, "How Artists Can Turn Childhood Pain into Creativity," **Greater Good Magazine,** May 8, 2018, https://greatergood.berkeley.edu/article/item/how_artists_can_turn_childhood_pain_into_creativity.

74 **flashes of insight** Karuna Subramaniam et al., "A Brain Mechanism for Facilitation of Insight by Positive Affect," **Journal of Cognitive Neuroscience,** https://direct.mit.edu/jocn/article/21/3/415/4666/A-Brain-Mechanism-for-Facilitation-of-Insight-by.

75 **"Creative people are not"** Amanda Mull, "6 Months Off Meds I Can Feel Me Again," **The Atlantic,** December 20, 2018, https://www.theatlantic.com/health/archive/2018/12/kanye-west-and-dangers-quitting-psychiatric-medication/578647/.

75 **"felt at home in darkness"** Sylvie Simmons, **I'm Your Man: The Life of Leonard Cohen** (New York: Ecco Press, 2012), 763.

75   **she showed subjects** Nancy Gardner,
     "Emotionally Ambivalent Workers Are
     More Creative, Innovative," **University of
     Washington News,** October 5, 2006, https://
     www.washington.edu/news/2006/10/05
     /emotionally-ambivalent-workers-are-more
     -creative-innovative/.

76   **ardent believer in Enlightenment values**
     Tom Huizenga, "Beethoven's Life, Liberty and
     Pursuit of Enlightenment," **Morning Edition,**
     NPR, December 1, 2020, https://www.npr
     .org/sections/deceptivecadence/2020/12/17
     /945428466/beethovens-life-liberty-and-pursuit
     -of-enlightenment.

76   **"I am well"** Joseph Kerman et al., "Ludwig
     van Beethoven," **Grove Music Online**
     (2001): 13, https://www.oxfordmusiconline
     .com/grovemusic/view/10.1093
     /gmo/9781561592630.001.0001/omo
     -9781561592630-e-0000040026.

76   **"I must confess"** Ibid., 17.

77   **"stood in front"** David Nelson, "The Unique
     Story of Beethoven's Ninth Symphony," In
     Mozart's Footsteps, August 2, 2012, http://
     inmozartsfootsteps.com/2472/the-unique-story
     -of-beethovens-ninth-symphony/.

77   **When the performance ended** Jan Caeyers,
     Beethoven, A Life (Oakland: University of
     California Press, 2020), 486.

78   **immersing oneself in creativity** Koenraad
     Cuypers et al., "Patterns of Receptive and
     Creative Cultural Activities and Their

Association with Perceived Health, Anxiety, Depression and Satisfaction with Life Among Adults: The HUNT Study, Norway," **Journal of Epidemiology and Community Health** 66, no. 8 (August 2012), https://doi.org/10.1136/jech.2010.113571.

78 **simple act of <u>viewing</u> beautiful art** Matteo Nunner, "Viewing Artworks Generates in the Brain the Same Reactions of Being in Love," **Narrative Medicine,** July 10, 2017, https://www.medicinanarrativa.eu/viewing-artworks-generates-in-the-brain-the-same-reactions-of-being-in-love.

78 **"The people who weep"** Mark Rothko, "Statement About Art," Daugavpils Mark Rothko Art Centre, https://www.rothkocenter.com/en/art-center/mark-rothko/statement-about-art.

83 **he told his rabbi** Simmons, **I'm Your Man,** 491.

83 **"It was part of this thesis"** Interview with Rick Rubin, "Leonard Cohen's Legacy with Adam Cohen: Thanks for the Dance," **Broken Record,** n.d., https://brokenrecordpodcast.com/episode-8-leonard-cohens-legacy-with-adam-cohen.

84 **he calls "self-transcendent experiences"** D. B. Yaden et al., "The Varieties of Self-Transcendent Experience," **Review of General Psychology** 21, no. 2 (June 2017), https://doi.org/10.1037%2Fgpr0000102.

84 **"This is love"** Scott Barry Kaufman, **Transcend: The New Science of Self-Actualization** (New York: TarcherPerigee, 2021), 198.

85 **"I was wondering"** Author interview with
    David Yaden, December 10, 2019.

85 **the "oceanic feeling"** J. Harold Ellens, ed., **The
    Healing Power of Spirituality: How Faith
    Helps Humans Thrive** (Santa Barbara, Calif.:
    Praeger, 2010), 45.

86 **"some of life's"** Yaden et al., "Varieties of
    Self-Transcendent Experience."

87 **"experience the most important"** D. B.
    Yaden and A. B. Newberg, **The Varieties
    of Spiritual Experience: A Twenty-First
    Century Update** (New York: Oxford University
    Press, forthcoming).

88 **themes grew more religious, spiritual, and
    mystical** D. K. Simonton, "Dramatic Greatness
    and Content: A Quantitative Study of 81
    Athenian and Shakespearean Plays," **Empirical
    Studies of the Arts** 1, no. 2 (1983): 109–23,
    https://doi.org/10.2190/0AGV-D8A9
    -HVDF-PL95; D. K. Simonton, **Greatness:
    Who Makes History and Why** (New York:
    Guilford Press, 1994); see also Paul Wong,
    "The Deep-and-Wide Hypothesis in Giftedness
    and Creativity," May 17, 2017, http://
    www.drpaulwong.com/the-deep-and-wide
    -hypothesis-in-giftedness-and-creativity/.

88 **intense "peak experiences"** Tom S. Cleary and
    Sam I. Shapiro, "The Plateau Experience and
    the Post-Mortem Life: Abraham H. Maslow's
    Unfinished Theory," **Journal of Transpersonal
    Psychology** 27, no. 1 (1995), https://www
    .atpweb.org/jtparchive/trps-27-95-01-001.pdf.

88 **"Meeting the grim reaper"** Amelia Goranson
et al., "Dying Is Unexpectedly Positive,"
Psychological Science (June 1, 2017), https://
doi.org/10.1177%2F0956797617701186.

89 **Estelle Frankel explores** Estelle Frankel,
**Sacred Therapy: Jewish Spiritual Teachings
on Emotional Healing and Inner Wholeness**
(Boulder, Colo.: Shambhala, 2004).

90 **"Happy Birthday" in C major** Dr. Vicky
Williamson, "The Science of Music—Why Do
Songs in a Minor Key Sound So Sad?," **NME,**
February 14, 2013, https://www.nme.com/blogs
/nme-blogs/the-science-of-music-why-do-songs
-in-a-minor-key-sound-sad-760215.

91 **"Dearest Marianne," it said** https://
theconversation.com/mythmaking-social-media
-and-the-truth-about-leonard-cohens-last-letter
-to-marianne-ihlen-108082.

93 **violin was her soul mate** Min Kym, **Gone: A
Girl, a Violin, a Life Unstrung** (New York:
Crown Publishers, 2017).

93 **"The instant I drew the first breath"** Ibid., 85.

94 **"the only instrument"** Conversations
conducted with the author throughout
their friendship.

96 **At first, she thought** Liz Baker and Lakshmi
Singh, "Her Violin Stolen, a Prodigy's World
Became 'Unstrung,'" **All Things Considered,**
NPR, May 7, 2017, https://www.npr.org/2017
/05/07/526924474/her-violin-stolen-a-prodigys
-world-became-unstrung.

CHAPTER 4:

How should we cope with lost love?

101 **"Though lovers be lost, love shall not"** https://
     genius.com/Dylan-thomas-and-death-shall-have
     -no-dominion-annotated.

116 **"to open your heart"** Steven C. Hayes, "From
     Loss to Love," **Psychology Today,** June 18,
     2018, https://www.psychologytoday.com/us
     /articles/201806/loss-love.

116 **"In your pain"** Tony Rousmaniere, "Steven
     Hayes on Acceptance and Commitment," n.d.,
     Psychotherapy.net, https://www.psychotherapy
     .net/interview/acceptance-commitment-therapy
     -ACT-steven-hayes-interview.

116 **Hayes is the founder** Steven C. Hayes and Kirk
     D. Strosahl, **A Practical Guide to Acceptance
     and Commitment Therapy** (New York:
     Springer, 2004).

116 **"When you connect"** Rousmaniere, "Steven
     Hayes on Acceptance and Commitment."

117 **seven skills for coping** Steven C. Hayes,
     "From Loss to Love," **Psychology Today,**
     June 18, 2018.

117 **acquisition of this skill set** M. E. Levin et al.,
     "Examining Psychological Inflexibility as a
     Transdiagnostic Process Across Psychological
     Disorders," **Journal of Contextual Behavioral
     Science** 3, no. 3 (July 2014): 155–63, https://
     dx.doi.org/10.1016%2Fj.jcbs.2014.06.003.

117 **give an impromptu speech** When Brett Ford

was a doctoral student at the University of California, Berkeley, in 2017, she and three fellow Berkeley researchers devised a three-part study to try to find out the relationship between accepting negative emotions and long-term thriving. Their findings, in Ford et al., "The Psychological Health Benefits of Accepting Negative Emotions and Thoughts: Laboratory, Diary, and Longitudinal Evidence," were published in the **Journal of Personality and Social Psychology** 115, no. 6 (2018), https://doi.org /10.1037/pspp0000157.

118 **greater sense of well-being** Lila MacLellan, "Accepting Your Darkest Emotions Is the Key to Psychological Health," Quartz, July 23, 2017, https://qz.com/1034450/accepting-your-darkest -emotions-is-the-key-to-psychological-health/; Ford et al., "Psychological Health Benefits of Accepting Negative Emotions and Thoughts."

118 **"Connecting with what matters"** Hayes, "From Loss to Love."

119 **"Leonardo da Vinci of the twentieth century"** Marshall McLuhan so called Fuller in R. Buckminster Fuller, **Buckminster Fuller: Starting with the Universe,** ed. K. Michael Hays and Dana Miller (New York: Whitney Museum of American Art, 2008), 39.

119 **her powerful memoir** Maya Angelou, **I Know Why the Caged Bird Sings** (New York: Random House, 2010).

120 **"Were they the same"** Ibid., 97.

121 **"We can all be stirred"** Oprah Winfrey,

foreword to Angelou, **I Know Why the Caged Bird Sings,** ix.

121 **"the most beautiful"** Richard Gray, "The Sorrow and Defiance of Maya Angelou," The Conversation, May 29, 2014, https:// theconversation.com/the-sorrow-and-defiance -of-maya-angelou-27341.

121 **it was "Providence"** Winfrey, foreword to Angelou, **I Know Why the Caged Bird Sings,** x.

121 **the "wounded healer"** Serge Daneault, "The Wounded Healer: Can This Idea Be of Use to Family Physicians?," **Canadian Family Physician** 54, no. 9 (2008): 1218–25, https://www.ncbi.nlm.nih.gov/pmc/articles /PMC2553448/.

121 **Chiron was injured** Neel Burton, M.D., "The Myth of Chiron, the Wounded Healer," **Psychology Today,** February 20, 2021, https:// www.psychologytoday.com/us/blog/hide-and -seek/202102/the-myth-chiron-the-wounded -healer.

122 **The bereaved mother** "Candace Lightner," https://www.candacelightner.com/Meet -Candace/Biography.

122 **survivor of a mass shooting** Catherine Ho, "Inside the Bloomberg-Backed Gun-Control Group's Effort to Defeat the NRA," **The Washington Post,** June 20, 2016, https://www .washingtonpost.com/news/powerpost/wp/2016 /06/20/everytowns-survivors-network-stands-on -the-front-lines-of-the-gun-control-battle/.

122 **mental health counselors** Lauren

Eskreis-Winkler, Elizabeth P. Shulman, and Angela L. Duckworth, "Survivor Mission: Do Those Who Survive Have a Drive to Thrive at Work?," **Journal of Positive Psychology** 9, no. 3 (January 2014): 209–18, https://doi.org /10.1080/17439760.2014.888579.

122 **record numbers of Americans** Adam M. Grant and Kimberly A. Wade-Benzoni, "The Hot and Cool of Death Awareness at Work: Mortality Cues, Aging, and Self-Protective and Pro-social Motivations," **Academy of Management Review** 34, no. 4 (2017), https://doi.org/10 .5465/amr.34.4.zok600.

122 **At Teach for America** Abby Goodnough, "More Applicants Answer the Call for Teaching Jobs," **The New York Times,** February 11, 2002, https://www.nytimes.com/2002/02/11/us /more-applicants-answer-the-call-for-teaching -jobs.html.

122 **One New York City firefighter explained** Donna Kutt Nahas, "No Pay, Long Hours, But Now, Glory," **The New York Times,** February 17, 2002, https://www.nytimes.com /2002/02/17/nyregion/no-pay-long-hours-but -now-glory.html.

122 **Actor Amy Ting** "Terrorist Survivor Enlists in Air Force," **Airman,** September 2002, 12.

123 **author and public defender** Jane Ratcliffe, "Rene Denfeld: What Happens After the Trauma," **Guernica,** November 18, 2019, https://www.guernicamag.com/rene-denfeld -what-happens-after-the-trauma/.

123   **"the king of normal"** Rene Denfeld,
        "The Other Side of Loss," The Manifest-
        Station, January 21, 2015, https://www
        .themanifeststation.net/2015/01/21/the-other
        -side-of-loss/.

123   **But she became** "Rene Denfeld," https://
        renedenfeld.com/author/biography/.

124   **"My kids bring me"** Denfeld, "Other
        Side of Loss."

125   **Loving-kindness meditation** Emma
        Seppälä, "18 Science-Backed Reasons to Try
        Loving-Kindness Meditation," **Psychology
        Today,** September 15, 2014, https://www
        .psychologytoday.com/us/blog/feeling-it
        /201409/18-science-backed-reasons-try-loving
        -kindness-meditation.

127   **India's most revered teachers** "Who Was
        Dipa Ma?," Lion's Roar, February 24, 2017,
        https://www.lionsroar.com/mother-of-light-the
        -inspiring-story-of-dipa-ma/.

128   **the mustard seed** Justin Whitaker, "The
        Buddhist Parable of the Mustard Seed," Patheos,
        November 29, 2016, https://www.patheos.com
        /blogs/americanbuddhist/2016/11/the-buddhist
        -parable-of-the-mustard-seed-grief-loss-and
        -heartbreak.html.

128   **"And that," Sharon told me** Author interview
        with Salzberg, August 3, 2017.

134   **woman named Dora Diamant** Jordi Sierra
        i Fabra and Jacqueline Minett Wilkinson,
        Kafka and the Traveling Doll (n.p.: SIF
        Editorial, 2019).

CHAPTER 5:
How did a nation founded on so much heartache turn into a culture of normative smiles?

143 **"The word 'loser'"** Garrison Keillor, "A Studs Terkel Lesson in Losing and Redemption," **Chicago Tribune,** n.d., https://digitaledition .chicagotribune.com/tribune/article_popover .aspx?guid=eeb0ab19-1be3-4d35-a015 -238d1dadab6c.

144 **"Just stay positive"** David, "Gift and Power of Emotional Courage."

147 **smile more than any other society** Olga Khazan, "Why Americans Smile So Much," **The Atlantic,** May 3, 2017, https://www.theatlantic .com/science/archive/2017/05/why-americans -smile-so-much/524967/.

147 **smiling is viewed as dishonest** Kuba Krys et al., "Be Careful Where You Smile: Culture Shapes Judgments of Intelligence and Honesty of Smiling Individuals," **Journal of Nonverbal Behavior** 40 (2016): 101–16, https://doi.org /10.1007/s10919-015-0226-4.

148 **"a little bit afraid"** "How Learning to Be Vulnerable Can Make Life Safer," **Invisibilia,** NPR, June 17, 2016, https://www.npr.org /sections/health-shots/2016/06/17/482203447 /invisibilia-how-learning-to-be-vulnerable-can -make-life-safer.

148 **Americans suffered from anxiety** "Any Anxiety Disorder," National Institute of Mental Health,

https://www.nimh.nih.gov/health/statistics/any
-anxiety-disorder.

148 **Journal of the American Medical Association**
Deborah S. Hasin et al., "Epidemiology of
Adult DSM-5 Major Depressive Disorder and
Its Specifiers in the United States," **JAMA
Psychiatry** 75, no. 4 (April 2018): 336–46,
https://dx.doi.org/10.1001%2Fjamapsychiatry
.2017.4602.

148 **over fifteen million** Benedict Carey and Robert
Gebeloff, "Many People Taking Antidepressants
Discover They Cannot Quit," **The New York
Times,** April 7, 2018, https://www.nytimes.com
/2018/04/07/health/antidepressants-withdrawal
-prozac-cymbalta.html.

148 **dead by morning** Sogyal Rinpoche, **Tibetan
Book of Living and Dying** (New York:
HarperOne, 2009), 22.

148 **We don't weave imperfections** "Intentional
Flaws," **The World,** PRI, July 2002, https://www
.pri.org/stories/2002-07-13/intentional-flaws.

148 **art form of wabi sabi** Emma Taggart, "Wabi-
Sabi: The Japanese Art of Finding Beauty
in Imperfect Ceramics," My Modern Met,
https://mymodernmet.com/wabi-sabi-japanese
-ceramics/.

148 **sympathy cards** Birgit Koopmann-Holm and
Jeanne L. Tsai, "Focusing on the Negative:
Cultural Differences in Expressions of
Sympathy," **Journal of Personality and Social
Psychology** 107, no. 6 (2014): 1092–115,
https://dx.doi.org/10.1037%2Fa0037684.

149 **prepare for their sons' departures** I can't recall for the life of me where I read this, but it has stuck with me.

150 **lost "their lives, loved ones"** Barbara Ehrenreich, **Bright-Sided: How the Relentless Promotion of Positive Thinking Has Undermined America** (New York: Henry Holt, 2009), 6.

150 **The fatality rate** Drew Gilpin Faust, **This Republic of Suffering: Death and the American Civil War** (New York: Vintage, 2008), xi.

151 **memory of ancient traumas** Andrew Curry, "Parents' Emotional Trauma May Change Their Children's Biology. Studies in Mice Show How," **Science Magazine,** July 2019, https://www.sciencemag.org/news/2019/07/parents-emotional-trauma-may-change-their-children-s-biology-studies-mice-show-how.

151 **doctrine of predestination** According to Puritan Reformed Theological Seminary's Joel R. Beeke and Paul M. Smalley: "The doctrine of predestination does teach that only God's elect will be saved. That does not imply that we can't know for certain whether we are saved. Rather, God's free gift of 'all things that pertain unto life and godliness, through the knowledge of him [i.e., Christ Jesus] that hath called us to glory and virtue' enables believers 'to make your calling and election sure' by growing in knowledge, faith, and practical holiness (2 Pet 1:3–10)." Joel R. Beeke and Paul M. Smalley, "Help! I'm Struggling with the Doctrine of Predestination,"

Crossway, October 19, 2020, https://www
.crossway.org/articles/help-im-struggling-with
-the-doctrine-of-predestination/.

151 **Calvinism seemed to loosen** Jenni Murray,
**"Smile or Die: How Positive Thinking
Fooled America and the World** by Barbara
Ehrenreich," **The Guardian,** January 9, 2010,
https://www.theguardian.com/books/2010/jan
/10/smile-or-die-barbara-ehrenreich.

151 **"hideous and desolate wilderness"**
Gov. William Bradford writing in **Of Plymouth
Plantation** in 1630. See Peter C. Mancall,
"The Real Reason the Pilgrims Survived," Live
Science, November 22, 2018, https://www
.livescience.com/64154-why-the-pilgrims
-survived.html.

151 **"Why should we grope"** Ralph Waldo Emerson,
"Nature" (1836), in **Nature and Selected Essays**
(New York: Penguin Books, 2003).

152 **"reconfiguration of the doctrine"** Maria
Fish, "When Failure Got Personal," SF Gate,
March 6, 2005, https://www.sfgate.com/books
/article/When-failure-got-personal-2693997
.php.

152 **Farmers "must be extensively engaged"**
Scott A. Sandage, **Born Losers: A History
of Failure in America** (Cambridge, Mass.:
Harvard University Press, 2006), 11.

153 **Some "have failed, from causes beyond the
control"** Ibid., 36.

153 **The "loser" became, in Sandage's words**
Harvard University Press, https://www

.hup.harvard.edu/catalog.php?isbn=
9780674021075.

153 **"nobody fails who ought not"** Sandage, **Born Losers,** 46, 17.

153 **"Failures that arise from inevitable misfortune"** Ibid., 46.

154 **New Thought movement** Christopher H. Evans, "Why You Should Know About the New Thought Movement," The Conversation, February 2017, https://theconversation.com /why-you-should-know-about-the-new-thought -movement-72256.

154 **"moonstruck with optimism"** William James, **The Varieties of Religious Experience** (London: Longmans, Green, 2009), 95.

155 **"look for the bright side"** Boy Scouts of America, "What Are the Scout Oath and the Scout Law?," https://www.scouting.org/about /faq/question10/.

155 **"You should force yourself"** Robert Baden-Powell, **Scouting for Boys** (1908; repr., Oxford: Oxford University Press, 2018), 46.

155 **"Are you a Misfit?"** Sandage, **Born Losers,** 261.

155 **"The go-ahead man"** Ibid., 337.

155 <u>**Think and Grow Rich**</u> Napoleon Hill, **Think and Grow Rich** (Meriden, Conn.: Ralston Society, 1937).

155 **"whenever a negative thought"** Norman Vincent Peale, **The Power of Positive Thinking** (New York: Touchstone, 2003).

155 **1929 stock market crash** Sandage, **Born Losers,** 262.

155 **A 1929 headline** Ibid., 262, 263.

156 **the word <u>loser</u>** Ibid., 266, 267.

156 **Charles Schulz once said** Stuart Jeffries, "Why I Loved Charlie Brown and the 'Peanuts' Cartoons," **The Guardian,** December 5, 2015, https://www.theguardian.com/lifeandstyle/2015 /dec/05/charlie-brown-charles-schultz-peanuts -cartoon-movie-steve-martino.

156 **"how many Charlie Browns"** Martin Miller, "Good Grief. Charles Schulz Calls It Quits," **Los Angeles Times,** December 16, 1999, https://www.latimes.com/archives/la-xpm-1999 -dec-15-mn-44051-story.html#:~:text=%E2 %80%9CAs%20a%20youngster%2C%20I %20didn,%2C%20adults%20and%20children %20alike.%E2%80%9D.

156 **"America is deeply divided"** Neal Gabler, "America's Biggest Divide: Winners and Losers," **Salon,** October 2017, https://www.salon.com /2017/10/08/americas-biggest-divide-winners -and-losers_partner/.

157 **The "prosperity gospel"** Kate Bowler, "Death, the Prosperity Gospel and Me," **The New York Times,** February 13, 2016, https://www .nytimes.com/2016/02/14/opinion/sunday /death-the-prosperity-gospel-and-me.html.

157 **This "gospel" was endorsed** David Van Biema and Jeff Chu, "Does God Want You to Be Rich?" **Time,** September 10, 2006, http:// content.time.com/time/magazine/article/0,9171 ,1533448-2,00.html.

157 **use of the term <u>loser</u>** Google Books Ngram

Viewer, https://books.google.com/ngrams/graph
?content=loser+&year_start=1800&year_end=
2019&corpus=26&smoothing=3&direct_url=
t1%3B%2Closer%3B%2Cc0.

157 **recast the war hero** Ben Schreckinger, "Trump
Attacks McCain," **Politico,** July 18, 2015,
https://www.politico.com/story/2015/07/trump
-attacks-mccain-i-like-people-who-werent
-captured-120317.

157 **rates of anxiety** Lauren Lumpkin, "Rates of
Anxiety and Depression Amongst College
Students Continue to Soar, Researchers Say,"
The Washington Post, June 10, 2021, https://
www.washingtonpost.com/education/2021/06
/10/dartmouth-mental-health-study/.

157 **American Civil Liberties Union** "We were
calling this a mental health crisis before the
pandemic. Now it's a state of emergency," said
Amir Whitaker, policy counsel of the ACLU
of Southern California. See Carolyn Jones,
"Student Anxiety, Depression Increasing During
School Closures, Survey Finds," EdSource,
May 13, 2020, https://edsource.org/2020
/student-anxiety-depression-increasing-during
-school-closures-survey-finds/631224.

158 **Holleran died by suicide** Kate Fagan, "Split
Image," ESPN, May 7, 2015, http://www
.espn.com/espn/feature/story/_/id/12833146
/instagram-account-university-pennsylvania
-runner-showed-only-part-story.

158 **"she was so overwhelmed"** Izzy Grinspan,
"7 College Students Talk About Their

Instagrams and the Pressure to Seem Happy,"
New York, July 31, 2015, https://www.thecut
.com/2015/07/college-students-on-the-pressure
-to-seem-happy.html.

159   **call "disenfranchised griefs"** Val Walker, "The
Loneliness of Unshareable Grief," **Psychology
Today,** December 2, 2020, https://www
.psychologytoday.com/us/blog/400-friends
-who-can-i-call/202012/the-loneliness
-unshareable-grief.

161   **They call this thing "effortless perfection"**
Author interviews with Luke, Paige, Heather,
and Nick, February 13, 2018.

163   **stress, melancholy, and longing** "American
Psychological Association Survey Shows
Teen Stress Rivals That of Adults," American
Psychological Association, 2014, https://www
.apa.org/news/press/releases/2014/02/teen
-stress.

163   **Anna Braverman** Author interview,
February 13, 2018.

164   **Princeton Perspective Project** Kinsey believes
that this quote comes from an interview she
gave for this project, which was an initiative
she co-led when she was an associate dean at
Princeton; however, we've been unable to track
down the original source.

164   **The term effortless perfection** Kristie Lee,
"Questioning the Unquestioned," Duke Today,
October 6, 2003, https://today.duke.edu/2003
/10/20031006.html.

164 **Stanford calls it "Duck Syndrome"** "The
     Duck Stop Here," Stanford University, https://
     duckstop.stanford.edu/why-does-duck-stop
     -here.

CHAPTER 6:
How can we transcend enforced positivity in the workplace, and beyond?

167 **"I was going to buy a copy"** This may be from
     one of Shakes's standup comedy routines.
167 **"emotional agility"** Series of interviews with the
     author, including on July 27, 2017.
168 **"Research on emotional suppression"** David,
     "Gift and Power of Emotional Courage."
169 **"If, as the Buddha is reported"** Peter J.
     Frost, "Why Compassion Counts!," **Journal
     of Management Inquiry** 8, no. 2 (June
     1999): 127–33, https://doi.org/10.1177
     /105649269982004.
170 **run by University of Michigan scholar Monica
     Worline** Author interview, October 31, 2016.
170 **"There's an unspectacular mundane suf-
     fering"** Author interview with Jason Kanov,
     February 15, 2017, and emails thereafter.
171 **Yet a 2009 study** Juan Madera and Brent Smith,
     "The Effects of Leader Negative Emotions
     on Evaluations of Leadership in a Crisis
     Situation: The Role of Anger and Sadness," **The
     Leadership Quarterly** 20, no. 2 (April 2009):

103–14, http://dx.doi.org/10.1016/j.leaqua
.2009.01.007.

172   **difference between angry and sad leaders**
Tanja Schwarzmüller et al., "It's the Base: Why
Displaying Anger Instead of Sadness Might
Increase Leaders' Perceived Power But Worsen
Their Leadership," **Journal of Business and
Psychology** 32 (2017), https://doi.org/10.1007
/s10869-016-9467-4.

173   **"feel accepted and valued"** Melissa Pandika,
"Why Melancholy Managers Inspire Loyalty,"
OZY, January 4, 2017, https://www.ozy.com
/news-and-politics/why-melancholy-managers
-inspire-loyalty/74628/.

173   **"If followers mess up"** Ibid.

174   **their "core wounds"** Author interview with Tim
Chang, December 16, 2019.

174   **"In Silicon Valley"** Ibid.

178   **"In the moment"** Author interview with Lara
Nuer, September 27, 2017.

179   **segment on the radio show** "How Learning
to Be Vulnerable Can Make Life Safer,"
Invisibilia, NPR, June 17, 2016, https://www
.npr.org/sections/health-shots/2016/06/17
/482203447/invisibilia-how-learning-to-be
-vulnerable-can-make-life-safer.

181   **well-known case study** Robin J. Ely and Debra
Meyerson, "Unmasking Manly Men," **Harvard
Business Review,** July–August 2008, https://hbr
.org/2008/07/unmasking-manly-men.

181   **For Rick, a similarly miraculous thing** My

description of Rick's story is based on the **Invisibilia** story, the Harvard case study, and my conversation with Rick himself on May 27, 2019.

182 **managers who disclose troubles** Kerry Roberts Gibson et al., "When Sharing Hurts: How and Why Self-Disclosing Weakness Undermines the Task-Oriented Relationships of Higher Status Disclosers," **Organizational Behavior and Human Decision Processes** 144 (January 2018): 25–43, https://doi.org/10.1016/j.obhdp.2017.09.001.

182 **the billing unit** Jane E. Dutton et al., "Understanding Compassion Capability," **Human Relations** 64, no. 7 (June 2011): 873–99, http://dx.doi.org/10.1177/0018726710396250.

184 **Sharing troubles turned out** Ibid., 7.

184 **"Businesses are often trying to shape themselves"** Email from Susan David, September 14, 2021.

184 **series of landmark studies** James W. Pennebaker, "Expressive Writing in Psychological Science," **Perspectives in Psychological Science** 13, no. 2 (March 2018): 226–29, https://doi.org/10.1177%2F1745691617707315.

185 **His depression lifted** Susan David, "You Can Write Your Way Out of an Emotional Funk. Here's How," **New York,** September 6, 2016, https://www.thecut.com/2016/09/journaling-can-help-you-out-of-a-bad-mood.html.

185 **people who wrote about their troubles** James W. Pennebaker, "Writing About Emotional Experiences as a Therapeutic Process," **Psychological Science** 8, no. 3 (1997): 162–66, http://www.jstor.org/stable/40063169.

186 <u>**three times**</u> **more likely** Stefanie P. Spera et al., "Expressive Writing and Coping with Job Loss," **Academy of Management Journal** 37, no. 3 (1994): 722–33, https://www.jstor.org/stable /256708.

187 **live with insight** Susan David, **Emotional Agility: Get Unstuck, Embrace Change, and Thrive in Work and Life** (New York: Avery, 2016).

189 **"comfortable sadness"** Author interview with Tim Leberecht, November 4, 2018.

193 **"there are ships sailing"** Fernando Pessoa, "Letter to Mário de Sá-Carneiro," posted by Sineokov, July 17, 2009, The Floating Library, https://thefloatinglibrary.com/2009/07/17/letter -to-mario-de-sa-carneiro/.

CHAPTER 7:

Should we try to live forever?

201 **"Someday when the descendants"** Eliezer Yudkowsky, **Harry Potter and the Methods of Rationality,** chap. 45, https://www.hpmor.com /chapter/45.

204 **"radical life extension"** "RAADfest 2017 to Feature World-Class Innovators on Super

Longevity," RAAD Festival 2017, https://www
.raadfest.com/raad-fest//raadfest-2017-to-feature
-world-class-innovators-on-super-longevity.

204 **"revolution against aging and death"** RAAD
Festival 2018, https://www.raadfest.com
/home-1.

204 **"longevity escape velocity"** Author interview
with Aubrey de Grey, conducted onsite at
RAAD Festival 2017. See also "David Wolfe,"
https://www.raadfest.com/david-wolfe, and
"radical life extension," https://www.rlecoalition
.com/raadfest.

206 **"Death gives as much"** This quote no longer
seems to be on the page, but I copied it down
several years ago.

212 **"All of a sudden"** This is from a transcript
of Dr. Mike West's presentation at RAAD
Festival 2017.

213 **The Epic of Gilgamesh** Joshua J. Mark, "The
Eternal Life of Gilgamesh," World History
Encyclopedia, April 10, 2018, https://www
.worldhistory.org/article/192/the-eternal-life-of
-gilgamesh/.

214 **"It's giving me chills"** Author interview with
Keith Comito, June 12, 2017.

218 **"I think it is absolutely true"** Author interview with Aubrey de Grey, conducted onsite at
RAAD Festival 2017.

218 **subjects who were reminded** H. A. McGregor
et al., "Terror Management and Aggression:
Evidence That Mortality Salience Motivates
Aggression Against Worldview-Threatening

Others," **Journal of Personality and Social Psychology** 74, no. 3 (March 1998): 590–605, https://doi.org/10.1037/0022-3514.74.3.590.

218 **politically conservative students** Tom Pyszczynski et al., "Mortality Salience, Martyrdom, and Military Might: The Great Satan Versus the Axis of Evil," **Personality and Social Psychology Bulletin** 32, no. 4 (April 2006): 525–37, https://doi.org/10.1177/0146167205282157.

219 **"big picture message"** "People Unlimited: Power of Togetherness to End Death," March 17, 2015, https://peopleunlimitedinc.com/posts/2015/03/people-unlimited-power-of-togetherness-to-end-death.

220 **"place where all the beauty came from"** Lewis, **Till We Have Faces,** 86.

220 **"our whole nature"** J.R.R. Tolkien, **The Letters of J.R.R. Tolkien,** ed., Humphrey Carpenter (Boston: Houghton Mifflin Harcourt, 2014), 125.

CHAPTER 8:
Should we try to "get over" grief and impermanence?

222 **". . . and, when the time"** Mary Oliver, **American Primitive,** 1st ed. (Boston: Back Bay Books, 1983), 82.

223 **"I concede that water"** Kobayashi Issa, quoted

in **Bereavement and Consolation: Testimonies from Tokugawa Japan** by Harold Bolitho (New Haven, Conn.: Yale University Press, 2003).

223 **"It is true"** Robert Hass et al., **The Essential Haiku: Versions of Basho, Buson and Issa** (Hopewell, N.J.: Ecco Press, 1994).

225 **tradition called <u>ars moriendi</u>** Atul Gawande, **Being Mortal** (New York: Henry Holt, 2004), 156.

226 **"shameful and forbidden"** Philippe Ariès, **Western Attitudes Toward Death** (Baltimore, Md.: Johns Hopkins University Press, 1975), 85, 92.

226 **"ethical duty to enjoy oneself"** Geoffrey Gorer, **Death, Grief, and Mourning** (New York: Arno Press, 1977), ix–xiii. Joan Didion writes about this in her book **The Year of Magical Thinking** (New York: Alfred A. Knopf, 2005).

228 **"Margaret, are you grieving"** Gerard Manley Hopkins, "Spring and Fall" in **Gerard Manley Hopkins: Poems and Prose** (Harmondsworth, UK: Penguin Classics, 1985); see also Poetry Foundation, https://www.poetryfoundation.org /poems/44400/spring-and-fall.

229 **it also has the power to help us to live in the present** Author interview with Laura Carstensen, June 11, 2018.

229 **the key isn't age** Gawande, **Being Mortal,** 99.

230 **They focus on smiling faces** Laura L. Carstensen et al., "Emotional Experience Improves with Age: Evidence Based on Over 10

Years of Experience Sampling," **Psychology and Aging** 26, no. 1 (March 2011): 21–33, https://dx.doi.org/10.1037%2Fa0021285.

231 **"We're also appreciating"** Author interview with Laura Carstensen, June 11, 2018.

234 **how few good years** Laura L. Carstensen, "The Influence of a Sense of Time on Human Development," **Science** 312 no. 5782 (June 2006): 1913–15, https://dx.doi.org/10.1126%2Fscience.1127488; Helene H. Fung and Laura L. Carstensen, "Goals Change When Life's Fragility Is Primed: Lessons Learned from Older Adults, the September 11 Attacks, and SARS," **Social Cognition** 24, no. 3 (June 2006): 248–78, http://dx.doi.org/10.1521/soco.2006.24.3.248.

235 **a short quiz** "Download the FTP Scale," Stanford Life-span Development Laboratory, https://lifespan.stanford.edu/download-the-ftp-scale.

236 **the religious traditions we've grown up with** David DeSteno, **How God Works: The Science Behind the Benefits of Religion** (New York: Simon & Schuster, 2021), 144, 147.

236 **"Remember, thou art mortal"** " 'Memento Mori': The Reminder We All Desperately Need," Daily Stoic, https://dailystoic.com/memento-mori/.

239 **Western scholars of grief** George Bonanno, **The Other Side of Sadness** (New York: Basic Books, 2010).

239 **"Another revelation: how much"** Chimamanda

Ngozi Adichie, "Notes on Grief," **The New Yorker,** September 10, 2020, https://www.newyorker.com/culture/personal-history/notes-on-grief.

240 **"The dominant experience is sadness"** David Van Nuys, "An Interview with George Bonanno, Ph.D., on Bereavement," Gracepoint Wellness, https://www.gracepointwellness.org/58-grief-bereavement-issues/article/35161-an-interview-with-george-bonanno-phd-on-bereavement.

240 **"Nonattachment is not against love"** Email interview with Sri Sri Ravi Shankar in 2017.

241 **"For a mother"** Van Nuys, "Interview with George Bonanno."

242 **"a sacred hush"** Author interview with Stephen Haff on or near October 27, 2017.

242 **"In this yogi-ridden age"** George Orwell, "Reflections on Gandhi," Orwell Foundation, https://www.orwellfoundation.com/the-orwell-foundation/orwell/essays-and-other-works/reflections-on-gandhi/.

243 **"circular pattern between life and death"** Author interview with Ami Vaidya, April 20, 2017.

246 **spiritual teacher Ram Dass's observation** "If you think you're enlightened go spend a week with your family," Ram Dass, "More Ram Dass Quotes," Love Serve Remember Foundation, https://www.ramdass.org/ram-dass-quotes/.

248 **"I like being with people"** Author interview with Lois Schnipper, December 9, 2016.

250   **between moving on and moving forward**
Nora McInerny, "We Don't 'Move On' from
Grief. We Move Forward with It." TED Talk,
November 2018, https://www.ted.com/talks
/nora_mcinerny_we_don_t_move_on_from
_grief_we_move_forward_with_it/transcript
?language=en#t-41632.

CHAPTER 9:

Do we inherit the pain of our parents and ancestors? And, if so, can we transform it generations later?

252   **What is silenced in** Françoise Dolto:
Kathleen Saint-Onge, **Discovering Françoise
Dolto: Psychoanalysis, Identity and
Child Development** (United Kingdom:
Routledge, 2019).

253   **Dr. Simcha Raphael** Author interviews on
October 13 and December 20, 2017, and Art of
Dying conference, New York Open Center,
October 17, 2017.

261   **"People say, when something cataclysmic
happens"** Rachel Yehuda, "How Trauma and
Resilience Cross Generations," **On Being
with Krista Tippett** (podcast), July 30, 2015,
https://onbeing.org/programs/rachel-yehuda
-how-trauma-and-resilience-cross-generations
-nov2017/.

262   **The survivors' children** Helen Thomson, "Study
of Holocaust Survivors Finds Trauma Passed On

to Children's Genes," **The Guardian,** August 21, 2015, https://www.theguardian.com/science /2015/aug/21/study-of-holocaust-survivors -finds-trauma-passed-on-to-childrens-genes.

262 **"preconception parental trauma"** Rachel Yehuda et al., "Holocaust Exposure Induced Intergenerational Effects on FKBP5 Methylation," **Biological Psychiatry** 80, no. 5 (September 2016): P372–80, https://doi.org/10 .1016/j.biopsych.2015.08.005.

263 **Yehuda's study was criticized** Seema Yasmin, "Experts Debunk Study That Found Holocaust Trauma Is Inherited," **Chicago Tribune,** June 9, 2017, https://www.chicagotribune.com/lifestyles /health/ct-holocaust-trauma-not-inherited -20170609-story.html.

263 **"reductionist biological determinism"** Rachel Yehuda, Amy Lehrner, and Linda M. Bierer, "The Public Reception of Putative Epigenetic Mechanisms in the Transgenerational Effects of Trauma," **Environmental Epigenetics** 4, no. 2 (April 2018), https://doi.org/10.1093/eep /dvy018.

263 **Yehuda's findings were later replicated** Linda M. Bierer et al., "Intergenerational Effects of Maternal Holocaust Exposure on **KFBP5** Methylation," **The American Journal of Psychiatry** (April 21, 2020), https://doi.org/10 .1176/appi.ajp.2019.19060618.

264 **water fleas subjected to the odor** Anurag Chaturvedi et al., "Extensive Standing Genetic Variation from a Small Number of Founders

Enables Rapid Adaptation in **Daphnia**," **Nature Communications** 12, no. 4306 (2021), https://doi.org/10.1038/s41467-021-24581-z.

264 **mice exposed to a harmless scent** Brian G. Dias and Kerry J. Ressler, "Parental Olfactory Experience Influences Behavior and Neural Structure in Subsequent Generations," **Nature Neuroscience** 17 (2014): 89–96, https://doi.org/10.1038/nn.3594.

265 **descendants of the traumatized mice** Gretchen van Steenwyk et al., "Transgenerational Inheritance of Behavioral and Metabolic Effects of Paternal Exposure to Traumatic Stress in Early Postnatal Life: Evidence in the 4th Generation," **Environmental Epigenetics** 4, no. 2 (April 2018), https://dx.doi.org/10.1093%2Feep%2Fdvy023.

265 **sons of released POWs** Dora L. Costa, Noelle Yetter, and Heather DeSomer, "Intergenerational Transmission of Paternal Trauma Among U.S. Civil War ex-POWs," PNAS115, no. 44 (October 2018): 11215–20, https://doi.org/10.1073/pnas.1803630115.

265 **children of Dutch women** P. Ekamper et al., "Independent and Additive Association of Prenatal Famine Exposure and Intermediary Life Conditions with Adult Mortality Between Age 18–63 Years," **Social Science and Medicine** 119 (October 2014): 232–39, https://doi.org/10.1016/j.socscimed.2013.10.027.

265 **racial discrimination can cause** Veronica Barcelona de Mendoza et al., "Perceived Racial

Discrimination and DNA Methylation Among African American Women in the InterGEN Study," **Biological Research for Nursing** 20, no. 2 (March 2018): 145–52, https://doi.org/10.1177/1099800417748759.

266 **"Answering that objection"** Curry, "Parents' Emotional Trauma May Change Their Children's Biology."

266 **"If it's epigenetic"** Ibid.

266 **"Research may unintentionally be received"** Rachel Yehuda, Amy Lehrner, and Linda M. Bierer, "The Public Reception of Putative Epigenetic Mechanisms in the Transgenerational Effects of Trauma," **Environmental Epigenetics** 4, no. 2 (April 2018), https://doi.org/10.1093/eep/dvy018.

267 **seems to produce measurable** Rachel Yehuda et al., "Epigenetic Biomarkers as Predictors and Correlates of Symptom Improvement Following Psychotherapy in Combat Veterans with PTSD," **Frontiers in Psychiatry** 4, no. 118 (2013), https://dx.doi.org/10.3389%2Ffpsyt.2013.00118.

267 **raising traumatized mice in therapeutic conditions** Katharina Gapp et al., "Potential of Environmental Enrichment to Prevent Transgenerational Effects of Paternal Trauma," **Neuropsychopharmacology** 41 (2016): 2749–58, https://doi.org/10.1038/npp.2016.87.

267 **"And then I remembered"** Yehuda, "How Trauma and Resilience Cross Generations."

268   **she'd visited Gorée Island** "Gorée: Senegal's
       Slave Island," BBC News, June 27, 2013,
       https://www.bbc.com/news/world-africa
       -23078662.

268   **"the last place our ancestors"** Email to author
       from Jeri Bingham, June 2021.

271   **"grief never left them"** Readers who would like
       to learn more about the relationship between
       inherited grief and the African American experi-
       ence might also like to read Joy Degruy, **Post
       Traumatic Slave Syndrome: America's Legacy
       of Enduring Injury and Healing** (Uptone
       Press, 2005).

271   **"I just have it"** Author interview conducted in
       July 2019.

274   **a sense of meaning** William Breitbart, ed.,
       **Meaning-Centered Psychotherapy in the
       Cancer Setting: Finding Meaning and Hope
       in the Face of Suffering** (New York: Oxford
       University Press, 2017), https://doi.org/10.1093
       /med/9780199837229.001.0001.

274   **His results have been inspiring** William
       Breitbart, ed., "Meaning-Centered Group
       Psychotherapy: An Effective Intervention
       for Improving Psychological Well-Being in
       Patients with Advanced Cancer," **Journal of
       Clinical Oncology** 33, no. 7 (February 2015):
       749–54, https://doi.org/10.1200/JCO.2014
       .57.2198; Lori P. Montross Thomas, Emily A.
       Meier, and Scott A. Irwin, "Meaning-Centered
       Psychotherapy: A Form of Psychotherapy for
       Patients with Cancer," **Current Psychiatry**

Reports 16, no. 10 (September 2014): 488, https://doi.org/10.1007/s11920-014-0488-2.

275 **find their "whys"** Wendy G. Lichtenthal et al., "Finding Meaning in the Face of Suffering," **Psychiatric Times** 37, no. 8 (August 2020), https://www.psychiatrictimes.com/view/finding -meaning-in-the-face-of-suffering.

276 **"If you were telling my story"** Author interview with William Breitbart, May 3, 2017.

281 **send a paper lantern** Dave Afshar, "The History of Toro Nagashi, Japan's Glowing Lantern Festival," Culture Trip, April 19, 2021, https:// theculturetrip.com/asia/japan/articles/the -history-of-toro-nagashi-japans-glowing-lantern -festival/.

281 **set out favorite foods** Amy Scattergood, "Day of the Dead Feast Is a High-Spirited Affair," **Los Angeles Times,** October 29, 2008, https://www .latimes.com/local/la-fo-dia29-2008oct29 -story.html.

282 **"Live as though"** I came across this quote via Ted Hughes's writing. Unfortunately, I haven't been able to track down its original source.

CODA:

How to Go Home

287 **"And did you get what"** Raymond Carver, "Late Fragment," from his last collection, **A New Path to the Waterfall** (New York: Atlantic Monthly Press, 1988).

293 **glamorous couple driving their convertible** Virginia Postrel writes wonderfully about the iconography of convertibles in her book **The Power of Glamour: Longing and the Art of Visual Persuasion** (New York: Simon & Schuster, 2013).

296 **a book on their experiences** Kenneth Cain, Heidi Postlewait, and Andrew Thomson, **Emergency Sex and Other Desperate Measures** (New York: Hyperion, 2004).

298 **learning how to ascend** I'm pretty sure I read this idea somewhere—that it wasn't mine originally. But I can't seem to locate the source.

299 **a "sacred psychology"** Houston, **Search for the Beloved**, 26.

INDEX

Page numbers in **bold** indicate illustrations.

ABOUT THE AUTHOR

Named one of the top ten influencers in the world by LinkedIn, SUSAN CAIN is a renowned speaker and author of the award-winning books **Quiet Power, Quiet Journal, and Quiet: The Power of Introverts in a World That Can't Stop Talking.** Translated into more than forty languages, **Quiet** has appeared on many best-of lists, spent seven years on the **New York Times** bestseller list, and was named the number one best book of the year by **Fast Company,** which also named Cain one of its Most Creative People in Business. Her TED Talk on the power of introverts has been viewed over forty million times. Please visit her at susancain.net.